The Hudson

The Hudson

An Illustrated Guide to the Living River

Stephen P. Stanne
Roger G. Panetta
Brian E. Forist

A Project of
Hudson River Sloop
Clearwater, Inc.

RUTGERS UNIVERSITY PRESS   NEW BRUNSWICK, NEW JERSEY

Library of Congress Cataloging-in-Publication Data

Stanne, Stephen P., 1950–
     The Hudson: An Illustrated Guide to the Living River /
Stephen P. Stanne, Roger G. Panetta, and Brian E. Forist.
        p.   cm.
     "A project of Hudson River Sloop Clearwater, Inc."
     Includes bibliographical references and index.
     ISBN 0–8135–2270–6 (cloth : alk. paper).
— ISBN 0–8135–2271–4 (pbk. : alk. paper)
     1. Natural history—Hudson River (N. Y. and N. J.)
2. Stream ecology—Hudson River (N. Y. and N. J.)   3. Hudson
River (N. Y. and N. J.)—History.   4. Hudson River (N. Y. and
N. J.)—Environmental conditions.   I. Panetta, Roger G.,
1939– . II. Forist, Brian E., 1956– . III. Hudson River
Sloop Clearwater, Inc.   IV. Title.
QH104.5.H83S74   1996
508.747′3—dc20   95–23674
                                                         CIP

British Cataloging-in-Publication information available.

Credits

Text: Chapters 1, 2, 3, 6, 11, and 12 by Stephen P. Stanne; chapters 7, 8, 9, and 10 by Roger G. Panetta; and chapters 4 and 5 by Brian E. Forist.

Illustrations: Unless otherwise credited, drawings for chapters 1, 2, 5, and 6, and all photographs by Stephen P. Stanne; drawings for chapter 3 by Cara Lee; and drawings for chapter 4 by Cynthia Saniewski.

Cover design and Hudson River map by Nora Porter.

Picture research for chapters 7, 8, 9, and 10 by Nora Porter.

Contents

Preface

In studying a river, the place to begin seems obvious: find its source. Take out a map and follow the twisting blue line as it narrows, heading upstream past each tributary, until it ends in a lake or wetland, or perhaps dwindles to nothing in a mountainside valley.

But those with a more historical frame of reference may want to start with discovery of the river by humans. From there one can follow the growth of human society and endeavor along the river over the ensuing centuries.

To a geologist, whose vision of time extends back millions of years, a few centuries are nothing, nor does a river's present source necessarily constitute its beginning. The river may be where it is because of forces operating on a scale much grander than the swirl of its currents.

To a biologist, leery of chicken-and-egg questions about what came first, the beginnings may not matter as much as a deeper understanding of one of the many diverse and fascinating groups of organisms that inhabit the river.

To a teacher, what's important about studying a river, particularly one that is the defining feature of an area's natural landscape and that has figured prominently in a region's—indeed, a nation's—history, is that it can support curricula in any or all of these disciplines, and many more besides. In addition, a local river has real shape and associations in students' lives and minds, an advantage a teacher can use to make inquiry and learning even more effective and substantive.

No better example exists than the Hudson River. Get up close and its teeming life and shifting currents provide a compelling introduction to the natural sciences, while artifacts along its shores provide a glimpse of our forebears' daily lives. Pull back a bit, study the landscape in which the river flows, and feel for yourself the inspiration that guided major developments in American art. Widen the field of view even more, place the Hudson in its geographical setting, and gain a clearer picture of American history while examining the river's pivotal role in Revolutionary War strategies or in providing a route of migration and commerce into the expanding frontier. Study the precedent-setting battles waged over Hudson River environmental concerns to understand our political and legal process, and realize that these controversies offer an interdisciplinary link back to the closeup view of the river's biology.

The Hudson was originally envisioned as a basic reference for teachers studying the Hudson River with their students. It remains that, but it also fulfills the larger role of providing information to anyone inclined to be a student of the river, whether or not the inquiry takes place in a formal classroom.

This is a book of elementary principles, providing an overview of the Hudson's natural and human histories between the head of tidewater at Troy and the briny ocean at its mouth. It is not a complete field guide; only common or distinctive species were selected for brief descriptions. The many forms of life to be seen in the river could be fully described only in a multivolume work. Besides, field guides concern themselves primarily with identification of organisms or objects, not so much with the physical phenomena and biological relationships that tie them together. This book does attempt to convey a sense of the great diversity of life in the Hudson, weaving descriptions of representative organisms into discussions of the ecological ties that bind them together.

Similarly, this book cannot cover all the basic tenets of the sciences that are applicable when studying the Hudson—from astronomy, botany, and chemistry all the way to zoology. But those interested in specific sciences will find examples from the Hudson to illustrate the workings of important phenomena, theories, laws, and principles from many disciplines.

The Hudson's content draws on the insights, research, and writing of, among others, historians, naturalists, scientists, and government officials. However, it is not intended to be an academic or scientific work; thus we have not cited the source of every fact or observation that originated in earlier works. Key references are acknowledged in the Sources section at the end of the book. The most encompassing and widely available of those references, along with other worthwhile books, are also cited in the annotated Suggested Readings section.

Any book dealing with science must confront the bugaboo of terminology. Scientists sort out phenomena, particles, organisms—whatever it is they study—and assign names or terms to the categories they create. In his authoritative *Freshwater Invertebrates of the United States*, Robert W. Pennak quotes Lewis Carroll's *Alice in Wonderland*:

> "What's the use of their having names," the Gnat said, "if they won't answer to them?"
> "No use to *them*," said Alice; "but it's useful to the people that name them, I suppose."

While the terminology created may seem daunting to the layperson, it is a necessity for scientists who must be very precise in their descriptions.

We have made an effort to limit terminology, but there are scientific terms that are very useful in discussing the Hudson River in any detail. Most will be defined where and when they first appear in the text, as well as in the appended glossary. While these twenty-five-cent words may twist the tongue and seem pretentious, they are often more efficient than wasting breath or text in repeated descriptive phrases or sentences. For instance, we will discuss algae that live self-sufficiently on the stems and leaves of underwater plants. Don't let the fact that we will discuss epiphytic algae put you off.

In studying history, a major obstacle is the memorization of dates, names of people and places, and similar facts. Like scientific terms, they have their place in discussions of the Hudson. But pay attention to them as you pay attention to minutes passing on a clock, reference points against which major themes of American history play out on the stage provided by the Hudson. Just as species descriptions illustrate biological diversity and junctures in the network of ecological relationships, so do accounts of specific events of the Hudson's history, with their associated dates, people, and sites, illuminate the interplay of far-reaching social, political, and cultural ideas and movements.

In years of leading teacher workshops dealing with Hudson River studies, we have learned that educators attend them not only—or even mainly—because they expect the practical reward of being able to enrich their curricula or programs. Most participate because they are fascinated by the Hudson and feel that it is a vital part of their lives and communities. For all those who dwell along the Hudson, it is our hope that this book will reinforce that fascination and strengthen their sense of the Hudson's vitality and importance.

Acknowledgments

The authors and Clearwater wish to acknowledge and thank the Hudson River Foundation, the Henry L. and Grace Doherty Charitable Foundation, and the Norcross Wildlife Foundation for grants in support of the research, writing, and production of *The Hudson*. The views expressed in this book do not necessarily reflect the beliefs or opinions of the donors, who assume no liability for the contents or use of information. Additional funding was provided through general support from the J. M. Kaplan Fund, the Joyce Mertz-Gilmore Foundation, and Clearwater's members.

The support of the entire Clearwater staff was critical to our production efforts. We would like to express special appreciation to Nora Porter and the late Ken Yeso, whose contributions of creativity, time, and energy to this project went far beyond any work listed in the credits. Thanks also to Hannah Kalkstein for her editing assistance, Bridget Barclay, Julie Neander, and Don Kent for research and review of chapters 11 and 12, volunteer Jane Kellar for her hours at the copy machine, intern Julia Wilson for her consistency checks, and John Mylod for his patience.

This book was greatly improved by the knowledge and critical eye of expert individuals outside Clearwater who generously donated time from their busy schedules to review chapters relevant to their fields of knowledge. We owe particular thanks to Nancy Beard, Citizen Participation Specialist, Hudson River Program, N.Y. State Department of Environmental Conservation (DEC) (chapters 11 and 12); Dr. Jonathan J. Cole, Aquatic Microbiologist at the Institute of Ecosystem Studies (IES) (chapters 2 and 3); Frances F. Dunwell, Special Assistant to the Commissioner for the Hudson River Valley and Hudson River Coordinator, DEC (chapters 11 and 12); Dr. Erik Kiviat, executive director of Hudsonia Ltd. (chapters 3 and 6); Thomas R. Lake,

Hudson River Fishermen's Association (chapter 5); Cara Lee, environmental director at Scenic Hudson (chapters 11 and 12); Dr. Michael Pace, Aquatic Ecologist at IES (chapters 2 and 4); Dr. David Strayer, Freshwater Ecologist at IES (chapter 4), and Dr. John Waldman, Research Associate at the Hudson River Foundation (chapter 5).

Equally generous and expert were the teachers who reviewed and helped to shape the book in ways benefiting those who teach about the Hudson. Our thanks go to Meg Clark-Goldhammer, Lisa Fitzgerald, Gary Post, Paul and Vincent Rubeo, Suzanne Tichner, and Al Vinck.

Other individuals patiently answered questions during our research: Dr. Joanna Burger, Rutgers University; Dr. Donald Cadwell, N.Y. State Geological Survey; Dr. Stuart Findlay, IES; Ward Freeman, U.S. Geological Survey; Tony Goodwin, Adirondack Mountain Club; Kathy Hattala, DEC; Andy Kahnle, DEC; Kate McCaig, Liberty State Park, N.J.; Russell Mt. Pleasant, DEC; Jim Rod, National Audubon Society; Larry Sarner, N.J. Department of Environmental Protection; and Dr. Russell Waines, State University of New York at New Paltz.

We are most grateful to the artists, photographers, and institutions (credited elsewhere) who, on a volunteer basis or for nominal fees, provided materials for use in illustrating this book. In addition, we would like to thank Val Ruge for providing access to her extensive collection of Hudson River prints and allowing us to use many images.

Clay Hiles and Dr. Dennis J. Suszkowski of the Hudson River Foundation, Dr. Terry Shtob, formerly of the Foundation, and Sam Kalkstein provided much appreciated general review and suggestions for improving this book. Thanks also to Uta Gore, river educator, Sr. Brigid Driscoll, president of Marymount College, and Dr. Bessie Blake, dean of the School of New Resources, College of New Rochelle, for their support of Hudson River studies.

Finally, thanks to Dr. Karen Reeds of Rutgers University Press for her patience and interest in seeing this project come to fruition, and to Paul Fargis of Stonesong Press for advice and assistance in the endeavor.

The Hudson

Chapter 1

A Physical Overview of the Hudson

The Chapter in Brief

The Hudson River flows 315 miles from Lake Tear of the Clouds in the Adirondacks to the Battery in New York City. Its course and shoreline topography result from erosion by water and glacial ice over the past sixty-five to seventy-five million years. The river is influenced by ocean tides to Troy, 153 miles north of the Battery, and by salt water as far north as Newburgh, 60 miles upriver. The lower Hudson is an estuary, a type of ecosystem that ranks among the most productive on the planet.

The Hudson's Origins

To begin a study of the Hudson River at its source, lay out a map of eastern New York State and trace the blue line north from New York Harbor along the cliffs of the Palisades, under the ramparts at West Point, through the sunset shadows of the Catskill Mountains, past the capital city of Albany, and on into the Adirondacks. There, at the confluence of two creeks near Henderson Lake, the name Hudson River disappears; the map offers the option of following Calamity Brook northeastward or the outlet from Henderson Lake westward.

Following the geographer's dictum that a river's source is the highest body of water feeding into it, turn northeast and face the heart of the High Peaks region. Continue upward along Calamity Brook, the Opalescent River, and little Feldspar Brook, reaching at last a tiny lake perched 4,322 feet up on the southwest side of Mount Marcy, New York State's highest peak at 5,344 feet. In 1872 Verplanck Colvin, an indefatigable explorer and surveyor of the Adirondacks, described this lake as a "minute, unpretending tear-of-the-clouds—as it were—a lonely pool shivering in the breezes of the mountains." Thus the Hudson's source was named—Lake Tear of the Clouds.

The Water Cycle

The clouds that so often cap the Adirondacks, the snow that falls on Mount Marcy's shoulder, the raindrops that dimple the surface of Lake Tear, the fog that condenses in tiny droplets on spruces lining Feldspar

Lake Tear of the Clouds, source of the Hudson, nestles high on the southwest shoulder of Mount Marcy, New York State's highest peak.

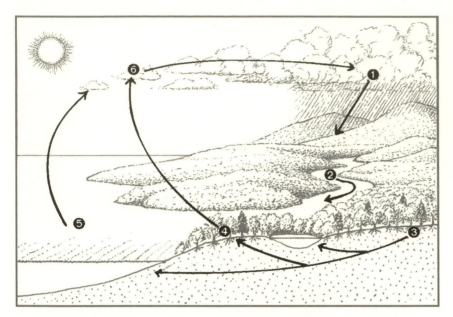

In this simplified illustration of the water cycle, rain falls to earth (1) and runs off into streams flowing seaward (2) or enters the ground (3). As groundwater moves toward the ocean, it feeds streams and lakes and is taken up by plants (4), from which it is transpired into the atmosphere as water vapor. Evaporation from the sea (5) and other surface waters also supplies water vapor to the atmosphere. There, the vapor condenses to form clouds (6) and eventually falls to earth again as precipitation.

the water cycle, that function is carried out by the sun, which provides energy to evaporate water and move it from place to place in the atmosphere, and by gravity, which causes precipitation to flow as runoff across the land and as groundwater under the land's surface.

An Arm of the Sea

From Lake Tear to the Battery at the southern tip of Manhattan, the Hudson follows a course 315 miles long. Joining it along the way are many tributaries, the largest being the Mohawk River, which flows in from the west at Cohoes. The area of land drained by the Hudson and its tributaries totals 13,390 square miles, mostly in eastern and northern New York State. Small portions of this area, the Hudson's watershed, reach into Vermont, Massachusetts, Connecticut, and New Jersey.

In length and watershed area the Hud-

Brook, and their union in the runoff that eventually becomes the Hudson—all are manifestations of a much larger "stream" of water. These visible forms are linked to water hidden in the ground and pulled up in the stems of plants to their leaves, from where it is transpired into the atmosphere. There it joins water vapor invisibly rising from great oceans and tiny puddles, moving with weather systems from continent to continent or from a valley to its bordering hills, and once more taking forms that we can see—clouds and precipitation. This unending movement of water, seen and unseen, constitutes the water cycle.

The water cycle is a circulatory system supporting life on earth much as arteries and veins support human existence. Like blood, water transports substances needed by living organisms of the Hudson and its valley. In our bodies, the heart is the pump that circulates blood through the system. In

Gathering waters from Adirondack tributaries, the Hudson rushes through its gorge at Blue Ledge, near the village of North Creek.

son does not rank highly among American rivers. Yet numbers do not tell the full story, as one can appreciate when gazing across wide bays at Newburgh, the Tappan Zee, and Haverstraw, the latter being where the Hudson is widest, about three and a half miles east to west.

Such expansive grandeur results from the fact that for nearly half its length, the Hudson is an arm of the sea. In plunging over a dam at Troy, the river falls to a level only two feet above that of the faraway Atlantic Ocean, entering a long narrow trough in which its flow is governed less by the pull of earth's gravity than by the pulse of ocean tides responding to the gravity of the moon.

The lowest portions of the Hudson's valley south of Troy were submerged when sea level rose at the end of the most recent

Bordered on the west by the northern portion of the Palisades, Haverstraw Bay is the widest spot on the Hudson.

The Troy Dam marks the upriver limit of tidal influence on the Hudson. A lock here allows boat passage via the river to and from the New York State Barge Canal (successor to the famed Erie Canal) and the Champlain Canal.

ice age. The deepest known spot of the river is at World's End near West Point, where a 1934 survey found bottom 216 feet down.[1] The Hudson's gorge through the Highlands is its deepest stretch, with many charted depths over 100 feet.

The Hudson is quite turbid, carrying large amounts of sediment that give it a muddy appearance. The sediment tends to settle and fill in certain stretches of the river, notably at Haverstraw Bay and from Kingston north to Albany. In these areas, the ship channel must be maintained by dredging—digging out bottom sediments—since under federal law, the channel between New York and Albany must be kept at least 32 feet deep. This allows large barges and ocean-going ships to reach the Port of Albany.

The Hudson Fjord

With its great depths and cliffs slanting steeply into the river, the Hudson's route through the Highlands reminds many observers of the strikingly scenic fjords of Norway. Fjords are troughs eroded below sea level, often to great depths, by glacial

Shaped by the Ice Sheets

Other aspects of topography along the Hudson's course reflect the enormous power of the Ice Age's continental glaciers. At the peak of glaciation, the metropolitan New York area was buried under as much as 3,000 feet of ice. So much water was frozen in ice sheets worldwide that the Atlantic Ocean was about 400 feet lower than it is today. To reach the sea the Hudson flowed an additional 120 miles across a wide coastal plain.

As glaciers began to melt 18,000 years ago, tremendous volumes of water were re-leased into the Hudson, carrying with them great loads of sediment, the remains of rock and soil pulverized by the moving ice. These surges of meltwater and accompany-ing turbidity currents (underwater land-slides generated by the buildup of sediment deposits) carved the Hudson Submarine Canyon, a deep gorge at the edge of the continental shelf southeast of New York Harbor. A submerged valley running across the continental shelf—a feature not seen off other East Coast rivers—links the Hudson's mouth to the canyon. This valley may have been cut when glacial meltwaters from the prehistoric Great Lakes and Lake Cham-plain, their St. Lawrence River outlet blocked by the ice sheets, flowed torren-tially down the Hudson to the Atlantic.

The glaciers also built up some land-scapes. Debris that had been eroded from areas to the north was piled up by the ice sheets at the limits of their advance. At this terminus the rate of melting equaled the speed of advance; like Cinderella, left with-out conveyance as her carriage turned back into a pumpkin, the debris brought south was dropped, forming rows of low hills, as ice turned to water. Such deposits consti-tute the backbone of Long Island and Brooklyn. The Hudson breaches one of these glacially created ridges, called a ter-

The Hudson's established channel through the Highlands was gouged to greater depths by glacial ice, which also steepened the slopes plunging down to the river.

ice. They are deepest not at their mouths but upstream, where the ice was thickest and its erosive power the greatest. A shal-lower, less eroded sill of bedrock is usually present at the mouths.

The bedrock underlying the lower Hudson is largely buried below layers of sediments, some deposited by the river, others dropped by the ice sheets or their meltwaters. These deposits fill a much deeper gorge scoured out by the glaciers. Drilling during construction of aqueducts and bridges across the river found that the deepest portions of this gorge lie at least 750 feet below sea level at the northern en-trance to the Highlands, and 740 feet down at the Tappan Zee. Nearer the ocean, geol-ogists have found a shallower sill: bedrock is less than 200 feet down at the Verrazano Bridge. Thus most geologists today agree that the Hudson is a fjord.

minal moraine, at the Narrows between Brooklyn and Staten Island.

Other shoreline features owe their origins to the continental glaciers. Meltwaters from the ice sheets collected behind glacial debris and melting ice masses in the region's valleys, creating large lakes such as Glacial Lake Albany.[2] Rivers swollen by meltwater carried gravel and sand into the lakes. There, as the currents slowed, the material was dropped to form deltas. Much of Croton Point is such a delta, built up by the ancestral Croton River.[3]

Glacial Lake Albany is thought to have lasted at least four thousand to five thousand years before draining. In its still waters, tiny particles of rock flour—soil and rock ground up by the glaciers—gradually settled to the bottom, forming deep beds of clay. Such beds later supplied the raw material for the brick industry that flourished along the Hudson.

Of Time and River Flowing

Though its origins are poorly known and disputed, the river's general course was probably set sixty-five to seventy-five million years ago, long before the great glaciers' advance. A gradual uplift of the earth's crust in this region began then, steepening the grades of streams and increasing their erosive power.

The region's landscape at the time was very flat, similar to that seen today near the coasts of the southeastern states. The rocks that would later be sculpted into the Catskills, Highlands, and Palisades were buried under coastal plain sediments, over which the ancestral Hudson made its way to the ocean. As its grade steepened, the river and its tributaries wore away those sediments, exposing and cutting into rock. A delicate balance between gradual uplift of the terrain and the erosive power of the current allowed the ancient Hudson to cut and maintain a gorge through hard, resistant rock such as the gneiss and granite that ultimately were exposed to form the Highlands.

Gaps in the ridges of the Palisades and New Jersey's Watchung Mountains suggest that until ten million to fifteen million years ago the Hudson followed a course different from its present route between the Tappan Zee and the Atlantic. It crossed the Palisades at the Sparkill Gap, located a few miles south of the Tappan Zee Bridge, and continued southwest across the Watchungs near Paterson, New Jersey. The river then paralleled the Watchungs south for about 15 miles before turning eastward and re-

At the low-lying Sparkill Gap, the Hudson once flowed westward through the Palisades and on to the sea past the site of present-day Paterson, New Jersey, instead of Manhattan.

crossing them on its way to the ocean. Later in prehistoric time the Hudson probably flowed south from the Sparkill Gap along the Hackensack Meadowlands to the sea.

It is possible that the river abandoned the Sparkill Gap as the headwaters of a small stream running east of the Palisades eroded its watershed, extending its boundaries to the north. At some point this erosion reached the ancestral Hudson, giving it a new, lower outlet to the sea. Eventually all the waters of the river were diverted into this new course past Manhattan Island and on to the ocean. Another hypothesis suggests that glacial deposits blocked the Sparkill Gap, forcing the Hudson to erode its present course east of the Palisades.

The geological handiwork of water and ice over millions of years created a waterway that offered immense advantages to the humans who eventually settled in its valley. In a time before railroads, superhighways, and jumbo airliners, water-based transportation was the easiest, fastest, most comfortable, and most capacious way of moving goods and people long distances. The river's surface was unbroken by rapids or waterfalls for over 150 miles inland. Its erosive power had created the gorge through the Highlands, the only sea-level passage through the Appalachian Mountain Range. This fact figured prominently in DeWitt

Clinton's vision for a water route linking America's expanding west to its Atlantic coast, a vision realized in the Erie Canal. And in the days before steamships, when vessels depended on the motive power of wind or muscle, the Hudson offered yet another boon to those trying to get from one place to another: tidal currents.

A River That Flows Two Ways

Tides were not always favorable to the sloops once so common on the Hudson—the currents would usually move in the direction opposite to the one desired for half of each day. But when there was little wind (frequently the case during Hudson Valley summers), vessels could anchor to wait out an ill tide, and then get a much-needed boost in the desired direction when the tide turned in their favor.

Tides occur in patterns set by a celestial dance involving the earth, the moon, and, to a lesser extent, the sun. The most obvious of these patterns is the daily tidal cycle along the Atlantic coast, in which two high tides and two low tides occur over roughly twenty-four hours. While a complete explanation of how tides work is beyond the scope of this book, a simple overview will be helpful in understanding the Hudson.

The effects of ocean tides in the Hudson are evident at Poughkeepsie, where the average high tide is three feet higher than the average low tide.

Moonrise over the Esopus Meadows just south of Kingston.

The Pull of the Moon . . .

The moon is large enough and near enough to exert considerable gravitational pull on the earth. In the oceans, this attraction literally causes water to bulge out toward the moon. This bulge remains positioned under the moon (actually a little behind it due to inertia and friction) as the earth spins on its axis. Thus, while beachcombers on the Atlantic coast watch the moon rise, they are being inexorably carried into a mound of water, evident in the rising tide lapping around their feet.

This bulge raises the ocean's level above the level of water in the Hudson; as a result, seawater starts rushing into the river. At the Battery on Manhattan's southern tip, strollers gazing out at the Statue of Liberty might notice that the Hudson's current is pushing northward, in from the sea toward the mountains, and that the water is rising along pilings lining the shore.

Hours later, after the beachcombers and strollers have gone to bed, the Atlantic

This diagram shows, in greatly exaggerated form, the tidal bulge created by the gravitational mechanics of the moon and earth (as viewed from above the North Pole). High tides occur on the portion of earth facing the moon and on the portion directly opposite.

Moon   Earth

6:00 P.M., Day 1: In between, where the lighthouse stands at 6:00 P.M. on day 1, the tide is low. But earth's rotation is carrying the lighthouse into the bulge under the moon . . .

12:00 A.M., Day 2: . . . and at midnight 6 hours later, the tower is largely submerged by a high tide.

6:00 A.M., Day 2: By 6:00 A.M. on day 2, earth's rotation has taken the lighthouse out of the bulge. A low tide laps at the tower's base.

 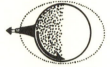

12:00 P.M., Day 2: At noon, the lighthouse reaches the crest of the bulge on the opposite side of earth and is again experiencing high tide.

6:00 P.M., Day 2: By 6:00 P.M., earth's rotation has brought the lighthouse back to where it was 24 hours earlier. During those 24 hours, the lighthouse went through two high tides, the typical pattern along the East Coast (see note 5).

coast has passed under the moon and reached the backside of the bulge. The tide is now falling, and as the ocean's level drops below the level of water in the river, the current at the Battery reverses and starts flowing toward the sea once more. The native tribes of the valley described this in one of their names for the river: Muhheakantuck, meaning "river that flows two ways."

For reasons best explained in cited references, a second tidal bulge forms at a point on the earth opposite the moon. In between the two bulges are areas where the ocean's level is lower, resulting in low tides. Thus, in the twenty-four hours it takes the earth to spin around its axis, a given point on the Atlantic coast will usually experience two high tides and two low tides, one following the other roughly every six hours.[4]

. . . and of the Sun

In addition to this daily rhythm, tides vary cyclically over the twenty-eight-day lunar month—the time the moon takes to circle once around the earth. The lunar month is marked by the phases of the moon. More extreme tides (higher highs and lower lows) occur when the moon is in its new or full phase; these are the spring tides. During the moon's first and last quarter, the difference between high and low tides is minimal; these are the neap tides.

Spring and neap tides reflect the interaction of the sun's gravitational attraction with the moon's. One might expect the sun to have greater tidal influence because it is so much bigger than the moon and exerts a correspondingly stronger gravitational force. However, this force decreases with distance, and the sun is much farther away from the earth than the moon. On balance, the sun's effect in raising tides is only about half that of the moon's.

Up and Down, Back and Forth

The rise and fall of the tides affects the river all the way to the dam at Troy, 153 river miles north of the Battery. In fact, the Hudson's maximum tidal range (the difference in level between average high and low tides) is observed at Troy: 4.7 feet. Tidal range is least along the mid-Hudson, averaging only 2.7 feet at West Point.

Like high and low tides, reversals in current direction follow roughly a six-hour schedule. The current draining the river south toward the ocean is called the *ebb;* that pushing north from the ocean is called the *flood.* Extreme rain and accompanying runoff will sometimes suppress the flood current.[5] Persistent, strong northerly or southerly winds can also affect the timing and strength of tidal currents.

An adventure like Huckleberry Finn's raft trip down the Mississippi would be quite a different experience on the lower Hudson. Instead of progressing steadily downstream, a rafter on the Hudson might admire the scenery while drifting south-

Spring tides occur when the moon is new or full. The sun, moon, and earth are all in line, so that the sun's pull works with the moon's to create a more extreme tidal bulge evident in higher high tides and lower low tides.

Neap tides occur at the moon's first and last quarters, when sun and moon are at right angles relative to earth. The moon raises the high tides alone, without help from the sun; thus these highs are lower than normal. However, the sun's pull does act on the low tide area of the bulge, causing higher low tides.

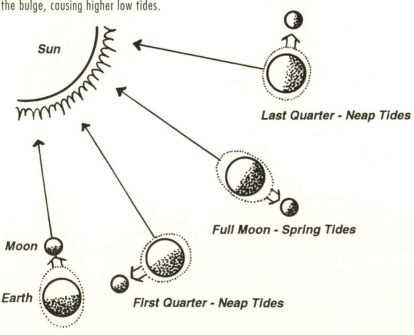

Sun

Last Quarter - Neap Tides

Full Moon - Spring Tides

Moon

Earth

First Quarter - Neap Tides

New Moon - Spring Tides

HUDSON RIVER TIDE TIME DIFFERENCES BETWEEN THE BATTERY IN MANHATTAN AND POINTS UPRIVER

	High water hrs. / mins.	Low water hrs. / mins.
George Washington Bridge	+ 0 50	+ 0 46
Tarrytown	+ 1 49	+ 1 57
Peekskill	+ 2 28	+ 3 03
Newburgh	+ 3 46	+ 4 03
Poughkeepsie	+ 4 34	+ 4 46
Kingston	+ 5 20	+ 5 34
Catskill	+ 6 41	+ 6 58
Albany	+ 8 55	+ 9 21

These differences are predictions from standard tide tables; they will vary depending on runoff and weather.

(Data from National Ocean Survey Tide Tables.)

ward on an ebb current for about six hours, then view the same scenery again as the flood current pushed the raft back upstream for the next six hours, and endure it yet again as the ebb current took over once more.

The velocity of the Hudson's currents varies depending on the strength of tidal forces at a given time, location along the river, and weather conditions. Currents are swiftest near the George Washington Bridge (average flood 1.9 mph; ebb 2.6 mph) and farther north around Catskill (flood 1.9 mph; ebb 2.4 mph). The ebb current is generally stronger than the flood; thus our Hudson River rafter would eventually reach New York Harbor. Starting at Troy, a very rough estimate of the time necessary for the trip is 126 days, the "flushing rate" of the system.

The flushing rate depends on the volume of fresh water flowing into and through the tidal Hudson. This flow varies greatly, largely on a seasonal basis. For example, spring's heavy rains and melting snow and ice increase runoff and the flushing rate during that season. But freshwater flow is usually only a small fraction of the water moving past a given point in the river; most of that movement is water being sloshed back and forth by tidal currents.

Tide information is available in tide tables or in almanacs accompanying the weather report in major newspapers. However, at any given time different parts of the river will be experiencing different tides. Since the Hudson's tides are generated in the ocean, there is an increasing lag in the timing of a specific event as one moves away from the sea. The crest of a high tide which occurs at the Battery at 12:00 noon will not reach Poughkeepsie until about 4:30 P.M., and Albany around 9:00. The accompanying table shows lag times based on high and low tides at the Battery.

The Hudson Estuary

Tides are not the only evidence of ocean influence in the Hudson. Swimmers escaping summer's heat with a dip in the river at Croton, or sailors hit with a faceful of spray as they tack across the Tappan Zee, might have their tastebuds surprised by the tang of salt water. They learn by experience that the lower Hudson is an estuary, a semi-enclosed coastal body of water freely connected to the sea, in which salty seawater is mixed and diluted with fresh water running off the land.

The Salt Front

Fresh Hudson River water contains some salt, typically about 20 parts per million (ppm).[6] In moving downriver one reaches a point where salinity starts to rise above that level. This is the salt front—the leading edge of seawater entering the river. While the term suggests a sharp line of demarcation, seawater at the front is greatly diluted and only slightly saltier than fresh water; the difference is not apparent to the eye or to most taste buds. Salinity increases downriver from the salt front, reaching about 35,000 ppm (more commonly expressed as 35 parts per thousand—ppt) of salt in the waters of the open ocean. By the way, the word "salt" is used loosely here; it includes all the dissolved chemicals in seawater. Sodium chloride—common table salt—accounts for about 78 percent of the mix; magnesium chloride another 11 percent or so.

Hudson River literature is somewhat inconsistent about what salt concentration actually defines the salt front's location. The Hudson supplies drinking water for a number of communities, and many studies related to this use locate the front where salinity reaches 100 ppm; a few refer to a lower standard of 50 ppm.[7] Ecologists studying estuaries have a different convention, defining water as fresh until the salt reaches a concentration of 500 ppm (0.5 ppt). The lower conventions are preferred in the former studies since public health laws set a limit of 250 ppm of chloride in drinking water supplies, mainly for reasons of taste.

The salt front's movements up and down the Hudson (and correspondingly the salinity at any point) show an annual pattern linked to seasonal weather conditions and resulting freshwater runoff. Spring's runoff surges against the salty ocean water, pushing it well downriver. As freshwater flow slackens through the summer months, salt water penetrates farther upriver, only to be driven seaward again as rainfall increases in late autumn.

Superimposed on this seasonal pattern are daily movements of the salt front with the ebb and flood tidal currents, the former causing the salt to retreat toward the Atlantic, the latter pushing it upriver.

So how far up the Hudson does the salt front travel? In a year with typical amounts and patterns of precipitation, the salt front reaches Newburgh Bay, 60 miles north of the Battery, during summer or early fall. Drought conditions reduce freshwater runoff, allowing the salt front to push farther north. In dry spells during the mid-1960s and in 1985, salinities exceeded 100 ppm at Poughkeepsie, 75 miles upriver. Spring runoff and major storms can push the salt front well below the Tappan Zee Bridge, and sometimes south to Manhattan.

Salinity from Top to Bottom

One would expect salinity in estuaries to increase as one moves from the salt front toward the ocean. Less obviously, salinity often increases from surface to bottom at a given place in an estuary. Fresh water is less dense than salt water; in an idealized estuary fresh water would flow seaward on top of a wedge of saltier water pushing in from the ocean.

In the Hudson estuary, such layering—also termed "stratification"—occurs in limited fashion according to runoff conditions, geographic location, and current velocity. During times of high freshwater flow, salin-

The volume of freshwater runoff into the Hudson determines the salt front's location. Typically, runoff is greatest—and the front is farthest south—in spring. Freshwater flow is least—and the front is farthest north—during the drier summer months. Ocean water at the salt front is greatly diluted by fresh water; salinity increases as one moves toward the sea.

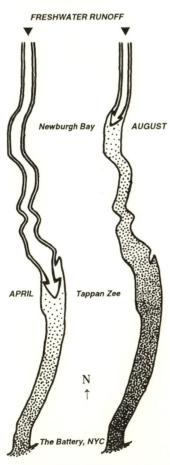

FRESHWATER RUNOFF

Newburgh Bay   AUGUST

APRIL   Tappan Zee

N
↑

The Battery, NYC

SALTY OCEAN WATER

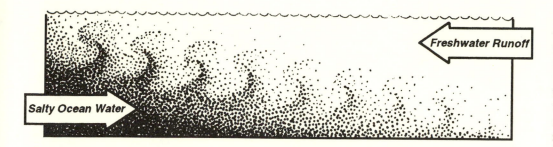

Salty Ocean Water

Freshwater Runoff

In many estuaries, fresh water flows seaward over denser salt water intruding inland. Though some layering can be observed in the Hudson from the Tappan Zee south, friction between the layers creates turbulence, which mixes them and moderates differences between salinities near the surface and in the depths. Such turbulence and mixing are intensified by the back and forth motion of tidal currents and by irregularities in the river's bed and course.

ity at the bottom is, on average, about 20 percent greater than at the surface. In low flow periods, the average difference is reduced to about 10 percent.

However, these averages mask the variation that occurs from place to place on the Hudson. Through the Highlands salinity is fairly uniform from top to bottom because turbulence disrupts the smooth flow of the layers and mixes them together. The turbulence is caused by the river's twisting course through the mountains and bottom irregularities like reefs and deep holes. The Hudson's waters generally remain well mixed into Haverstraw Bay. From the southern end of the Tappan Zee to New York Harbor, the channel straightens out and current velocities increase, promoting stratification. In this stretch of the river salinities at the bottom can be three or four times greater than those near the surface.

Salinity and Productivity

In many estuaries, the layering of outgoing fresh water over intruding salt water contributes to high biological productivity. The richest estuaries rank among the most productive ecosytems on the planet, matching tropical rain forests and coral reefs. They are typically more productive than either the freshwater systems draining into them or the oceans beyond their mouths. Estuaries frequently generate or collect

more nutrients and organic material than they can use, a surplus eventually exported to the benefit of nearby coastal waters.

In some estuaries, stratification of fresh and salt water promotes high productivity through creation of a nutrient trap. The landward movement of seawater underneath less dense fresh water tends to keep nutrients in an estuary, and friction between the layers creates turbulence which circulates nutrients upward toward well-lit surface waters. There algae and other tiny organisms can readily take advantage of these vital substances and grow in great abundance.

However, recent research suggests that this physical trapping phenomenon does not play an important role in promoting productivity in the Hudson estuary. Scientists have discovered that the most productive regions of the estuary are not located where stratification of salt water and fresh water is greatest.

Nonetheless, the Hudson estuary is clearly a productive ecosystem; the huge rafts of waterfowl floating on its surface and tremendous schools of striped bass that annually appear in its waters are eloquent evidence of this. The factors that do account for this wealth of life and the ways in which this biological productivity is defined and measured are the subject of the next chapter.

Chapter 2

Energy Flow and Nutrient Cycles in the Hudson

The Chapter in Brief

Ecologists often describe ecosystems in budgetary terms, tracking inputs, outputs, and available quantities of energy and nutrients. Solar energy, captured by green plants, is bound up in food molecules that travel through food webs made up of herbivores, carnivores, and detritivores. In the Hudson, much of the energy stored by plants enters food webs as detritus after the plants die. Energy is *not* recycled through food chains, but is ultimately converted into forms unusable by living creatures. Carbon, nitrogen, and phosphorus *are* recycled. Most of the detritus, carbon, nitrogen, and phosphorus available to organisms in the Hudson estuary comes from sources outside the estuary; human sewage is a major source of these substances. Growth of organisms can be controlled by scarcity of a single limiting factor, even if other vital substances are present in abundance.

Ecological Budgets

Budgets and the bottom line often dominate headlines. How much money is coming in? From what sources? How much is going out? To where? What limits does lack of resources place on society?

Over the past few decades many scientists have adopted a budgetary perspective in looking at nature's structure and function. They use budgets to track and describe the flow of energy and vital nutrients in ecosystems, functional units encompassing interacting living organisms and all aspects of the physical environment inhabited by these organisms. The study of relationships between living organisms and their environments constitutes the science of ecology.

In *Fundamentals of Ecology*, Eugene Odum notes that the words "ecology" and "economics" have the same root—the Greek word *oikos*, meaning "house"—and he points out that "economics deals with financial housekeeping and ecology deals with environmental housekeeping." Perhaps the most basic item in a household budget is food, and the most important task

of human housekeeping is keeping oneself or one's family fed. The flow of food is also key to ecological housekeeping—and a good place to start discussion of Hudson River ecology.

Food Chains: A Deli-style Approach

On a cloudless September morning the rising sun clears the hills along the Hudson's eastern shore and shines down on the shallows of the Green Flat just north of Saugerties. Its rays light a bed of wild celery, the plant's long, tapelike leaves gently undulating in the current. On many leaves are green, hairlike growths of algae. As sunlight enters each algal cell, the tiny plant's photosynthetic machinery starts humming, converting light energy into the chemical energy of sugar and other molecules that build and maintain protoplasm.

Nosing along one of the wild celery leaves is a half-inch-long amphipod, browsing on the algae, digesting plant protoplasm and converting it into animal tissue. The amphipod's algal food also fuels muscular

activity, as when the creature launches itself off the leaf, swimming away from the bright sun and toward a thicker, more shadowy patch of vegetation.

A bluegill sunfish, alert and hungry, spots the amphipod spiraling downward and with a quick burst of speed intercepts it, gobbling it down whole. Still hungry, the sunfish slowly swims downcurrent to explore a couple of sticks reaching upward through the surface and out of its watery world.

With only the slightest motion of its head, the great blue heron zeroes in on the bluegill approaching its legs. Experienced, not over-eager, the bird waits patiently for the fish to come within range, spears it with a motion too quick for the eye to follow, pulls the bluegill out of the water, and swallows it. A quick shake of its head, a few steps toward a likely looking patch of pondweed, and the heron resumes the alert wait familiar to anglers everywhere.

Producers and Consumers

The example above describes one of many food chains in the Hudson River ecosystem. The food chain concept allows us to understand important aspects of organisms' roles in ecosystems.

The various meals in this Hudson River food chain, and in almost every food chain in earthly ecosystems (including those that put food on our tables) are repackaged solar energy. Whether a diet includes amphipods, steak, algae, or tofu, the energy contained in those items came from sunlight.

Green plants like the algae in the example above have earned the label "primary producers," since only they can capture solar energy and convert it into chemical energy, stored in the compounds that make

up living protoplasm. Animals and other organisms that cannot make food directly from light must meet their energy needs by consuming these compounds; thus in ecological jargon they are labeled "consumers."

Amphipods and other plant eaters, familiarly called *herbivores*, are primary consumers since they are able to use the chemical energy stored in plant tissue. This energy must be modified through incorporation into animal tissue before it can be used by predators like the bluegill sunfish and great blue heron. Such animals, commonly known as *carnivores*, are categorized as secondary and tertiary consumers according to how far removed they are from the primary producers.

Weaving Food Chains into Food Webs

While it is useful to draw connections between a producer, primary consumer, secondary consumer, and so on to illustrate a food chain, most organisms belong not to one but to many food chains. Bluegills eat (in addition to amphipods) insects, worms, and small fish. Sunfish, in turn, are menu items not just for great blue herons but also for kingfishers, bass, and other predators, whose diets include many kinds of fish, amphibians, and other small creatures. Draw lines connecting all these organisms and the result is a complicated web showing who eats whom—a food web.

Cloth woven of many threads is much stronger than a single strand of thread. So it is in ecosystems, where an interwoven web of food dependencies is more stable than a few independent food chains. If one element drops out of a food chain—perhaps a disease kills off bluegills—then the chain is cut with dire results for consumers

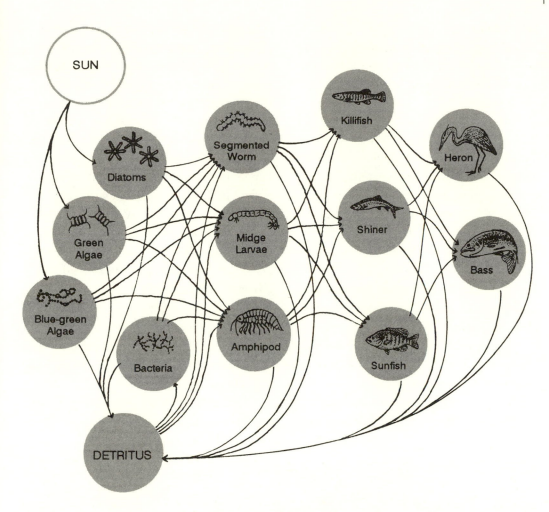

Complicated as it looks, even this food web linking Hudson River organisms is greatly simplified. Sunfish and shiners, for instance, eat a greater variety of creatures than can be shown here, and a host of other animals eat algae.

higher up on the chain. If one organism disappears from a food web, those creatures that eat it may turn elsewhere for nourishment. Of course, while food webs are less fragile than linear food chains, removal of several members can wreak havoc even with such interwoven networks.

Grazing Food Chains

In the food chain described above, the primary consumer is the amphipod eating living green plants, a situation characteristic of grazing food chains. Other examples would be muskrats chewing on cattails in the Tivoli North Bay, copepods eating algal cells drifting in the Tappan Zee, and white-tailed deer grazing on saltmeadow cordgrass in the Piermont Marsh.

One might well ask how another sort of food chain could exist. Aren't green plants at the base of almost all food chains? The answer is yes; however, in some ecosystems, including the Hudson estuary, their energy is not used by herbivores chewing on living plants, but later, as plant tissues die and decompose.

Detrital Food Chains

Imagine a Hudson River cattail marsh at the end of the growing season. Winter is coming; the cattails are turning brown. Looking at this scene in terms of food, we might think, "What a waste! Here's an abundant crop going uneaten, fated to be plowed under when winter's ice scours the marsh. Think of all the starving muskrats in China!"

Besides the fact that there are no muskrats in China, this view of uneaten food, of limited value at a family dinner table, reflects an incomplete understanding of the workings of an estuarine ecosystem. While little of the living plant tissue here was grazed by herbivores during the growing season, there are hordes of organisms ready to feast on those brown cattail leaves as they bend, tatter, and break apart in the clutches of ice and wind. Green or brown, they are a source of food energy.

Dead and decaying organic material—plant parts, bodies of animals, undigested food excreted by living organisms—is called *detritus*. Like living tissue, this material contains energy ultimately derived from

sunlight. Detritus becomes food for small invertebrate animals grouped under the label *detritivores* and for *decomposers*—the bacteria and fungi. As they feed they carry out the process of decomposition. From a human viewpoint, this process might seem to be chiefly a matter of cleaning up unsightly remains. Ecologically the process is important as a means of freeing up nutrients and carbon in detritus and making them available for reuse in the ecosystem.

Detritivores are abundant in the Hudson—mussels, clams, small crabs, worms, and amphipods among them. But, you may ask, wasn't the amphipod acting as an herbivore in the food chain example earlier in this chapter? Yes; the feeding habits of some animals include plant and animal material, sometimes both dead and alive. Such animals are called *omnivores*.[1]

Larger detritivores break decaying material into smaller pieces and alter it in pas-

This decaying plant material in a Hudson River marsh is one example of detritus.

sage through their digestive systems so that it becomes more susceptible to bacterial and fungal breakdown. Detritus that supports large numbers of bacteria is preferred by many detritivores. They obtain additional nourishment from eating the bacteria with the decaying organic matter, just as peanut butter adds nutrition to the cracker on which it is spread.

While carrying out the process of decomposition, these small invertebrates and bacteria provide another pathway through which energy can move up a food chain; the invertebrates become food for predators like the sunfish. Ecologists distinguish food chains in which the links between producers and consumers include detritus as detrital food chains.

Food Chains: A Gourmet Approach

Food chains are sometimes simplistically described as cycles—endless circles in which matter incorporated into plant tissue passes through herbivores and carnivores, is decomposed, and is taken up by plants once more. Molecules of organic matter passing through a food chain are rearranged and ultimately broken down, with their building blocks being recycled back into the system.

While true, such a description ignores the most important function of food chains: they are pathways by which chemical energy in food molecules is distributed throughout ecosystems. This energy *cannot be recycled;* it is ultimately transformed into heat energy of no further use to organisms in an ecosystem.

Energy flow through food chains obeys the two laws of thermodynamics. The first law states that, though energy may change form, be transferred from one location to another, or be used to do work, it is nei-

ther created nor destroyed; none is lost or gained in any of these processes. The second law states that in any energy transfer or transformation, some of the energy assumes a form not useful in doing any more work.

Energy "Loss" at the Molecular Level

These laws affect food chains in several ways. Food chains do not create energy; they only transform solar energy into chemical energy, contained in the forces that bind molecules together, and route it through a succession of further transformations. Energy is not destroyed when food is eaten along this route; the molecules are altered in ways that release energy or transfer it to bonds in different chemicals. After each transformation the total amount of energy remains the same, but a certain portion has become low-grade heat energy no longer usable in the food chain.[2]

Since the total amount of energy transformed into heat increases with each step in the chain, the available amount of useful chemical energy dwindles as we get farther away from the primary producers—green plants. Putting the food chain in budgetary terms, the top consumers get the smallest piece of the food energy pie.

Energy "Loss" at the Organism Level

The impacts of thermodynamics at the molecular level may seem abstract. It is easier to understand how energy is also lost to a food chain by the activities of the organisms in the chain, starting with green plants. They must use much of the solar energy they capture to meet their own growth and maintenance needs. Only the remainder is available to food chains.

Think also of what happens to the

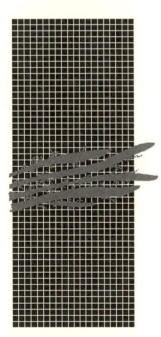

As energy moves through a food chain, the amount available to organisms at each successive level decreases. Ecologists show this graphically as a pyramid of energy, in which the greatest quantity of energy is found in the plants at the bottom, and only a small amount remains for predators at the top.

energy contained in the amphipod meal eaten by the bluegill sunfish (and allow a little more time between that meal and the bluegill's demise at the feet of the heron). Some of the energy contained in the amphipod is in body parts that the fish cannot digest; this energy is lost through excretion of digestive wastes. Of the energy assimilated by the fish, much is used up in activity: swimming, opening its gill covers to breathe, and making chemicals which its body needs to function. What is left builds tissue; it is this small remainder that goes to the heron when it eats the sunfish.

Ecologists have estimated that in going from one level to the next higher one in a food chain, the amount of food energy available is reduced by a factor of ten. Thus in the algae-amphipod-sunfish-heron example above, only one-thousandth of the energy available from the algae would ultimately reach the heron.[3]

Productivity and the Hudson's Energy Budget

With such reductions occurring as energy flows through food chains, it helps to start off with a big budgetary pie—a large stock of chemical energy collected by the producers. This energy pie is called *primary production;* the rate at which energy is stored is called *primary productivity*. The magnitude of this productivity has a major role in determining the diversity and numbers of organisms that an ecosystem can support.

In the Hudson, the greatest portion of the primary production pie comes from the smallest of the producers—tiny algae called phytoplankton that drift on the river's currents.

Cutting Budgetary "Waste"

As mentioned in chapter 1, estuaries like the Hudson can be very productive envi-

ronments, in part because they use net production (total capture of solar energy minus the amount of energy used by plants to meet their own needs) very efficiently.

Detrital food chains are one means by which this is accomplished. In some ecosystems detritus is lost to inaccessible "sinks"—buried deep in sediments, perhaps. The Hudson, though, is inhabited by numerous and diverse bottom-dwelling detritivores. Like skilled pinball players keeping that silver ball in play, these organisms keep the energy and nutrients of detritus circulating in the ecosystem and minimize the burial and loss of these valuable commodities deep in the river bottom.

Budgetary Subsidies

The contributions of detrital food chains to the Hudson's energy budget loom even larger when scientists look at the sources and quantities of organic matter available to consumers in food webs here. The estuary receives a subsidy in the form of organic material washed into the Hudson from its watershed, and detritivores and decomposers are the agents through which that material becomes part of the food web.

This subsidy is considerable, exceeding the amount of organic matter available from primary production in the Hudson itself. Detritus from the watershed above the Troy dam and from tributaries reaching the river below that dam accounts for 45 percent of the organic matter entering the estuary. It is estimated that only 19 percent comes from green plants growing in the estuary.[4]

The timing of that 19 percent contribution from estuarine plants may make it more significant than its size alone would indicate. This contribution comes during the warmer months of the growing season, when biological activity in the estuary reaches a peak and needs fuel. Populations of invertebrates like the amphipod are exploding, and countless young fish hatched after spring spawning runs are growing and eating hungrily.

Much of the detritus from the watershed enters the river in spring runoff, when high flows tend to carry it out of the estuary rapidly, reducing its value to the system. Nonetheless, this detritus represents an enormous amount of food energy, giving detrital food chains a major role in the Hudson ecosystem. In the mid-Hudson, production by bacteria—the store of chemical energy stockpiled among countless numbers of these tiny cells as they consume detritus—is at least four times greater than production by algae.

Tidal currents in estuaries provide another energy "subsidy." In a Hudson River marsh, for instance, the currents bring food into the system and carry wastes away. Many animals—mussels and barnacles, for instance—can live well staying in one spot, not using up any energy in movement. Thus a fairly high proportion of their energy intake goes into building tissue and subsequently becomes available to creatures—waterfowl, for example—farther up the food chain.

The Bottom Line
So what is the bottom line? How much energy is available to the Hudson's food webs? This figure is difficult to measure in such a large, variable, and dynamic system, which benefits from the productivity of several plant communities—phytoplankton, submerged aquatic vegetation, and marshes (see chapter 3)—and from organic material washed in from the watershed.

There are some measurements of primary productivity by phytoplankton. There are also site-specific figures for cer-

tain marshes and beds of submerged vegetation. Estimating from this data, primary productivity in the Hudson is thought to total about 46,200 tons of organic carbon per year.

Contribution of organic material from other sources is thought to total about 223,300 tons of carbon annually. Thus about 269,500 tons of organic carbon are available per year to the Hudson's consumers.

But why are these figures given in units of weight of organic carbon? Isn't this discussion about energy? Remember that food chains distribute chemical

Primary production by phytoplankton is lower in the freshwater tidal Hudson and in New York Bay than in other nearby estuary systems. But primary production is only part of the picture. Detritus entering the river nourishes immense numbers of bacteria, which are a major source of energy for organisms farther up the food chain. The freshwater tidal Hudson ranks highest among these estuaries in bacterial production.

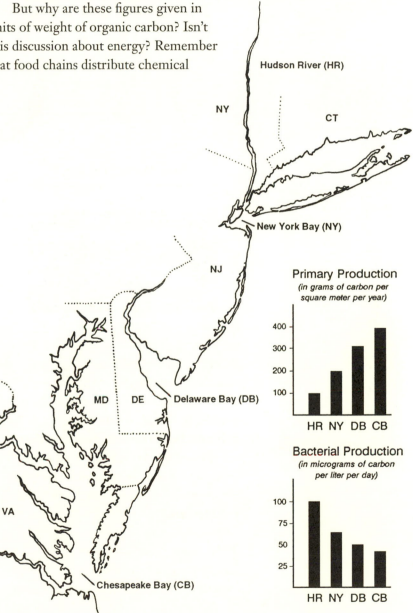

Hudson River (HR)

NY

CT

New York Bay (NY)

NJ

MD   DE   Delaware Bay (DB)

VA

Chesapeake Bay (CB)

Primary Production
(in grams of carbon per square meter per year)

400
300
200
100

HR NY DB CB

Bacterial Production
(in micrograms of carbon per liter per day)

100
75
50
25

HR NY DB CB

This pie chart shows the tidal Hudson's income budget—its sources of organic carbon. The largest source is detritus from the river's watershed. While sewage is the next largest source of organic carbon, construction of treatment plants since researchers gathered data supporting these estimates has no doubt lowered its contribution. Primary production by plants growing in the Hudson estuary accounts for the remainder. (*Microphotograph by Dennis O'Leary/Micro-Optical Methods.*)

THE HUDSON'S INCOME BUDGET
Sources of Organic Carbon

from sewage 36%

from rooted aquatic vegetation 2%

from watershed 45%

from phytoplankton 17%

energy—the forces binding food molecules together—among the organisms in an ecosystem. Carbon atoms are the basic building blocks bound together in these molecules. By measuring amounts of carbon, scientists size up the amount of energy available from these molecules and from the organic material of which they are the constituents.

The Carbon Cycle

Unlike energy, carbon atoms can be recycled through food chains. In describing

this carbon cycle, the best place to jump in is the point where solar energy and atoms of carbon, along with other elements, are brought together through photosynthesis by green plants.

During photosynthesis, carbon in the compound carbon dioxide (chemical formula CO_2) is chemically combined with hydrogen from water molecules (H_2O) to form the compound glucose ($C_6H_{12}O_6$). Molecular oxygen (O_2) is released during the process. The presence of light and chlorophyll—the chemical that makes green plants green—is required for photosynthesis to occur.

The carbon in glucose can move along two paths. Glucose is a form of sugar that can be quickly digested and broken down to provide energy. It is also a building block used in constructing more complex compounds, a process that involves linking together more carbon atoms.

Plants and animals make use of the energy in glucose through respiration, a process that is essentially the reverse of photosynthesis. Oxygen is used in breaking glucose apart, releasing energy, carbon dioxide, and water. Carbon dioxide released by respiration can be reused in photosynthesis, thus cycling carbon atoms back into the food chain.

Use of glucose and its carbon atoms in building more complex molecules can delay the cycling of carbon. This delay might be as long as the life of the sunfish in our food chain example, up to the point where the blue heron uses the energy in molecules of sunfish tissue, or where bacteria and other detritivores use the undigested remains of the fish to meet their metabolic needs. Respiration by the heron and detritivores ultimately will break down the complex molecules, releasing carbon dioxide for reuse in photosynthesis.

Nutrient Budgets and Cycles

While the element carbon is the most important building block of living tissue, other elements are required in lesser amounts. The most significant of these nutrients are the elements nitrogen and phosphorus.[5] Their abundance or scarcity is often key to determining the productivity of a particular ecosystem. For example, nitrogen and phosphorus are the most important ingredi-

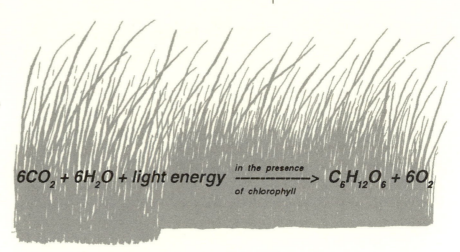

$$6CO_2 + 6H_2O + \text{light energy} \xrightarrow[\text{of chlorophyll}]{\text{in the presence}} C_6H_{12}O_6 + 6O_2$$

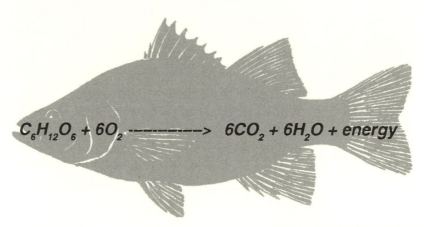

$$C_6H_{12}O_6 + 6O_2 \dashrightarrow 6CO_2 + 6H_2O + \text{energy}$$

Photosynthesis and respiration cycle oxygen as well as carbon. Oxygen released by photosynthesis is used in respiration, producing carbon dioxide to be taken up during photosynthesis, which makes oxygen available again. This oxygen cycle is one of the most oft-cited examples of the interdependence of plants and animals.

ents in fertilizers applied by homeowners trying to establish lush green lawns and by farmers eager to increase crop yields.

Nitrogen, Nitrogen Everywhere, But . . .

In trivia contests and science exams, people are often surprised to find out that the most abundant gas of the atmosphere—79 percent of it, in fact—is not oxygen or carbon dioxide but nitrogen. However, this form of nitrogen (N_2) cannot be used by most living things. To be useful biologically it must be *fixed:* combined with oxygen and hydrogen to form compounds such as ammonia (NH_4^+) and nitrate (NO_3^-) which are taken up by living organisms.

Fixation can occur in a variety of ways. In the atmosphere, nitrogen is combined with the hydrogen and oxygen of water using the energy of lightning and cosmic rays. The resulting ammonia and nitrate fall with rain into the Hudson, as does a much larger contribution of nitrates from air pollution.

Natural atmospheric fixation supplies very limited amounts of usable nitrogen to most ecosystems. A more important source is fixation by living organisms, especially bacteria that live on the roots of plants known as legumes, other bacteria living freely in the soil, and blue-green algae (actually a specialized group of bacteria, called *cyanobacteria*, which photosynthesize in much the same way as do green plants—see

chapter 3). Blue-green algae are common in the Hudson, but their contribution to the estuary's nitrogen budget, though not known for certain, is probably small.

As is the case with the river's carbon budget, most of the usable nitrogen available to the Hudson ecosystem is not fixed in the river itself. Large amounts of nitrate enter the estuary in runoff from the watershed. However, the greatest inputs of nitrogen to the Hudson River come from human sources, especially wastewater from municipal sewage systems (chiefly in and around New York City and Albany), and deposition from atmospheric pollution caused by burning fossil fuels.

The Nitrogen Cycle

Once in the estuary, nitrogen is taken up by plants and cycled through the food chain. Like carbon, it is bound up in different molecules at each step, and either excreted

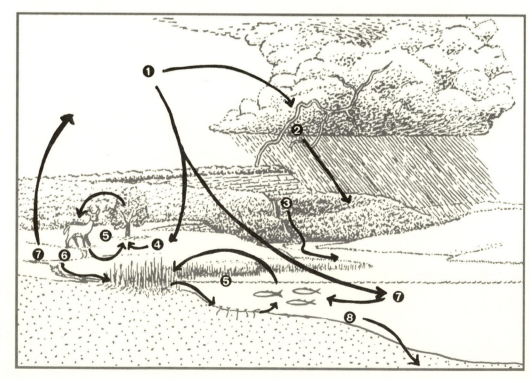

In the nitrogen cycle, here shown in simplified form and without accounting for human inputs, the main reservoir is gaseous nitrogen in the atmosphere (1). Some nitrogen is fixed by lightning and other atmospheric processes (2) to reach ecosystems in rainfall and runoff (3), but most is fixed by microorganisms: soil bacteria, bacteria associated with leguminous plants, and blue-green algae (4). Fixed nitrogen is taken up by plants and cycled over and over in food webs (5). Nitrogen in runoff (6) from terrestrial ecosystems is a major source of this nutrient in aquatic systems. Fixed nitrogen may be transformed back into a gas by bacteria (7) or buried deep in sediments (8).

in waste products or incorporated into tissue that is ultimately broken down by decomposers. In both cases the nitrogen is then available for reuse in the ecosystem.[6]

The greatest amounts of biologically useful nitrogen enter the Hudson with spring runoff. Since this is also the beginning of the growing season, the nutrient is in high demand by plants, which bind up a large amount of nitrogen until fall, when their tissues die and decomposers release the nutrient.

Fixed nitrogen exits the Hudson ecosystem in several ways. Much of the excess supply is exported into the New York Bight, an area of the Atlantic Ocean between Long Island and New Jersey and reaching seaward to the edge of the continental shelf some 80 to 120 miles offshore. And while the abundant detritivores of the Hudson's bottom keep much of the nitrogen in play in the food chain, this nutrient can be in-

corporated into decay-resistant tissue and buried deep in sediments out of the reach of the decomposers. Finally, some fixed nitrogen is bacterially altered back to the molecular form (N_2) which enters the atmosphere.

The Phosphorus Cycle

Phosphorus is often the critical nutrient controlling productivity in freshwater ecosystems, simply because it is less abundant and available than nitrogen and carbon. Unlike those elements, phosphorus does not circulate in the atmosphere as a gas. Thus the sources from which an ecosystem can obtain phosphorus (when humans are not present) are limited: erosion, weathering, and leaching of rock containing phosphate; and reuse of phosphate already present in organic matter.

In the Hudson, organic detritus is an important natural source of phosphorus,

Phosphorus is not found in a gaseous form; it weathers from rock, reaching ecosystems in runoff (1) or leaching into soil (2) to be taken up by plants and cycled and recycled through food webs (3). Runoff from ecosystems on land (4) is the most important source of phosphorus in aquatic systems. Eventually it is lost deep in sediments (5), which eons later may be solidified into rock and lifted above water, exposing the nutrient to weathering once more.

Human activities have increased the amounts of biologically useful nutrients entering the environment, degrading the health of ecosystems by providing too much of a good thing.

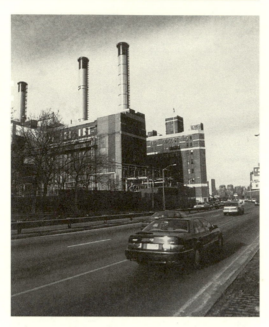

Used too freely, fertilizers containing phosphorus and nitrogen may increase crop yields or make grass more lush at the expense of nearby waterways that receive runoff from farms and lawns.

High-temperature combustion—in automobile engines and power plants, for example—fixes nitrogen, which eventually falls from the atmosphere into terrestrial and aquatic ecosystems.

Dense urban populations may discharge large volumes of sewage into aquatic systems, over-enriching them with nitrogen, phosphorus, and organic carbon.
(Courtesy New York City Department of Environmental Protection/Marion Bernstein.)

just as it is for carbon and nitrogen. And like these other nutrients, phosphorus is released by the decomposers, quickly taken up by plants, and moved through the food chain until it becomes part of detritus again and is released once more by the detritivores. Like nitrogen, phosphorus is taken up by plants at the start of the growing season and released with dieback in the fall. The Hudson ecosystem loses phosphorus to sediments and to the Atlantic.

Research suggests that phosphorus may be in short enough supply to limit the growth of algae in the Hudson north of Poughkeepsie, particularly in late summer and fall. In other sections of the estuary, however, phosphorous is in ample supply due to contributions from the region's human population.

Human Subsidies to the Hudson's Nutrient Budgets

Millions of people live in the Hudson Valley, people at the top of food chains which bring in vast quantities of foodstuffs from around the world. Their digestive wastes—sewage discharged into the river—are major contributors of nitrogen, phosphorus, and organic carbon to the Hudson estuary, particularly in the densely populated metropolitan area of New York City. Additional nutrient contributions that people make to the river include runoff from fertilized fields and lawns, laundry water containing phosphate detergents, and nitrate, originally emitted in automobile exhaust, which enters the river from the atmosphere.

It is logical to think that such subsidies benefit the Hudson ecosystem; after all, these nutrients are vital to the growth of plants and animals. But more is not always better. The increased productivity made possible by greater supplies of nitrogen and phosphorus may lead to algal blooms which ultimately can deplete a waterway's oxygen supplies, killing much of the life in the water.[7] The near "death" of Lake Erie a few decades ago is an oft-cited case of overenrichment by nutrients in pollution. Closer to the Hudson, recent episodes of serious oxygen depletion in the New York Bight and in western Long Island Sound are thought to be linked to such overenrichment.

Sewage has caused severe oxygen depletion in parts of the Hudson, though algal blooms due to its nitrogen and phosphorus content have not been at fault except perhaps in localized areas. Instead, sewage discharges have directly nourished populations of bacteria, elevating them to the point where their activities have reduced dissolved oxygen levels (see chapter 12).

Limiting Factors

Plants and animals depend on many nutrients for growth and health. Of these many nutrients, the one in lowest supply relative to the needs of a given organism or group of organisms in an ecosystem is a *limiting factor*. No matter how abundant the other nutrients may be, populations of the given organism will not be able to grow beyond the levels allowed by the limiting factor.

Nutrients are not the only examples of limiting factors. The Hudson's turbidity limits the penetration of sunlight into the water, which in turn limits populations of algae (and primary productivity). The river's turbulence may also play a role here, swirling algae to depths where there is not enough light for photosynthesis and thus limiting their growth. Scientists estimate that the average algal cell in the tidal freshwater Hudson may spend from eighteen to twenty-two hours of each twenty-four-hour day in light too dim to support photosynthesis.

Other examples of limiting factors include current velocity, the type of material found on the river bottom, and the presence of certain predators. The next chapter will discuss habitats and the limiting factors characteristic of different habitats.

Chapter 3

The Hudson's Habitats and Plant Communities

The Chapter in Brief

Habitats created by erosion, deposition, and other forces support distinct communities of plants and animals according to the mix of physical and chemical factors present, including depth, light penetration, extent of tidal flooding, salinity, and exposure to waves and ice. The effects of these factors are often modified by the living organisms of the community occupying each habitat. In open water, phytoplankton drift near the surface where light is sufficient for their growth. Wetlands covered by shallow water or intermittently flooded by tides contain stands of submerged vegetation, marshes, and tidal swamps. The types of plants dominating each of these communities are distinctive, identifying the community and determining its contribution to the Hudson's overall productivity.

What Is a Habitat?

To a commuter idled in traffic on the Mid-Hudson Bridge, the river might seem featureless, save for a few boats or buoys. A picnicker at Tallman Mountain State Park, looking out over the Piermont Marsh between bites of potato salad, might see only an undistinguished expanse of "grass." But in both cases closer study reveals a variety of habitats created by the chiseling of erosion, the soft sculpting of sediment deposition, and the energies of living organisms, all working on the material supplied by the region's geological development.

A habitat is the environmental setting that supports an individual organism or a community of organisms—a group of populations living in a particular area and interacting with one another. The habitat of an individual organism includes other organisms found in the environment as well as nonliving elements.

To many, the obvious differences between the river's habitat types are structural—features such as landforms, substrate (the type of material on the bottom), and water depth. Other factors may be less apparent but equally important in determining which, if any, plant communities de-

velop in a given site. For example, at first glance the Piermont Marsh might look much like the Tivoli North Bay Marsh. However, the Piermont site is flooded by brackish water; the Tivoli marsh by fresh water. As a result, the marsh communities at these sites have a different mix of plant species, and since the diversity of rooted plants increases as salinity decreases in estuaries, the Tivoli North Bay marsh also has a greater diversity of such plants than Piermont.

The plant communities that develop in each habitat often mediate its functions within the Hudson River ecosystem. These might include contributing energy to the river's food web, cycling nutrients, buffering the impacts of stressful forces, and providing shelter or other necessities for the Hudson's animal life.

The Channel

The term "channel" describes the deep, open-water portion of the river. Its extent and depth vary greatly along the tidal Hudson. Near Poughkeepsie the Hudson is a channel virtually from bank to bank; narrow shoals tucked along each shore quickly drop off to depths of 50 to 60 feet. On the

27

other hand, much of Haverstraw Bay, the river's widest spot, is less than 20 feet deep, and its deepest regions are naturally only 25 to 30 feet deep. A channel 32 feet deep, 600 feet wide, and over 2.5 miles long is dredged through the bay to allow passage of large ships and barges.

The channel generally experiences the full force of tidal currents in the Hudson. Otherwise, its depth and large volume of water moderate the extreme conditions—summer heat, winter ice scour, and wave action, for example—that assail the shallows. Some fishes take refuge in this habitat when such extreme conditions exist.

The channel's depths are not the Hudson's most biologically productive habitat. A key factor here is light penetration, or rather, lack of it due to the Hudson's turbidity. The euphotic zone—the depth of water to which there is enough light for plants to grow—is quite shallow, generally 5 to 10 feet but ranging from 2 feet in late winter to 13 feet in fall.[1] The point where the bottom rises into the euphotic zone marks the shoreward limit of the channel habitat. With insufficient light for plant growth below this point, productivity in the channel's depths is low.

Life at the Very Bottom: The Benthic Community of the Channel

Though plants cannot grow at the channel's bottom, a diverse community of animals known as *benthos* (bottom dwellers) lives just above, on, and in the bottom sediments. With green plants absent, herbivores are lacking here but there are many detritivores feeding on particles of detritus drifting in the water or deposited on and in bottom sediments. Clams and worms are examples of such organisms, which in turn feed carnivores including fish and crabs. The animals of the channel's benthic community are described in chapters 4 and 5.

Life Adrift: The Planktonic Community

In thinking of the Hudson's plant communities, one pictures leaves, stems, and branches waving in the currents or reaching skyward through the water's surface. But out in the open water, drifting in the euphotic zone near the surface, are the real pastures of the Hudson—countless microscopic plants capturing the sun's energy, using that energy to live and grow, and providing food in turn for zillions of tiny animals that graze here. This is the plankton community of the Hudson—plants and animals which, being weak swimmers or

The Hudson's channel is often not in the middle of the river. This ship, bound for Rensselaer with a cargo of gypsum, is hugging the west side of the river as it approaches the Rip Van Winkle Bridge. The map shows why: the channel runs along that shore to avoid shoals in the middle and along the river's east bank. *(Map from National Ocean Survey Chart 12347.)*

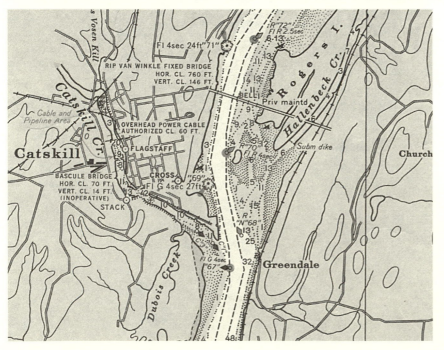

unable to move on their own at all, drift at the mercy of the currents. Animals of this community are called *zooplankton;* they are described in chapter 4. The rootless plants of the community are called *phytoplankton.*

In the Hudson estuary, phytoplankton produce more—an estimated seven to eight times more—of the carbon available to herbivores than do rooted plants such as cattail. These tiny plants obviously make up in numbers and rapid growth what they lack in size. Though present throughout the year, their numbers and productivity peak in summer and are lowest in winter; approximately 90 percent of the lower Hudson's annual primary production occurs from May through October. This productivity peak results from many factors, including the increased light available in summer's longer days and the warmer temperatures of those months. Under particularly favorable conditions, an extremely rapid period of growth called a *bloom* may occur.

Another factor accounting for this summer productivity peak is the minimal freshwater flow through the estuary at that time. Phytoplankton, which drift on the currents, are not washed out of the river as quickly in summer. Similarly, their populations tend to be most abundant in bays, shallows, and other areas where downstream flushing action is minimal.

The most abundant organisms in the Hudson's phytoplankton community are microscopic, single-celled algae and cyanobacteria, which drift as solitary cells or in colonies with more or less distinctive patterns of growth. Most often they reproduce asexually by simply splitting into two cells, each possessing the same genetic material and thus being a copy of the other. Cells may undergo this fission process several times a day, allowing phytoplankton populations to build rapidly, given the right conditions.

The plants we lump together as algae are genetically an extremely diverse group; indeed, most of the genetic diversity in the entire plant kingdom is within this group. For example, the genetic differences between diatoms and green algae (described below) are far greater than those between grasses and trees or pumpkins and corn. And the group commonly labeled blue-green algae are actually photosynthetic bacteria quite different from other plants; they are more properly known as cyanobacteria. So although we talk about algae as a group, keep in mind that the blue-greens are about as different from the diatoms as intestinal bacteria are from oak trees.

Botanists classify the major groups of plants into a series of divisions that are equivalent to phyla in the classification of animals. The algae most common in the Hudson, green algae and diatoms (sometimes categorized as yellow algae), belong to separate divisions—Chlorophyta and Bacillariophyta, respectively. Though the major groups of algae are sometimes designated by color—yellow, green, red, etc.—members of each group vary widely in their actual hue.

Diatoms. Of the algae found in the Hudson's phytoplankton community, diatoms appear with the greatest regularity. Diatoms characteristically have a cell wall made of silica. This wall is formed into two pieces that fit together like the two halves of a pillbox.

Diatom populations peak in early summer and fall, though they are exceeded in abundance then by blooms of green and blue-green algae. Though overall numbers are less in the colder months, diatoms dominate the phytoplankton community during that period.

Green Algae. Green algae are characterized by an abundance of the green pigment chlorophyll localized in cell parts called

Representative Genera of Diatoms

Melosira cells, long and cylindrical, sometimes join end-to-end to form tubelike chains. Often there is a constriction in each cell where the two halves of the cell wall overlap. Frequently the half above the constriction is intricately ornamented, whereas the lower half is not. Many marine and freshwater *Melosira* inhabit the estuary, different varieties becoming prominent as the year progresses.

Asterionella species form starlike colonies in which a number of elongated individual cells are joined together at one end by a gelatinous mass. Freshwater and saltwater species are present.

Cyclotella cells commonly appear as solitary small disks decorated with radial grooves near their edges. Most *Cyclotella* are marine, but representative species are found throughout the estuary, some appearing one after the other in distinct progression during the growing season.

Representative Genera of Green Algae

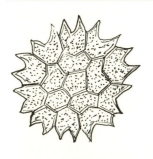

Pediastrum is colonial, with anywhere from 2 to 128 individual cells often arranged in a circular, geometric pattern. Several species occur in the river, some dominant in the phytoplankton community near Poughkeepsie during summer.

Scenedesmus species are also colonial, cells arranged side by side in multiples of 2: 4, 8, and sometimes 16 or 32. The genus is widespread in fresh water; some two dozen species have been found in the Hudson.

Ankistrodesmus, needle-shaped and usually somewhat curved, appears as solitary cells or in loosely formed masses without any particular growth pattern. This group is most common in summer and north of the Tappan Zee Bridge.

chloroplasts. Their cells also have distinct nuclei, as do diatoms. Green and blue-green algae dominate the Hudson's phytoplankton community in summer. Though most common in fresh water, there are some saltwater species of green algae.

Cyanobacteria (Blue-green Algae). Like the rest of the bacteria (more formally called *procaryotes*), cyanobacteria lack most true cell organelles such as nucleii or chloroplasts. However, the photosynthetic machinery of these special bacteria is very much like that in algae and the rest of the plant world. Their chlorophyll pigments are generally localized near the cell wall.

Representative Genera of Cyanobacteria (Blue-green Algae)

Anacystis species occur in fresh and brackish reaches of the river. They form amorphous, free-floating colonies in which spherical cells are embedded in a gelatinous substance.

Anabaena is filamentous, growing in solitary strands or in colonial masses. It is common in fresh and brackish portions of the Hudson estuary.

Blue-greens (Cyanophyta) are very numerous in the Hudson, both as phytoplankton and on mud, pilings, and other surfaces. Most species grow in colonies that form long strands, a habit of growth called *filamentous.*

Dinoflagellates. While included here as members of the phytoplankton community, dinoflagellates (division Pyrrophyta) actually show characteristics of both plants and

Representative Genera of Dinoflagellates

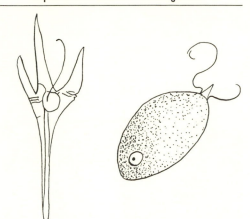

Ceratium might remind you of a science-fiction spaceship. The plates of its cell wall form two or three horns of different lengths sticking out in one direction and a single horn projecting in the opposite one. Most *Ceratium* species are saltwater organisms; one freshwater form is found in the Hudson.

Prorocentrum lives in saltier portions of the estuary. A spine projecting from one end of the cell identifies the forward end of this organism.

animals. These one-celled organisms possess two whiplike flagella which give them mobility. Many species have chlorophyll and carry on photosynthesis. Others are predators that feed on other dinoflagellates. Some can provide for their nutrition in either fashion.

Some dinoflagellates produce poisons toxic to many marine organisms and to humans. Blooms of such dinoflagellates are often the cause of the notorious red tides, during which people must avoid eating shellfish or other organisms that may have accumulated the toxins. These blooms seem to depend on the presence of particular nutrients, and some scientists believe that contributions of nutrients from sewage and other human sources are increasing the frequency of red tides and other problematic algal blooms along our coasts.

Reefs

No coral lives in the Hudson; the term *reef* applies to rock outcrops in the riverbed. Reefs are limited in extent here, and their rocky substrate is inhospitable to rooted plants, so their contributions to the river's overall energy budget are minimal. Anglers favor them, since fish will seek shelter around them. The Hudson's reefs are perhaps best known as sites of shipping accidents involving oil spills; an infamous

This reef extends northward from Esopus Island off Hyde Park. At low tide it is a favorite perch for gulls, cormorants, and other birds. *(Map from National Ocean Survey Chart 12347.)*

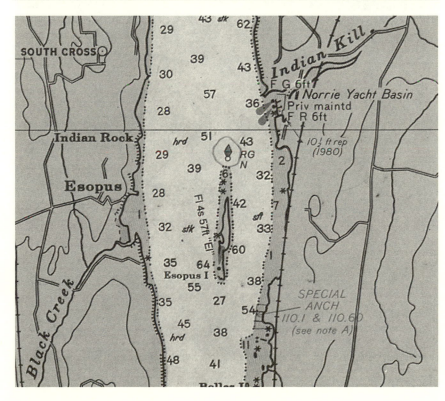

example is Diamond Reef, an underwater tower of rock reaching from 60-foot depths to within 5 feet of the surface midriver near New Hamburg.

Flats and Bays

Tidal flats are expanses of mud or sand in the river's shallows. Portions of these areas may be regularly exposed by falling tides, but the term also includes shoals that remain submerged even at low tide. Along shore, flats can occur as narrow belts or broader expanses like the Esopus Meadows, extending over half a mile into the river. North of Kingston, flats are sometimes found midriver, requiring mariners to pay heed to buoys marking the navigational channel.

In Croton Bay, nestled inside the long peninsula of Croton Point, the river's tidal currents are slowed, allowing sediment to accumulate. Portions of the bay's flats are exposed by very low tides. *(Map from National Ocean Survey Chart 12343.)*

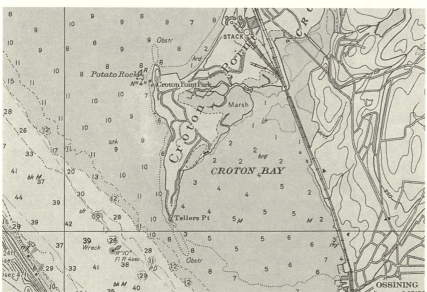

While the extent of ice formation on the Hudson varies with the severity of its winters, in most years there is ice north of the Highlands. Carried back and forth by tidal currents, ice floes scour river flats like these at Esopus Meadows.

Open river flats can be difficult habitats for rooted plants to colonize, being buffeted by the full force of storm waves, boat wakes, and scour by floating ice. These forces stress and uproot plants; thus one may see only bare mud on portions of such flats exposed at low tide. Plant communities most often found here are submerged rooted plants, epibenthic algae, and occasionally low marsh vegetation.

Flats are often broadest near points or breakwaters that jut out into the channel. The water shoreward of the tips of such features moves more slowly than water in the channel. As water slows, its ability to carry sediment decreases; particles settle out on the bottom. This effect is most marked in coves or small bays located between two adjacent headlands. The more sheltered conditions here often allow marsh and swamp plant communities to become established.

Sediment deposition in many coves along the Hudson has accelerated since they were cut off from the main river by railroad causeways constructed in the mid-1800s. This is only one of many impacts humans have had on these habitats. Such impacts, further discussed in chapter 11, are of particular concern because shallow-water habitats are among the most productive in the Hudson ecosystem.

Wetland Communities

The term "wetlands" broadly refers to shallow-water habitats and plant communities that develop there. New York State's Environmental Conservation Law, for example, defines freshwater wetlands as "lands and waters of the state which contain any or all of the following: (a) lands and submerged lands commonly called marshes, swamps, sloughs, bogs, and flats supporting aquatic or semi-aquatic vegetation" and goes on to specify plant species fitting into those categories. Separate regulations governing tidal wetlands use a similar definition.

In wetlands, different plant communities and species grow in response to the frequency and degree of flooding by water. It

may seem too obvious to point out that flooding depends on the height of the substrate above or below the water's surface, but it is important to realize that seemingly minor differences in elevation can make a big difference in the mix of plants growing in a given area.

The Hudson's water level fluctuates with the tides. Their daily and monthly rhythms—and to a much lesser extent the effects of flooding due to heavy precipitation—set growth conditions for wetland plants. Descriptions of where given wetland plants are found often refer to zones of tidal flooding as follows:[2]

> *Subtidal*—below low-tide level; submerged
>
> *Intertidal*—between average low- and high-tide levels; this zone will be alternately submerged and exposed to air over the course of a day; often subdivided into lower and upper zones, the dividing line being the *mean tide level* (the average of high and low water height)
>
> *Irregularly flooded*—above average high-tide level, this area is flooded occasionally by spring high tides and storm-driven tides
>
> *Upland*—area beyond the reach of all but the highest storm-related tides.

Upland
Irregularly Flooded
Upper Intertidal
Lower Intertidal
Subtidal

storm & high spring tides
mean high tide
mean tide level
mean low tide

Wetland plant communities may develop in all of these zones. However, in the Hudson, rooted vegetation is scarce at depths greater than 3 feet (at mean low water). The upland limit is land beyond the reach of the highest tides and floods, where plants adapted to drier soils will dominate.

Over time, many wetlands can evolve into dry land through a process known as ecological succession. Succession is often described as an orderly change in species composition and community type over time. In wetlands, stands of rooted aquatic plants slow currents, allowing sediment and organic material to be deposited, and building the substrate to a higher and drier level. Their own detritus also contributes to this process, setting the stage for their demise as other plant species adapted for drier conditions move in.

However, ecologists have become somewhat uncomfortable with a broadly applied view of succession as an orderly and quite predictable process. In many communities there are a variety of factors—severe disturbances such as fire and storms, for example—which alter, retard, or interrupt the process so regularly that the notion of orderly change has little basis in reality. In the case of the Hudson, no one has demonstrated that tidal wetland communities develop into dry land as predicted in the usual descriptions of wetland succession.

Algal Communities

Many of the algae found in the phytoplankton community can also be found growing in shallow-water benthic communities within the euphotic zone. Colonies of algae can become visible when they attach to and build up on substrates in the water. The dark greenish band sometimes seen on mud banks in the intertidal zone is composed of epibenthic algae—those that grow on the river bottom. The hairy green growth covering the stems and leaves of underwater plants is also formed by algae; this habit of growth is described as *epiphytic*.[3]

Blue-green algae are particularly prominent on mudflats in the intertidal zone. Many blue-greens are very hardy, able to endure extremes of temperature and wetting or drying. This hardiness gives them a real advantage in colonizing this habitat with its changeable conditions.

Attached algal communities, especially in the Hudson, have not received as much study as rooted plant communities. Generalizations about such communities here are thus a little risky. Scientists doing research in estuaries in Georgia estimated that "mud algae" accounted for as much as a third of annual primary production there, making up for what they lack in size by their ability to carry on photosynthesis even in the colder months when rooted plants have died back. But that figure might well be lower in the Hudson estuary, where winters are more severe. Other studies of algae in the soil of tidal marshes suggest that the algal communities reach peak diversity and densities just before and after the growing season for rooted vegetation, which probably shades algae out. Epiphytic algae, on the other hand, reach maximum densities during the growing season when they are abundant on the leaves and stems of submerged vegetation.

Submerged Aquatic Vegetation

These rooted plants grow completely submerged in the subtidal zone. Limp and sometimes buoyant rather than stiff and woody, their leaves and stems are supported by the water and float upward toward the surface and light.

While the productivity of submerged

Dense stands of submerged aquatic vegetation provide excellent habitat for tiny invertebrates and the small fish that feed on them.

aquatic vegetation is not as high as that of emergent marsh plants such as cattails, dense stands of the former can provide a substantial fraction of the river's energy budget. They are an important habitat for many invertebrates—insect larvae, crustaceans, and snails among them. Young fish are often abundant among these plants, finding both a ready supply of invertebrate cuisine and shelter from larger fish also looking for meals. The leaves, stems, and underground parts of many submerged aquatic plants are prime foods for ducks

Representative Species of Submerged Aquatic Plant Communities

Wild celery (*Vallisneria americana*) has long (to 3 feet, but usually less) ribbonlike leaves that grow in tufts, often closely spaced in dense stands. Though considered a freshwater plant, wild celery is found downriver to the brackish Tappan Zee. This plant is a favorite waterfowl food.

Water chestnut (*Trapa natans*), not the esteemed vegetable of Chinese cuisine, is an introduced species. Its rosettes of floating leaves often crowd together in mats, sometimes miles long, which choke freshwater shallows, limit boat access, and shade out other submerged vegetation. Its seed is the sharp-spined, nutlike "devil's head" found in vast numbers on the river's banks. On the plus side, water chestnut beds may harbor large populations of invertebrates and young fish.

Eurasian water milfoil (*Myriophyllum spicatum*), another nonnative species, is considered a pest like water chestnut. Often growing in dense stands in fresh water, it replaces native plants that are more important as food for waterfowl. Milfoil's bushy stems and feathery leaves are habitat for great numbers of invertebrates and young fish.

Pondweeds commonly grow mixed in with a variety of other plants rather than in single-species stands. Some rank highly as waterfowl food. Pondweeds come in many forms; those shown in the next three illustrations, selected from kinds widely distributed both in fresh and brackish water, illustrate this variability.

Curlyleaf pondweed (*Potamogeton crispus*), a species introduced from Europe, has few stems and its leaves have a curly, wavy margin.

Clasping pondweed (*Potamogeton perfoliatus*) has oval leaves, the bases of which clasp around the plant's stem.

Horned pondweed (*Zannichellia palustris*) has linear, threadlike leaves.

and geese. According to *An Atlas of the Biological Resources of the Hudson Estuary,* "there is evidence that the greatest faunal productivity per unit area in the estuary occurs in association with submerged aquatic vegetation and is surpassed only by the sewage-dependent faunal communities off Manhattan."

This community and others in the Hudson have been seriously impacted by the introduction of nonnative species from other parts of the country and the world. The water chestnut and zebra mussel (see chapter 4) are only the most infamous of a long list of such aliens. Some native species have adapted their diets to include the newcomers—the water lily leaf beetle eats water chestnut, and scaup ducks eat zebra mussels—but cannot keep these exotics in check. Human attempts to control water chestnut's invasion of the submerged aquatic vegetation community have included spraying of herbicides and removal by mechanical means. The former is ecologically problematic, the latter expensive. Small areas such as boat landings can be cleared by hand.

Marshes and Swamps

Growing in the intertidal zones of the Hudson's more sheltered flats and bays are *emergent* plants—those which push their leaves and stems above the water's surface. Where trees and other woody plants dominate, the wetland community is called a *swamp;* where cattail, reeds, and other herbaceous (nonwoody) plants dominate, the community is a *marsh.*

Marshes are probably the most productive wetland communities (per unit area) in the Hudson. They are fertilized by tidal currents, which bring in nutrients needed during the growing season. The nutrients are taken up in plant tissues during spring and summer. While some are retained in underground parts of these plants, a large percentage of these stored nutrients is released back into the river during fall and winter as leaves, stems, and other aboveground tissues die back.

Low Marsh. Low marsh occupies the lower intertidal zone, where plants must endure extremes from complete submersion to baking in the hot sun.[4] In winter, this zone is scoured by ice; in warmer months, carp and snapping turtles do a fair amount of digging into the bottom in some locales. Few plants are adapted for this regime, so that species diversity in this community is lower than in adjacent shallows or higher marsh. Those that colonize this area most successfully are freshwater species; in saltier sections of the estuary the lower intertidal zone is largely devoid of rooted vegetation, excepting a few stands of saltwater cordgrass.

The above-ground parts of most of these plants die back and decay rapidly in fall and may be a major source of nutrients to the estuary at that time. By winter the flats on which they grow appear bare.

Spatterdock is the dominant plant in this area of low marsh at Kingston Point. The photograph was taken at low tide; at high tide, these plants will be completely submerged.

Representative Plants of Low Marsh Communities

Spatterdock (*Nuphar lu-teum*) forms extensive stands low in the intertidal zone in fresh water. It has large, heart-shaped leaves up to 3 feet long by late summer and sports a single yellow flower on a long stalk. Spatterdock offers cover but is not grazed much by larger marsh animals; the seeds are eaten by various creatures. It supports invertebrates eaten by fish, birds, and other animals.

Pickerelweed (*Pontederia cordata*) leaves are similar to spatterdock's but smaller and more elongated. Like spatterdock, the plant forms dense stands, but usually higher in the lower intertidal zone. In summer a spike of small, closely packed violet blue flowers crowns the plant. Its rhizomes are eaten by muskrats, the seeds by ducks and other birds. This freshwater plant also grows in downriver sites where tributaries lower the salinity.

Arrow-arum (*Peltandra virginica*) has arrow-shaped leaves with a pattern of veins unlike that of pickerelweed, with which it often grows. The fruiting structure, commonly found floating in the Hudson, is an oval ball full of green berries with clear, jellylike coatings. Ducks eat the berries and shoots of arrow-arum. Also found in the upper intertidal zone, this plant is very sensitive to wave action, even that produced by small boats.

Common three-square (*Scirpus pungens*) is most common in the northern reaches of the tidal Hudson, where flats are more likely to have the sandy substrates it prefers. This plant, grasslike in appearance and up to 4 feet tall, is one of many sedges found along the river. Sedges are distinguished from grasses by their stems, which are triangular in cross section.

Wild rice (*Zizania aquatica*) grows to 10 feet or more in fresh and slightly brackish water, most commonly near the mean tide level and with a more diverse mix of plants than occurs lower in the marsh. Though this grass can form dense stands, its abundance has varied along the Hudson over the past few decades. Wild rice is an excellent wildlife food. There have been efforts in the past to raise wild rice commercially here, notably in the Constitution Island Marsh.

High Marsh. High marsh is found in the intertidal zone above the mean tide level. This is the community many people visualize when they hear the word "marsh": a wetland dominated by reed and grasslike plants, perhaps suggesting a rankly growing corn, wheat, or hay field. The comparison is an apt one, for this wetland community rivals the productivity of intensively cultivated field crops. While muskrats, geese, insects, and other creatures may significantly graze high marsh plants locally or periodically, most of this productivity enters the Hudson's energy budget through detritus food chains. The tough leaves and stems of many high marsh plants make them unappealing

Representative Plants of High Marsh Communities

Saltmeadow cordgrass (*Spartina patens*), also called salt hay grass, was once a common livestock food. The species is usually found above the mean high tide level, where it may be flooded only a few times a month. Up to 3 feet tall, it often grows in distinctive, matted whorls resembling cowlicks. This *Spartina* requires salty water and is present upriver to the Croton Marsh.

Saltwater cordgrass (*Spartina alterniflora*) tolerates fresh water better than *Spartina patens*; small stands are found as far upriver as Iona Island Marsh. This species, up to 5 feet tall, also occurs lower in marshes than saltmeadow cordgrass, to mean tide level and sometimes lower in the intertidal zone. Growing along tidal channels and marsh edges facing the open Hudson, it provides food and habitat for birds, fish, and crustaceans.

Swamp rose-mallow (*Hibiscus moscheutos*), up to 6 feet tall, is not a dominant high marsh plant but has found a niche among the more abundant grasses and grasslike species. In summer the rose-mallow has showy pinkish or white flowers 4–6 inches across. Though found in freshwater marshes elsewhere, along the Hudson it is most common in brackish marshes from the Highlands south.

Purple loosestrife (*Lythrum salicaria*) is a Eurasian immigrant that competes with more valuable native species in disturbed wetlands. Eaten by deer and insects, loosestrife has a bushy form which provides songbird nesting sites. In midsummer, spikes of pinkish purple flowers crown the 5–7-foot-tall plant. Dense stands of loosestrife are most common high in the upper intertidal zone of freshwater marshes and around the landward edges of brackish marshes.

Narrow-leaved cattail (*Typha angustifolia*) is a dominant plant in marshes as far south as Piermont. Cattail rhizomes are a prime muskrat food, and many birds and animals find shelter and nest sites in dense cattail stands. Average height is about 6 feet.

Common reed (*Phragmites australis*) is also known as giant reed, reed grass, and by its generic name *Phragmites*. Its stalks, up to 14 feet tall, are tipped with a feathery flower cluster, purplish in late summer, fading to a silvery tan later. *Phragmites* populations are increasing along the estuary, often at the expense of cattail, which is a better provider of food and habitat for animals. The reed quickly colonizes areas of exposed soil high in the intertidal zone and has capitalized on human disturbances of wetlands.

This photograph of the Tivoli North Bay marsh, taken at low tide, shows the cattail-dominated high marsh community thinning out in the lower intertidal zone along the channel, which must endure longer periods of flooding.

to most herbivores. But after being fragmented by waves, ice, and wind, these tissues become prime food for invertebrates, bacteria, and fungi, which feed animals higher in the river's food webs.

Most of the dominant high marsh plants have strong underground networks of rhizomes (underground stems); these stabilize the underlying soil against erosion by currents and waves.[5] The tough, closely growing stems and leaves also absorb the punch of waves and resist winter storms and ice, often remaining standing through their rounds with that difficult season. Partly because of this buffering ability, the Hudson's high marsh communities offer breeding, nesting, and wintering habitat for many birds and mammals. In similar marshes on open coasts buffeted by severe storms, this shock absorber role is particularly important even to humans, whose shortsighted filling and development of marshes can both destroy the buffer and put structures directly in harm's way.

Tidal Swamps. In many of the Hudson's marshes the upper intertidal zone ends against a steep slope, making the transition from wetland to dry land very abrupt. But in some of the river's freshwater marshes the landward slope is more gradual, and a tidal swamp community dominated by woody plants can be found near the average high tide level and higher into true upland.[6] Its elevation is high enough so that plants here usually endure only brief periods of flooding at high tide. The woody species typical of this community will also grow singly or in clumps on small bits of such high ground elsewhere in the marsh.

The Hudson's freshwater tidal swamp communities have not received much study, but they contain a rich assortment of plant and animal species. Of the many herbaceous plants found among the more prominent trees and shrubs, quite a number grow widely in the upper intertidal zone but are seldom dominant anywhere.

The trees and shrubs of this tidal swamp border a small marsh near Norrie Point in Hyde Park.

Representative Plants of Tidal Swamp Communities

Red maple (*Acer rubrum*) or swamp maple has red flowers that impart a hazy rose color to wet woodlands in early spring. In early fall, its foliage turns brilliant red. Large specimens can exceed 100 feet in height.

Red ash (*Fraxinus pennsylvanica*) and black ash (*Fraxinus nigra*) have compound leaves with several leaflets on one stalk. Red ash leaves have 5–9 leaflets (usually 7), each attached to the main stalk by its own little stem; black ash has 7–11 leaflets lacking such stems. Wood from these trees is used in basket making.

Willows (*Salix* species) take forms ranging from the 70-foot-tall black willow tree to the shrubby pussy willow. Many hybridize, making species identification difficult. Generally, willow leaves are long, narrow, and arranged alternately along branchlets. Species that become large trees usually have several thick, irregularly shaped branches reaching skyward from their bases instead of one trunk. Their bark is rough and deeply furrowed.

Smooth alder (*Alnus serrulata*), is a tall (to 20 feet) water-tolerant shrub in the birch family. Its bark pattern is the reverse of familiar birch bark, with light dots on a dark gray background. Alders have distinctive catkins—scaly spikes that bear inconspicuous flowers lacking petals. The catkins persist through the winter, the more oval ones (which bear female flowers) looking much like small, dark pine cones.

Silky dogwood (*Cornus amomum*) is typically densely branched, each branch tapering to twigs covered with silky hairs and usually dull reddish purple in color. This shrub's leaves are arranged opposite one another along the branches. Clusters of bluish berrylike fruits develop from small white flowers at the tips of the branches.

Jewelweed (*Impatiens capensis*) or touch-me-not is an herbaceous plant found throughout the upper intertidal zone. Three to five feet tall and somewhat shade tolerant, it is prominent in the tidal swamp community. The tubular orange flowers, about an inch long, develop into a pod that, when ripe, will burst open at a touch, explosively scattering the seeds.

Tributaries

The Hudson's tributaries vary greatly in size and impacts on the main stem, and a complete description of their ecology is beyond the scope of this book. However, they are of major importance to the Hudson, delivering much of the detritus and nutrients that sustain the estuary's food webs and serving as critical habitats for many river organisms on a seasonal or localized basis.

The Rondout Creek, a major tributary of the Hudson, enters the river at Kingston. Many largemouth bass move from the Hudson into the Rondout for the winter.

Many fishes ascend tributaries to spawn— alewife and white sucker, for instance. Other species, notably largemouth and smallmouth bass, move from the open river into the mouths of larger tributaries for the winter. Fresh water from tributaries entering the brackish section of the estuary allows plants with low tolerance for salt water to maintain a foothold in those areas.

A Caveat

Having taken many pages to distinguish and describe various habitats and plant communities found in and along the Hudson, we must now add a caveat. When you actually get into a canoe and paddle through these communities, you may find that the distinctions between them are not always as clear as might be inferred from the text. The diversity of microhabitats in marshes, for instance, allows plants typical of one community to appear interspersed among the species of another community. Our ten-

dency to draw lines separating the natural world into discrete categories is helpful and often necessary behavior, but realize that in real ecosystems these lines are sometimes blurred or arbitrary.

For example, New York State's tidal and freshwater wetlands laws differ in procedural points, making their application problematic on the Hudson, which is both tidal and fresh for much of its length. The regulatory solution was to draw a line at the Tappan Zee Bridge: for legal purposes, wetlands above the bridge are freshwater wetlands; below, tidal wetlands. As tidal currents carry them back and forth under the bridge, the algae of the phytoplankton community do not notice any difference.

So while learning to make distinctions between communities, remember to appreciate the ways in which they are inextricably linked together and the often subtle gradients along which one community is transmuted into another.

Chapter 4

The Hudson's Invertebrate Animals

The Chapter in Brief
The Hudson River is home to diverse ecological communities, of which invertebrate animals are important members. Invertebrates in the zooplankton community are major consumers of phytoplankton and are in turn food for larger organisms. Some are planktonic at all stages of their life cycles, others may be planktonic at one or two life stages. At the bottom of the river, invertebrates dominate another life zone, the benthos. The benthic invertebrates include many detritivores as well as herbivores, carnivores, and omnivores. Zooplankton and benthic communities include representatives of nearly every invertebrate phylum.

Animals without Backbones

Invertebrates are animals without backbones, an apparently simple definition. But dig a little deeper—beyond large, showy invertebrates such as butterflies, crabs, and lobsters—and they start to look complicated. Most are small and hard to study casually. Many have a daunting multiplicity of appendages and sensory organs—or seemingly none at all. Names are often in unfamiliar Latin and Greek rather than plain English. Their behavior patterns may seem alien or even repulsive compared to that of more familiar warm, fuzzy creatures. And there are so darn many: 97 percent of the world's animal species are invertebrates.[1]

In ecosystems, including the Hudson River, these animals play roles that correspond in importance to their numbers. They are vital links in food chains. For instance, relatively few of the Hudson's fish subsist primarily on plants; the food energy captured through photosynthesis reaches fish mainly in the form of invertebrates that dine on plants and detritus. A number of invertebrates show up on human menus as well: lobsters, crabs, clams, oysters, and squid. And once one has gotten beyond an initial dislike for creepy-crawly critters and their strangeness, one finds among them some fascinating creatures of great beauty.

A Collection of Communities

In the previous chapter we grouped plants by habitat into fairly distinct communities. Animals can be similarly divided based on the space they occupy in the Hudson. Looking at a cross section of the river, organisms can be placed into three categories.

Living at the river bottom are the *benthos*, or *benthic* organisms: those that burrow in the sediments as do worms and clams; those, like amphipods and starfish, that creep and crawl over mud, rocks, rooted plants, and other objects found there; and those that can swim but usually stay on or near the bottom—the blue crab, for example.

Above the river's bottom is the *water column*. Of the animals found there, some are not able to propel themselves strongly enough to make headway against the current—jellyfish, for example. These are called *zooplankton* (as opposed to phytoplankton, the plant plankton described in the last chapter).

Also found in the water column are the *nektonic* creatures, free-swimming animals capable of traveling faster than the currents of the river. Most fishes are nektonic; one notable nektonic invertebrate—the squid— enters the estuary.

Note that these categories are based on how and where organisms live rather than on taxonomy. They include both vertebrates and invertebrates.

While the definitions of benthos and plankton are fairly clear, precise assignment of the taxonomic groups of invertebrates to one or the other category can be tricky. Most amphipods and water mites, for instance, are benthic creatures, yet there are a few planktonic species in each group. Other invertebrates spend one period of their lives as plankton and another as benthos. In addition, many benthic invertebrates do swim above the substrate, and are often swept up by the Hudson's currents and taken on an unplanned joyride in the water column as more or less "accidental" plankton. Thus placement of the various invertebrate groups in the zooplankton or benthos sections of this chapter indicates their occurrence in general rather than absolute fashion.

A Key Link in the Chain: Zooplankton

The profusion of phytoplankton and detritus found within the Hudson estuary supports an abundance of zooplankton. It is estimated that a coastal estuary provides such a rich habitat for zooplankton that a cubic meter of water may contain several million individuals. Forms of zooplankton include many species of protozoans, crustaceans, comb jellies, true jellyfish, and larval forms of fish, mollusks, and insects.

Many organisms are planktonic in their early life stages and become nektonic or benthic as they grow. Barnacles are a good example; their larvae ride the currents before cementing themselves to rocks and docks. As the young of such creatures hatch from eggs and take up the drifter's life, they create seasonal variation in the makeup of the Hudson's zooplankton community. Early summer, for instance, finds the river laden with freshly hatched planktonic fish larvae. There is also seasonal variation among organisms that are permanently part of the zooplankton: populations of various species of copepods and water fleas peak at different times of year.

Not only is there seasonal variation in the presence of zooplankton, there is great geographic variation as well. Some species are found only in the freshwater stretches of the river, others in brackish water, and still others only in the saltier areas. Some, tolerant of diverse conditions, are found throughout much of the estuary.

Comb Jellies

Among the most fascinating plankton in the saltier regions of the estuary are the prolific ctenophores, or comb jellies. Like jellyfish, they are graceful when supported by water, and amorphous blobs when removed. How-

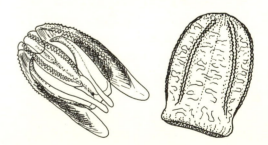

Leidy's Comb Jelly (*Mnemiopsis leidyi*)
Also called the sea walnut, this comb jelly's body is 1–4 inches long and has a slight brown or pinkish tint. The species is often abundant in summer in New York Harbor and is common as far north as Yonkers. The somewhat larger Beroe's comb jellies (*Beroe* species) *right* are also occasionally found in the lower estuary.

ever, comb jellies lack the stinging cells possessed by true jellyfish and are in a phylum all their own—the Ctenophora.

Comb jellies are shaped like an egg with one end hollowed out to form a digestive cavity. The outside of the body has eight comblike rows of cilia, tiny hairs which are in constant motion, propelling the animal slowly through the water. As these cilia move, an iridescent refraction of light can be seen. At night, an eerie green chemically produced light emanates from these cilia. Like insects to a street light, copepods and other creatures are attracted to this odd glow and consumed. Ctenophores have been observed to eat five hundred copepods in one hour.

True Jellyfishes

True jellyfishes are members of the phylum Cnidaria. The familiar jellyfish, an umbrella with tentacles hanging below, is actually one of the two forms in which a single species may exist. This free-floating form is called a *medusa*, after the snake-haired monster of Greek mythology. The second form is attached to the bottom of the estuary; in this benthic form, known as a *polyp*, the creature resembles a plant. Successive generations often alternate between the two forms. The larger species are simply called jellyfish; small species are called *hydrozoans*, their planktonic forms *hydromedusae*, and their polyp forms *hydroids*.

Jellyfishes are opportunistic carnivores, entangling and capturing any prey that happens by in their numerous tentacles. The tentacles are armed with special stinging cells called *nematocysts*, coiled springs waiting to go into action. In some species, the nematocysts inject a powerful neurotoxin into the body of the prey, paralyzing the animal before it is eaten by the jellyfish. The species described here, primarily residents of marine environments, enter New

Representative Species of Larger Jellyfishes

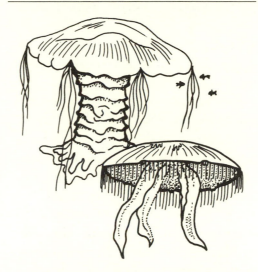

Lion's mane (*Cyanea capillata*) (*top*) is commonly called the red jelly because of the reddish orange color of its cap, which generally reaches a diameter of 8 inches. Young butterfish (*Peprilus triacanthus*) often live among its numerous tentacles, protected from predators. The fish are immune to the poison of the jellyfish and actually feed on their tentacles.

Moon jelly (*Aurelia aurita*) or white jellyfish (*bottom*) is typically 4–6 inches across. The tentacles form a short fringe around the nearly flat bell. In spring when the moon jelly is sexually mature, the gonads appear as four distinct rings looking like craters on the moon. Reportedly, their sting is barely noticeable.

Representative Species of Hydromedusae

Clapper hydromedusa (*Sarsia tubulosa*) has a long stomach tube dangling below the umbrella-shaped body, resembling the clapper in a bell. The medusa is no more than one-half inch across.

Bougainvillia species are similar in appearance to *Sarsia tubulosa* but lack the long stomach tube. Their tentacles are located in four distinct clusters symmetrically arranged around the bottom of the medusa.

York Harbor and are occasionally found in the lower reaches of the Hudson.

Planktonic Arthropods

The phylum Arthropoda contains more species (about 80 percent of all classified species) and more individuals than any other group of animals. Arthropods (including such beasts as spiders, insects, crabs, and lobsters) have jointed legs and an exoskeleton, a hard shell made of chitin. As they grow, they must shed the old shell and grow a new one. It is during this molt that many arthropods are most vulnerable to predators. Of the five classes of arthropods—crustaceans, horseshoe crabs, sea spiders, true spiders and their kin (arachnids), and insects—crustaceans dominate the Hudson River zooplankton community.

Copepods. The most numerous Hudson River crustaceans are the copepods. Copepods are tiny (rarely more than one-sixteenth of an inch long) with bodies that are somewhat pear shaped and distinctly segmented. The head bears a single eye and two antennae; the latter serve as sensory devices and also create a water current that brings food to the mouth. Body segments behind the head bear mouthparts and swimming legs.

Two major groups of copepods are found in the Hudson: the calanoids and the cyclopoids. Most of the river's copepods are filter-feeding calanoids dependent on phytoplankton. Female calanoid copepods carry a single bundle of eggs, looking much like a bunch of grapes, at the base of the tail; they resemble tiny exclamation points darting through the water. Typically, the calanoids prefer saltier water, each species requiring a particular salinity level.

Cyclopoid copepods, named after the mythical one-eyed Cyclops monster, prefer fresh water. They have biting mouthparts and are more apt to be predatory or even cannibalistic. Female cyclopoids usually carry twin bundles of eggs, one bundle on each side of the tail.

Calanoid copepods are a significant food source for young fishes in the saltier reaches of the estuary. Larval striped bass, one of the Hudson River fish most important to people, are almost entirely dependent on copepods. In fresh water, cyclopoid copepods are an important food source for newly hatched fish during a brief period in spring, a role assumed later in the year by water fleas.

Water Fleas. Water fleas or cladocerans are often lumped together under the name "daphnia," though *Daphnia* is actually but one of many genera of cladocerans. While they are crustaceans, cladocerans have a bivalve shell that makes them look somewhat like swimming clams. A pair of large antennae are their chief means of locomotion, though they have small legs used to create a current carrying food to the mouth. Their

Representative Species of Copepods

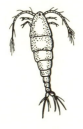  

Eurytemora affinis is a calanoid copepod abundant from March to May, before the river warms appreciably and where salinity is low (5–10 ppt). *Eurytemora* is an important food for many larval fishes, including striped bass and white perch.

Acartia tonsa is generally found in warmer water and at slightly higher salinities (10–20 ppt) than *Eurytemora*. Common downriver in summer, *Acartia* replaces *Eurytemora* as food for young-of-the-year fish.

Cyclops is the genus containing the typical cyclopoid copepods. Many hard-to-distinguish species are found in the river.

large eyes distinguish them from their benthic relatives, the ostracods. Most are less than a tenth of an inch long.

Like the calanoid copepods in saltier water, cladocerans are of key importance to food webs in freshwater portions of the Hudson. One of the dominant varieties, *Bosmina*, attains its greatest numbers at just the time of year when larval fish populations are peaking, making it an important food source for these youngsters.

Larval Crustaceans. Several species of benthic crustaceans are planktonic in their early life stages. Significant among these are barnacles, lobster, and crab. They are primarily marine during their larval phases, though they are often found up into the Tappan Zee. Untold numbers of these creatures' eggs can hatch in a short period of time, during which they may dominate plankton samples. The adult benthic forms of these species will be discussed later.

Planktonic Insects. Insects are the most familiar of the arthropods, their six legs typically distinguishing them from crustaceans and other classes in the phylum. A relatively small percentage of the estimated one million species of insects are adapted for aquatic life, and most of these inhabit fresh

Phantom Midge Larvae (*Chaoborus* species)
These larvae—nearly transparent, slender, and typically one-fourth inch long—move with a distinct jerking action. Eyes and mouthparts are visible in the head region. One pair of conspicuous air sacs is located just behind the head, another near the tail. The larvae are predatory, catching other tiny invertebrates with prehensile antennae. Adults resemble mosquitoes but do not bite or feed at all.

Representative Species of Water Fleas

Bosmina longirostris is abundant in fresh water, reaching peak densities between Hudson and Kingston, typically in June. This cladoceran also occurs in brackish water up to salinities of 8 ppt.

Diaphanosoma species are a bit larger than *Bosmina*. Its head is small compared to its body. *Diaphanosoma* is most common during August and September in fresh and low-salinity water, absent in winter and spring.

Moina species are found in saltier regions of the Hudson, most abundantly in the Tappan Zee and only in summer. It is absent from samples taken in other seasons.

Some Larval Crustaceans of the Plankton Community

Barnacles have two planktonic phases found in brackish and marine waters. The first phase—the nauplius—is triangular in shape, with distinct horns on the corners in the head region, a single eye, and three pairs of hairy legs. The second—the cypris—develops a bivalve shell somewhat obscuring the legs, though the eyespot is still visible.

Northern lobster (*Homarus americanus*) larvae are strange spiny things that only vaguely resemble their parents. By their fifth molt the young are about one inch long, look much more like a lobster, and settle into the benthic community.

Crab larvae are initially called zoeae. They look like a creature from outer space: one twenty-fifth of an inch wide, transparent, adorned with odd spines, two large eyes, and several hairy little legs. After several molts, another larval form emerges—the megalops—which more closely resembles an adult crab.

water. Of these, only the larvae and pupae (a resting stage of development similar to the cocoon of moths) of a few phantom midges regularly appear as zooplankton, and even these spend more time in the sediments of the benthic community than drifting in the water column. Larvae of their close relatives, the mosquitoes, drift on the currents but breathe air through the water's surface. Other insects become accidental plankton when currents sweep them up off the bottom.

Life Down Under: The Benthos

The benthic community in the Hudson is highly diverse, with representatives from nearly every invertebrate phylum. Ecologically, they fill a variety of niches. Some are stationary filter feeders, others are active predators, able to travel with some facility over the river bottom. Many are detritivores, organisms eating dead organic material—in a fashion, the garbage collectors of the estuary. Most benthic invertebrates found in fresh and slightly salty reaches of the Hudson are very small, exceptions being crayfish and the blue crab. In the more saline waters of New York Harbor a variety of larger species are found.

Benthic organisms are present in the river in all seasons. Most year-round resident fish (carp, shiners, perch, sunfish, etc.) depend on this food source, as do the young of many migratory species once they grow beyond the larval stage. Thus the most abundant of these invertebrates, particularly the amphipods, play key roles in supporting fish populations in the Hudson.

Sponges

While sponges are most familiar in the saltwater setting of New York Harbor and Raritan and Sandy Hook Bays, they are abundant in the freshwater Hudson too. Assigned to the phylum Porifera, sponges are the simplest forms of multicellular animals, strange masses of tissue held rigid by tiny calcium-laden spines called *spicules*. Some scientists believe a sponge mass to be one organism; others, a colony consisting of many individual organisms.

Tiny pores on the surface of a sponge

Representative Species of Sponges

 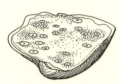

Redbeard sponge (*Microciona prolifera*) comes in bright shades of red or orange and grows in a form looking suspiciously like thick, fleshy fingers. It occurs in relatively shallow waters, below the tide line, and has been found in salinities as low as 15 ppt. The redbeard sponge can grow to 8 inches high and 12 inches wide.

Boring sponge (*Cliona* species) is actually an interesting sponge; its name comes from its growth habit. This species frequents oyster beds, growing on shells in forms ranging from a light crust to a large mass completely engulfing the host. After entirely dissolving a shell, the boring sponge, sulfur-yellow in color, can live independently, growing more than 8 inches high.

bring water into the animal's body, where it flows through a network of canals while food and oxygen are filtered out. Water and waste products pass out through larger pores on the sponge's surface.

Sea Anemones and Hydroids

Many jellyfish kin in the phylum Cnidaria are part of the estuary's benthic community, where salinity is high. These include the sea anemones and hydroids—the polyp phases of the small jellyfish called hydrozoans. The former spend most of their lives in the benthic community and do not go through a medusa stage; the latter are, for the most part, temporary bottom dwellers. Like jellyfish, these benthic organisms all have tentacles—some sticky, some armed with nematocysts—used to trap prey. They

Representative Species of Sea Anemones and Hydroids

Snail fur (*Hydractinia echinata*) polyps encrust snail shells occupied by hermit crabs. Out of the water, these hydroids look like an indistinct brown fuzz. Under water, their extended tentacles surround the shell in a soft, pinkish cloud.

Tubularian hydroids (*Tubularia* and *Ectopleura* species) are found in more saline areas of the estuary. They look much like plants with clear stalks and delicate pink blossoms, the "blossoms" being the tentacles. Prey is stung with nematocysts, paralyzed, and digested by the hydroid.

White or ghost anemone (*Diadumene leucolena*), our most commonly seen anemone, grows on rocks, docks, and the backs of a variety of hard-shelled animals. Out of water it is an amorphous white, pink, or olive blob no more than one-half inch in diameter. When its 40–60 tentacles emerge under water, the animal looks like a beautiful flower.

can retract during low-tide periods of exposure to air.

Segmented Worms

The segmented worms (phylum Annelida) are well represented in the benthic community of the Hudson. Most significant are the bristle worms and earthworms, known to scientists respectively as *polychaete* and *oligochaete* worms.[2]

Bristle worms vary a great deal though they are most often distinctly segmented, have a head of sorts, and possess bristles or little legs helpful in movement. Polychaete worms are most abundant and diverse in salt water.

Almost all aquatic earthworms have bristles too, but they lack a distinct head segment. Among the benthos of the Hudson's freshwater reaches, oligochaete worms are numerically dominant. They play an important role in mixing the sediments of the river bottom and in the exchange of nutrients and toxic pollutants between water and sediment. Some of these worms, notably *Tubifex* and *Limnodrilus*, can survive

indefinitely in waters with little or no dissolved oxygen. Their dominance in a given benthic community can be an indicator of organic pollution; the most concentrated populations occur in areas heavily polluted with sewage.

Another class of segmented worms, the leeches, are most common in freshwater reaches of the river. They lack bristles, are

Representative Species of Segmented Worms

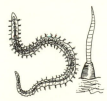

Red-gilled mud worm (*Scolecolepides viridis*), one of the estuary's most abundant invertebrates, has two distinct tentacles on the head, red gills, and prominent bristles along the body, which can be up to 4 inches long. This polychaete constructs a tube of detritus particles bound together with mucus and set vertically into the bottom. With only its head protruding, the worm filters detritus from passing water. It is eaten by crustaceans and fish.

Tubificid worms (family Tubificidae) are oligochaetes, which, like terrestrial earthworms, feed mostly on detritus. As their name suggests, many species dwell in tubes, their mouths down in the mud and their tails projecting out of the other end into the water.

flattened from top to bottom, and possess a sucker at each end of the body. Though infamous as "bloodsuckers," many kinds are predators or scavengers rather than parasites.

Snails and Clams

Snails, whelks, mussels, clams, and oysters—all mollusks of the phylum Mollusca—are among the most familiar invertebrates of the Hudson's benthic community. Though the best known are creatures of brackish and salty water, ninety-two species have been reliably recorded from the fresh waters of the Hudson River drainage basin, and about two dozen of these are common in the freshwater Hudson itself.

Two features found in mollusks and nowhere else in the animal kingdom are the *mantle* and the *radula*. The mantle is a special fold in the body wall that secretes the calcium carbonate shell so prominent among clams and snails. The radula, characteristic of snails but lacking in clams, is a tonguelike organ bearing rasplike teeth. It is variously adapted depending on the feeding habits of particular mollusks. Most mollusks have a foot, a flexible muscular mass responsible for the creeping movement of snails and the burrowing of clams.

Gastropods. The snails and their kin are called *gastropods*. They typically have one spiral-shaped shell and an oozing foot that can be quite large. Some members of this group have an *operculum*, a leathery door that closes the opening of the shell once the foot has been retracted. Unlikely as it may seem for such slow-moving creatures, a number of gastropods—moon snails and whelks, for example—are predators, feeding on even slower mollusks such as clams.[3] Others feed on algae, rooted vegetation, and detritus.

Representative Species of Gastropods

Atlantic moon snail (*Polinices duplicatus*) or shark's eye has a smooth tan or gray shell up to 3 inches across. The enormous foot can be retracted and sealed into the shell. Moon snails are found in more marine sections of the estuary, primarily below low-tide level. Their egg masses, often discovered on beaches, are called sand collars as they resemble a starched shirt collar 5–6 inches in diameter.

Channeled whelk (*Busycon canaliculatum*) shells, up to 9 inches long, have distinct channels in their coils; inside they are yellowish to tan in color. Whelks are found in New York Harbor from the low tide line to a depth of about 50 feet. Their egg cases, cast up on beaches, look like a string of coins made of parchment. Each coin, about 1 inch in diameter, is a capsule containing from 20 to 100 eggs.

Atlantic slipper shell (*Crepidula fornicata*) occurs in the saltiest areas of the estuary. Its shell (up to 1.5 inches long) forms an oval cup, the half open underside suggesting a bedroom slipper. They typically live in stacks in which the bottom individual is female and those on top are male. As the stack gets taller, those close to the bottom eventually become female as well. Slipper shells feed on algae. They often hitchhike on the underside of horseshoe crab shells or on other mollusks.

Seaweed snails (*Hydrobia* species) are found in brackish water weed beds. These animals are no more than one-fourth inch long. The smooth shells are nearly translucent and yellowish brown in color.

Freshwater snails number over 45 species in the Hudson basin; many are common. *Valvata tricarinata* (*left*), about one-fourth inch in diameter, is abundant on tidal mudflats, where it feeds on algae and detritus. It has an external plumelike gill. *Bithynia tentaculata* (*right*), about three-eighths inch long, prefers hard substrates in the intertidal zone, sometimes covering the undersides of rocks.

Representative Species of Bivalves

Blue mussel (*Mytilus edulis*) *top,* the common edible mussel, inhabits saltier regions of the lower estuary. It attaches to hard substrates: rocks, piers, scattered shells, or other mussels, forming colonies. The smooth shell—blue-black outside, violet inside—may be up to 4 inches long. The ribbed mussel (*Modiolus demissus*) *bottom,* a solitary dweller of brackish marshes, has rough ribs radiating outward from the narrow end of the shell.

American oyster (*Crassostrea virginica*) shells, up to 10 inches long, vary greatly in appearance and shape. The bottom shell, usually more cuplike than the top, binds to a hard substrate: rock, broken shell, or another oyster. Empty shells, indicators of once flourishing populations, are common from the Tappan Zee south. A few live oysters remain, and their numbers may be increasing.

Soft-shelled clams (*Mya arenaria*), or steamers, have thin shells 3–4 inches long with an elongated oval shape. They live in stiff mud in the intertidal zone and under water to depths of 20 feet. Their long siphon draws in food and water and spits water when the clams are disturbed. Hard clams (*Mercenaria* species), the wampum clams once used as money by native peoples, have thick shells up to 4 inches wide and broadly oval in shape, with brilliant purple coloring inside.

Pearly mussels (family Unionidae) typically have an oval shell—variable in color outside, pearly inside—up to 6 inches long. Their larvae are parasites of fishes, to which they must attach within a day or two of release from the mother. They spend one to several weeks on a fish, metamorphose into juvenile mussels, and then fall free to settle on the bottom. Shad and herring serve as hosts for *Anodonta implicata,* one of the most abundant of this family in the Hudson.

Zebra mussel (*Dreissena polymorpha*), like the gypsy moth and other infamous nonnative species, is likely to cause trouble, clogging municipal and industrial water intake pipes, for instance. This small (up to 2 inches) freshwater bivalve hitchhiked to North America in the ballast water of ships from Europe. It infested parts of the Great Lakes by the late 1980s, appeared in the Hudson in 1991, and by 1993 had reached an estimated population of 240 billion here.

Bivalves. Clams and other bivalves make up the largest group of mollusks in the Hudson River estuary. As the name implies, each has two shells (valves) joined by strong muscles. The shells close tightly for protection and moisture retention when the animal is exposed to the air. With shells open, a bivalve takes in water, extracting oxygen for respiration and feeding on phytoplankton and detritus. Many species can also extrude a muscular foot used in locomotion and burrowing.

These animals are very efficient filter feeders. In 1993, phytoplankton concentrations in the freshwater Hudson were down 85 percent from historical levels; in 1994 they were about 70–75 percent lower. Scientists attributed this decline to the feeding activity of the zebra mussels rapidly infesting the river. Such declines could have serious impacts on native bivalves, zooplankton, and other organisms sustained by phytoplankton, and subsequently on creatures further along the Hudson's food webs.

While the saltwater clams and oysters are the most familiar members of this group, freshwater clams and mussels are also diverse and abundant in the Hudson. Twenty-three species of pearly mussels have been recorded from the Hudson basin, along with another twenty-three species of fingernail clams. Between the Troy Dam and Castleton, pearly mussels reach densities of 125–200 individuals per square meter. In 1993, the average density of zebra mussels in the Hudson was 1,400 per square meter; up to 30,000 per square meter cover some rocky areas of the river bottom near Poughkeepsie.

The Real Creepy-Crawlies: Benthic Arthropods

Many benthic arthropods are found in the Hudson. In fresh water they are mostly insects and tiny crustaceans. Once the water turns salty, the diversity of insects decreases while that of crustaceans increases greatly. The three other classes of arthropods lacking or not numerous in the plankton community (arachnids, horseshoe crabs, and sea spiders; the latter omitted here) join insects and crustaceans among the benthos.

 Water Mites. Water mites look very much like tiny spiders the size of a pinhead, and in fact are classed as *arachnids*, along with the spiders. They are red or brown in color, and use their eight legs to propel themselves in a rolling manner. Water mites consume their prey, often larger than themselves, by boring a hole in the animal's body and sucking out the liquids held inside. They are mostly restricted to freshwater habitats. Like other small benthic invertebrates, mites are occasionally swept off the bottom and suspended in the water column; there are also a few truly planktonic species.

Horseshoe Crabs. The world's five species of horseshoe crabs, more closely related to spiders than crabs, stand in a class all their own. Their body plan has survived virtually unchanged for over 350 million years; it features a helmetlike body and spiky tail. Though fearsome-looking, the tail is not a sword, nor does it have a venomous sting; it enables the crab to right itself when flipped over by waves.

On the horseshoe crab's underside are five pairs of legs, the first adapted as claspers in the male and the last pair with splayed ends for digging. The mouth is set between the legs, the bases of which break up the animals' food, chiefly clams and worms. Behind the legs are five pairs of book gills, flat appendages that look like the pages of a book. They flap back and forth to create a current for breathing and to propel the animal through the water. On the upper shell are two large, sophisticated compound eyes and several tiny simple eyes.[4]

 Ostracods. Ostracods are even more clamlike in appearance than their relatives the cladocerans. They are crustaceans, though their distinct bivalve shells suggest kinship with clams. Under magnification, the antennae used for locomotion are visible. Without magnification, ostracods resemble tiny animated seeds. For this reason they are sometimes called "seed shrimp." While found in both freshwater and marine habitats, the freshwater species are the better known.

Isopods. Most aquatic isopods resemble their more familiar terrestrial relatives, the sowbugs and pillbugs. These crustaceans are

 Atlantic Horseshoe Crab (*Limulus polyphemus*)
This is the only horseshoe crab of North American waters and is present in New York Harbor. It breeds on some beaches there in May and June. These animals are fairly long-lived; they do not reach sexual maturity until age 10. Females, larger than males, reach a length of 2 feet, including the tail.

Representative Species of Isopods

Edotea triloba has the typical isopod shape and is present from New York Harbor to Haverstraw Bay.

Cyathura polita has an elongated body and its first pair of legs are clawlike. It is one of the Hudson's most abundant benthic species, present from the George Washington Bridge north.

generally flattened from top to bottom and have seven pairs of legs. Isopods eat detritus as well as living plants and animals; a few are parasites of fish. Fish, ducks, and predatory invertebrates include isopods in their diets. While each species has particular salinity requirements, the group is represented throughout the estuary.

Amphipods. Amphipods, also called side-swimmers or scuds, are small, shrimplike animals, typically no more than half an inch long, with bodies compressed from side to side. While they occasionally appear in the plankton community, amphipods are most abundant as benthic creatures throughout the Hudson. Healthy populations of some species in New York Harbor exceed 20,000 individuals per square meter.

In addition to their numerical importance, amphipods are a vital part of Hudson River food webs. These crustaceans feed on all kinds of plant and animal matter, including detritus, algae, tiny invertebrates, and dead animals. In turn, they are a major food source for the estuary's fish. Examination of

fishes' stomach contents has shown that amphipods form a significant part of the diets of Atlantic sturgeon, Atlantic tomcod, white perch, and young striped bass from the Hudson.

Barnacles. Barnacles are benthic as adults, only vaguely resembling their planktonic larvae or their crustacean relatives. They are sessile, attached (essentially by their heads) to piers, rocks, boats, or any somewhat solid substrate. A shell is formed of six calcareous (containing calcium carbonate) plates. Two are overlapping end plates that open and close, allowing six jointed legs to extend beyond the shell, filtering food from the water. Barnacles flourish in saltier areas of the estuary and are found as far upriver as Newburgh Bay.

Shrimplike Crustaceans. Several members of the class Crustacea have a long body, distinct tail region, and often large pincers. These include the crayfishes, lobsters, and the

A Representative Amphipod—
Gammarus
Amphipods in this genus are extremely abundant and readily observed; one study determined that they seasonally constituted more than 30 percent of all animals in slightly salty (0.5–5.0 ppt) parts of the river.

Representative Species of Shrimplike Crustaceans

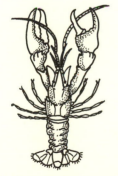

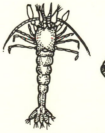

Crayfish (order Astacidae) are the only crustaceans found exclusively in fresh water. Crayfish resemble small lobsters, usually no more than 6 inches long. They frequent shoreline shallows and wetland areas of the estuary.

Northern lobster (*Homarus americanus*) is the saltwater cousin of the crayfish. Those found in New York Harbor are typically 8–12 inches long; giants caught offshore can reach a length of 3 feet, weighing in at 45 pounds.

Sand shrimp (*Crangon septemspinosa*) *left* and common grass or shore shrimp (*Palaemonetes pugio*) frequent shallows from the Tappan Zee south. The former, up to 2.5 inches long, may be translucent or gray in color. Females bear egg masses on the underside of the tail. The smaller grass shrimp is nearly transparent. Both are favorite foods of many fish.

most familiar of the shrimp. Together with the crabs, these crustaceans are grouped in the order Decapoda; counting the claws, all have ten pairs of legs.

Crayfish and lobsters are opportunistic feeders, scavenging the benthic region for anything but the most putrid of fare, including members of their own species. The smaller shrimp are omnivorous, feeding on tiny invertebrates, plants, algae, and detritus.

Representative Species of Crabs

Hermit crabs (*Pagurus* species) are among the smallest crabs residing in New York Harbor, and perhaps those that kids love best. They make their homes in abandoned snail shells, which when outgrown are discarded in favor of new, larger shells.

Red-jointed fiddler crab (*Uca minax*) is found in salt marshes north to Piermont. Their squarish shell can be up to 1.5 inches wide. Males sit near their burrows waving a distinctive outsized claw at passersby, courting female fiddler crabs.

Rock crab (*Cancer irroratus*) has a smooth shell up to 5 inches wide and pentagonal in shape. To the outside of each eye the shell is edged with nine toothlike projections. This crab is common in New York Harbor.

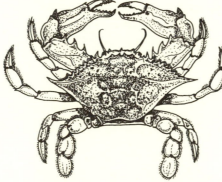

Spider crab (*Libinia emarginata*) has a round shell no more than 4 inches in diameter, but its spidery legs can reach a foot in length. Found in the harbor, these slow-moving scavengers are also called decorator crabs since they are often festooned with algae, hydroids, sponges, barnacles, and other living things that may help in camouflage.

Blue or blue-claw crab (*Callinectes sapidus*) is large and feisty, its shell up to 9 inches wide point to point, its strong blue claws up to a foot in length. Paddle-like rear legs make this crab an able swimmer. In summer, adult males travel well into fresh water, regularly reaching Poughkeepsie and in some years Albany. Females are more common downriver, though they too move north in summer. Both sexes retreat to deeper, saltier water in winter.

Crabs. The true crabs are crustaceans with a broad body, a tail folded underneath as a protective plate, and stout claws. Most are scavengers, but some (particularly the blue crab) are active predators, and the fiddler crabs eat bacteria, algae, and plant detritus.

As with all arthropods, the crab's shell does not grow. As the crab gets larger, it periodically sheds its old exoskeleton, and a new one underneath swells and hardens. Soft-shelled crabs are freshly molted crabs whose shells have yet to harden, a process that takes several days in adult blue crabs.

Gender can be determined by looking at the underside of a crab. Sexually mature females have a very broad tail plate that protects the eggs they carry until hatching. Immature females have a narrower, more triangular plate. The male, regardless of maturity, has a narrow plate, shaped like a pencil.

Benthic Insects. Most insects of the Hudson's benthic community are larvae that develop into winged, air-breathing adults. Some go through a pupal stage as do caterpillars turning into moths or butterflies. Others, called nymphs, have a form similar to that of the adult. They skip the pupal stage, simply leaving the water and undergoing one or more molts during which they take on adult characteristics.

Benthic insects are primarily found in freshwater sections of the Hudson. The wormlike larvae of little flies known as chironomid midges are particularly abundant and important. They are a major food of

Representative Species of Benthic Insects

 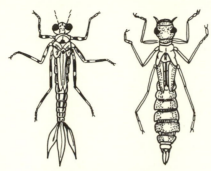  

Mayfly nymphs (order Ephemeroptera) have external gills along the abdomen and three (sometimes two) long tails. They spend 1–4 years in the benthos, feeding primarily on algae and detritus and being eaten by larger insects and fish. After emerging from the water as adults, mayflies mate and die in a few hours or days.

Dragonfly and damselfly nymphs (order Odonata) are voracious predators most common in silty areas and among plants in quiet waters. They capture prey (insects, small crustaceans, even tiny fish) using a double-hinged lower lip armed with spines. Dragonfly nymphs tend to have stout abdomens; damselfly nymphs are more slender with three tail-like gills.

Caddis fly larvae (order Trichoptera) are known for their case-building habit, though not all species build cases. Those that do spin a silklike tube and weave pieces of vegetation, tiny twigs, or grains of sand into it. The larva lives in the case, head and legs emerging as it feeds or moves about. Caddis larvae diets vary according to species; carnivores, herbivores, and detritivores are all represented.

Midge (order Diptera) larvae of the family Chironomidae creep or loop over the substrate, feeding on algae, higher plants, and organic detritus. The adults are tiny delicate flies that often appear in such swarms that they are bothersome even though they don't bite.

many fishes, including young shortnose sturgeon and young American shad.

Sea Stars

Members of the phylum Echinodermata— spiny skinned animals like starfish (more properly called sea stars) and sea urchins— are restricted to marine habitats. Only one species, a sea star, is commonly found in the estuary, and it only in New York Harbor.

Like other echinoderms, sea stars possess a water-vascular system linked to hundreds of tube feet that act like tiny suction cups. These animals feed on bivalves by attaching their tube feet and slowly and persistently pulling the shells apart. When its prey is open, the starfish turns its stomach inside out into the bivalve, and secretes enzymes and digestive juices that dissolve the animal's tissues. Because the sea star feeds voraciously on clams, mussels, and oysters,

it is seen as a pest by folks who make their living harvesting shellfish.

Starfish have an amazing ability to regenerate lost tissue. Any portion of a sea star that contains part of the central disk can regenerate anything it is missing. In this fashion a sea star missing one arm will replace the missing piece, and the severed arm can grow four new ones.

Animals with Backbones— Sort Of: The Tunicates

The phylum Chordata includes animals that have a spinal cord or some form of central nervous system. There are two subphyla. Vertebra, the animals with backbones, includes the fish, amphibians, reptiles, birds, and mammals. These will be discussed in later chapters. Urochordata includes some unusual little animals called tunicates that have a primitive nerve cord,

Common Sea Star (*Asterias forbesi*) Yellowish orange to deep purple in color, this sea star typically has five arms around its central disk. On the disk is a bright orange spot often thought to be an eye. In reality this sieve plate or madreporite filters the seawater that fills the animal's water-vascular system. The actual eyes are located at the end of each arm. This sea star is generally about 4–6 inches in diameter.

Representative Species of Tunicates

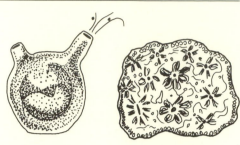

Sea grapes (*Molgula manhattensis*) look like peeled grapes. This sea squirt can reach a height of 1.5 inches, though most are under an inch. Two siphon tubes protrude from the body: one brings water, food, and oxygen in, the other expels wastes. The sea grape is tolerant of rather polluted water and lives in profusion in New York Harbor, often in great clusters.

Golden Star tunicate (*Botryllus schlosseri*) colonies resemble a blob of gelatin up to 4 inches long. The animals, only about one-sixteenth inch long, are arranged in starlike groupings of 5–20, each individual being one point of the star. Each has its own intake siphon but there is a communal discharge siphon at the star's center. The gelatinous mass may be golden yellow with deep purple stars speckled with gold or white, or this color pattern may be reversed.

or notochord, in their tadpole-like larval states.

The sea squirts may be the most familiar tunicates: small saclike animals with a tough, translucent outer coat—the tunic—and siphons that squirt water when the animal is disturbed. Most tunicates are marine animals; a few penetrate into brackish environments.

Long-finned Squid (*Loligo peali*) This is the only squid found within the Hudson estuary, entering New York Harbor. Its body can be up to 19 inches long, though most in the area are smaller, up to 12 inches.

A Nektonic Invertebrate: The Squid

Squid are mollusks with internal shells. The distinct head contains two very sophisticated eyes, comparable to those of vertebrates. The squid's mouth has a pair of strong parrotlike beaks surrounded by eight arms and two tentacles, all with suction cups, which secure prey including fish, crustaceans, and other squid.

The squid can move swiftly by expelling water from its body cavity to achieve a sort of jet propulsion. This mollusk can change color to blend in with its surroundings or eject a black inky substance to obscure the view of predators, affording the squid an easy getaway.

Of Taste Treats and Food Chains

Many bivalve mollusks are well-known taste treats. The abundant and delectable blue mussel shows up in marinara sauce at many an Italian restaurant, and in garlic sauce in Chinese eateries. The soft-shelled clam is steamed in heaping quantities at clambakes or often served as an appetizer. The hard clam is called many different names (quahog, cherrystone, littleneck, chowder clam) and is used in as many ways.

Over 90 percent of commercial shellfish species (those harvested for profit rather than recreation) are dependent on estuaries at some point in their life cycles. However, harvests in the Hudson estuary are limited by sewage pollution. As filter feeders, these bivalves draw in and concentrate the pathogens (disease-causing bacteria and viruses) present in sewage. Clams are harvested from portions of lower New York and Sandy Hook Bays, but prior to being marketed they must be treated with ultraviolet light to kill pathogens or be moved to cleaner waters where they purge themselves of such organisms.

When it comes to oysters, one either loves them or hates them. Raw oysters on the half-shell appeal to some and repulse others. Evidently they appealed to the first human inhabitants along the Hudson; shell middens—the refuse heaps left after their repasts—are common at Croton Point and other upriver sites. There used to be 350 square miles of oyster beds in New York Harbor and upriver as far as Croton, yielding more than a million and a half bushels of oysters per year until 1839. Even into the 1890s, oyster bars were very common in the New York City area. Patrons could eat their fill for a few cents.

Seed oysters (nickel-sized young) were once gathered from Haverstraw Bay and the Tappan Zee and transferred to saltier waters for growth to harvesting size. Hurricane rainfall in 1955 caused a lengthy discharge of fresh water over these upriver beds, killing off the oysters. And beds throughout the estuary have suffered from dredging, filling, and silting, while sewage pollution has rendered remaining oysters unfit for human consumption. Those interested in restoring the Hudson's oysters could take heart from successes in nearby Oyster Bay on Long Island Sound, where oysters and the fishery have been preserved through wise management, mariculture techniques, and observation of environmental laws.

Other mollusks eaten by people include whelks and squid. An Italian dish—scungili—is made of the rubbery foot of the whelk. Calamari is the Italian name for squid, often fried and served with a spicy red tomato sauce. The black ink from squid is used as a coloring agent and flavoring for pasta.

Many crustaceans are very popular food items. Lobster rides high on many lists of delicacies, and the population in New York Harbor supports one of the area's remaining commercial fisheries. Unlike the classic lobster fishery utilizing a buoy for each pot, the harbor fishery uses a string of traps dropped in sequence from the boat. The trapline is later checked for the catch.

Crabs, of course, are a prized catch. The blue crab is the desirable species found in the Hudson; a literal translation of its scientific name, *Callinectes sapidus*, is "beau-

In New York City, both oysters and oyster bars are less common than they used to be. But these succulent shellfish are among the many invertebrates that still earn high ranking on many lists of culinary delights.

tiful swimmer with a most agreeable flavor." While a small commercial fishery exists in the estuary, most of the catch is taken by recreational crabbers.[5] Commercial crabbers can recognize crabs ready to molt, and keep them in holding pens until they do. These freshly molted blue crabs are the soft-shelled crabs found on restaurant menus.

Horseshoe crabs are not used for food and were once considered of little use to humans except occasionally as bait. In 1977, limulus amebocyte lysate, a substance found in the crab's blood, came into wide use. It triggers blood clotting in the presence of certain bacteria and contaminants, a reaction which is used to test the purity of intravenous drugs and, experimentally, in diagnosing some diseases.

We humans are not the only predators that find invertebrates delectable. They are food for many species of fish, waterfowl, and other animals. Though often overlooked because of the splendor of the Hudson's fishes, the invertebrates are just as valuable in the grand mosaic of the ecosystem.

Chapter 5

The Hudson's Fishes

The Chapter in Brief

Over 200 species of fishes have been found in the Hudson River system, many in abundance. A highly productive critical zone in the estuary serves as a nursery for young fish. All fishes share certain adaptations for aquatic life; individual species have particular adaptations for specific habitats and activities. Fishes exploit the variety of habitats and salinity conditions existing within the Hudson, and some migratory species travel throughout the system and beyond. They can be categorized according to preferred habitats, though their mobility makes such groupings somewhat imprecise. A number of the river's fishes support valuable recreational and commercial fisheries in the Hudson and in coastal waters, but PCB contamination has had negative impacts on these fisheries

"This River Is Rich in Fishes"

From our perch in the late twentieth century, it's easy to lament or dismiss descriptions like the one quoted above from a seventeenth-century writer, Adriaen Van der Donck, as one more faded picture from the paradisical "good old days." But in spite of the wear and tear of human abuse of the Hudson, that image from bygone days has not faded as much as one might think. The river still supports abundant and diverse populations of fishes.

As of 1995, experts put the number of fish species recorded in the Hudson River drainage basin at 206. Of these, perhaps 50 are common to abundant in the tidewater Hudson. At the other extreme are 77 strays, wanderers from coastal waters that have been observed here less than five times apiece. The numbers of individual fishes in the river are also impressive. For example, researchers have estimated that the Hudson's yearly spawning runs of American shad in the late 1980s numbered three to four million fish.

Estimating fish populations in an ecosystem as large and complex as the Hudson

is an inexact science. By using standardized sampling methods year after year, fisheries scientists can track relative abundance, noting years when they catch many or few of a particular species and trying to correlate those data with trends in other factors such as fishing pressure or pollution. But determining the absolute number of fish at any given time is difficult. In addition, that number may change greatly from year to year, season to season, or month to month. Shad populations have apparently dropped since their peak in the 1980s. And note the age qualifier in a recent estimate that adult Hudson River striped bass number about

Biologists from New York State's Department of Environmental Conservation net, measure, and release Hudson River striped bass during the fish's spawning run each spring. Using data from scale samples, scientists determine the age structure of the striper population, an indicator of its prospects for the near future.
(Photo by Cara Lee.)

one million fish. The entire population may swell suddenly by tens of millions in late spring as bass eggs hatch, then drop rapidly through summer and fall as these young-of-the-year fish encounter predators and other hazards.

The Hudson River Nursery

The numbers of adult shad and striped bass in the Hudson are grand; its 7-foot sturgeon are awesome. But a real understanding of its abundant fish life and one of the ecosystem's most important roles begins with little fish—the teeming offspring of the big grownups that catch our attention. A Hudson River angler once took a group of striped bass experts from all around the country out fishing for fun on the Hudson. They caught lots of stripers, almost all young fish less than a foot long. When the angler apologized for their small size, the scientists told him they were just as happy to be seeing all these little fish. In many of the estuaries they studied, they only caught big, old fish—impressive, yes, but without the young ones, the prognosis for the future of stripers in those estuaries was poor.

The lower Hudson estuary is a particularly favorable nursery for fish. In fact, the portion of the estuary where the salinity ranges from 0.6 to 11 ppt is recognized as a "critical zone" vital to the survival of fish in their first year of life. The geographical location of this zone varies from season to season and year to year due to changes in

freshwater runoff. But in spring and summer, when recently hatched fish abound, the critical zone typically stretches through the Tappan Zee and Haverstraw Bay. The broad expanses of shallow water here allow a maximum input of the sunlight needed by phytoplankton, and relatively slow currents in these bays allow the tiny plants to build up in large concentrations.

These concentrations of phytoplankton support great numbers of zooplankton. Their abundance is critical to the estuary's newly hatched fish, for it is these tiny invertebrates upon which the fish depend for food. In addition, the turbid waters of the Hudson help to hide young fish from their predators.

Relatively few fish species actually spawn in the brackish water of the critical zone. Of the Hudson fishes most abundant and important to humans, the majority are *anadromous*—spending their adult lives in salt water but returning to fresh water to lay eggs—or are marine spawners. Their young are weak swimmers; they hitchhike on the appropriate river currents to reach the critical zone. The young of many marine spawners move upriver on the incoming flow of dense salt water near the river bottom; the young of anadromous species travel downriver on the outgoing fresh water nearer the surface. Eventually these fish will swim out into the Atlantic. The portion of their lives spent in the estuary may be short, but it is critical to these species' suc-

The *critical zone* is an area of low salinity (0.6–11.0 ppt) water important as a nursery for young fish. The young of species that spawn in fresh water—striped bass, for example—move down the Hudson to this zone; the young of marine spawners such as menhaden move upstream into this area.

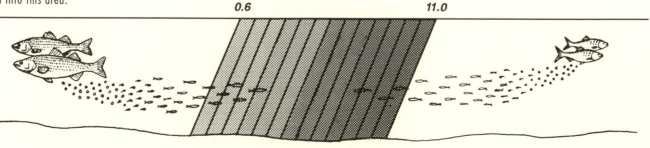

0.6   11.0

cess. Scientists estimate that 65 percent of commercially important finfish along our coast are dependent on estuaries, many during this early phase of their development.

In freshwater regions of the Hudson, marshes and vegetated shallows serve as a nursery for many resident fish species. These habitats provide some of the advantages of the brackish water critical zone: abundant plant growth supports large concentrations of the tiny invertebrates eaten by young fish, and vegetation provides cover from predators.

What Makes a Fish a Fish?

Ask a group of children what makes a fish a fish and some typical responses will be: "They breathe water"—a reference to their gills; "they have fins and scales"—most do; "they're slimy"—frequently true; and "they're cold-blooded"—which is to say they do not metabolically maintain a set body temperature. By the way, the word "fish" itself can be singular—referring to an individual, or plural—referring to these animals collectively. The plural form "fishes" refers to an assemblage of two or more different species.

Looking at these and other characteristics, most scientists recognize three classes of fishes. Members of the class Agnatha (lampreys and hagfishes) lack jaws.[1] Representatives of Chondrichthyes (the sharks, skates, and rays) have true jaws, cartilaginous bones, and plate gills.[2] The largest class, Osteichthyes (the bony fishes) includes those species with true jaws, bony skeletons, and covered gills. Many of these also bear scales.

Fishes are the most primitive of vertebrates, first evident in fossil records dating back 425 million years. Their appearance preceded that of humans' apelike ancestors by some 400 million years, other verte-

brates by about 100 million years. The first fishes, members of the class Agnatha, lacked jaws, as did their invertebrate predecessors. No bones are present in their remains, indicating they had a cartilaginous skeleton which decayed rather than being preserved as fossil (today's lampreys have similar features). From these evolved the sharklike species of cartilaginous fishes, and then bony fishes, which gave rise to amphibians, from which sprang reptiles and eventually mammals and birds. Many organ systems and basic life functions common to the "higher animals" first evolved in fish. With this in mind, a study of fish is a look at our own heritage, distant though it may be.

Supplying the Breath of Life: Gills

Water contains much less oxygen by volume than does air (by about twenty-five times). The need for an efficient method of oxygen extraction is met by fish gills,

These simplifed drawings of a sunfish's head show the main external and internal features of its gills.

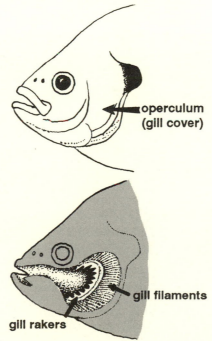

operculum (gill cover)

gill filaments

gill rakers

which can remove at least twice as much oxygen from a given volume of water as land animals' lungs can extract from the same volume of air.[3]

In most species gills are made of several parts including an operculum or gill cover, gill filaments, and gill rakers. The operculum functions like a pump. It seals as the fish opens its mouth to take in water. The mouth then closes and the operculum opens, allowing the water to pass the gill filaments as it flows out.

Gill filaments act much like the human lung. They are feathery structures, lined with blood vessels very close to the surface. As water passes across the filaments, oxygen is absorbed into the blood stream and pumped throughout the fish's body by the heart.

At the forward end of the gills are rows of gill rakers, toothlike appendages that filter impurities out of the water. In many species these strainers trap floating

The gill rakers of the American shad are long, fine, and closely spaced, allowing the fish to filter its food, primarily zooplankton, from the water as it swims.

plant and animal material which is then swallowed as food. A menhaden will swim through rich plankton swarms with its mouth open, filtering close to seven gallons of water each minute. During that time, the fish can swallow several cubic centimeters of food, mainly diatoms and small crustaceans. Fishes that feed primarily by filtering plankton have more highly adapted, finer gill rakers than those with predatory feeding habits.

That Slimy Skin

The body of a fish is covered with two layers of skin, the outer called the *epidermis*, the inner simply the *dermis*. Scattered throughout the epidermis are openings of mucus glands, from which a slippery body slime is secreted. This mucus has several functions. Most significantly, it acts as an antiseptic, killing bacteria and fungi, and thus protecting the animal from disease. The mucus sloughs off rapidly, so that parasitic plants and animals find it difficult to become established on the fish's body. It seems logical that the mucus would also act as a lubricant, reducing body friction and enabling fish to pass more quickly through the water, but in experiments with fish-shaped models, unslimed models fell through a column of water just as fast as slimed models.

Coloration

A given fish species may vary greatly in color from individual to individual; even an individual fish may change its color radically from time to time. Variable coloration can serve the purposes of camouflage and advertisement. Many fishes are colored and patterned to blend well with their surroundings. Most possess color-changing cells called *chromatophores*, located in the dermis beneath the scales. These cells give a fish the ability to match new backgrounds as it moves. Flounder are particularly noted for their color-changing abilities. Studies have been done with flounder placed on black, white, and checked surfaces. On black, the fish become very dark. An opposite response takes place on white. On the checks, the fish exhibit a pronounced mottling, variable with the size of the checks.

Fish are typically dark above, gradually changing to light or silvery below. As a result, a fish tends to merge visually with the background of light in the water. Sunlight is absorbed and scattered as it passes into the water, creating a dark background. The dark back of a fish blends into this background as seen by a predator from above. The light underside matches light coming down from the water's surface, making the fish less visible to a predator below.

Some fishes have color variations that help them to attract mates. Brilliant colors are a form of advertisement, luring a prospective partner. Human knowledge of this trait gives anglers an advantage at times, as fishing lures have been designed to mimic the attractive coloration of ready mates.

When the typical fish's dark back and light underparts are illuminated by the sun—lighting its back and shadowing the belly—the fish takes on a uniform color which blends into the watery background. This phenomenon is called *obliterative countershading.*

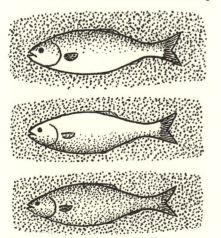

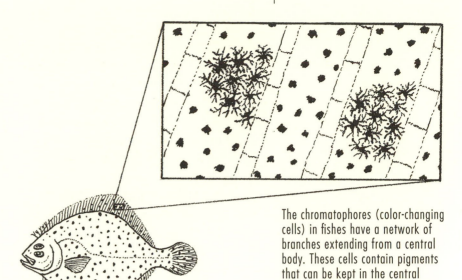

The chromatophores (color-changing cells) in fishes have a network of branches extending from a central body. These cells contain pigments that can be kept in the central body, reducing intensity of color, or dispersed throughout the cell and the branches, intensifying it. Each black dot on this flounder results from dispersal of the pigment melanin within each of a group of adjacent chromatophores.

Scales

The skin of most fishes is covered with some sort of scales. They are arranged on the fish's body in an overlapping pattern quite like the shingles on a roof. This assists in streamlining the body, affording it easier passage through the water. The scales also act as a protective layer, covering the body of the animal like a suit of armor. They vary in size; eels have scales so small as to be nearly invisible, while large carp have scales over an inch in diameter.

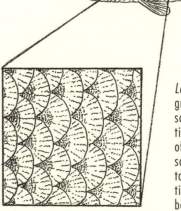

Left: The patterns of growth rings on a fish's scales often allow scientists to determine the age of that fish. *Right:* Fish scales overlap each other to form a flexible, protective body covering, as can be seen on this carp.

Scales grow with the fish, often leaving rings to mark periods of growth. A number of rings are created in a single year, spaced closely during times of slow growth, typically winter, and farther apart during periods of rapid growth. Assuming that each band of narrowly spaced rings represents one winter, researchers can estimate the age of a fish.[4]

A few fishes have no scales at all, the Hudson's catfish and lampreys among them. These tend to be bottom dwellers and secrete a lot of mucus, a necessity in the bacteria-rich environment they call home.

To Float or Not to Float

Many fishes have a swim bladder in their abdominal cavity. This unique organ is filled with air taken from the water's surface, or with other gases passed through the blood stream.[5] The swim bladder acts as a buoyant apparatus, enabling a fish to remain suspended without effort. If required to maintain position by constant muscular effort, a fish might use up more energy than it has simply staying in place. The swim bladder allows a fish to reserve energy for forward movement and such pursuits as finding food, escaping predators, and reproducing.

Anglers may see evidence of the swim bladder if they pull in a fish hooked at considerable depth. The fish's belly may be swollen due to expansion of the balloonlike organ as the fish nears the surface where there is less water pressure to restrict the size of the bladder. If a fish is brought up fast enough that its swim bladder cannot adjust, injury may result.

The swim bladder is found in those fish that occupy a niche suspended in the water column. Generally speaking, fish that reside at the bottom of the estuary, flounder for instance, lack this organ.

Swim bladders have auxiliary functions. They are used in some species as a sound-producing mechanism. Special muscles attached to the bladder's wall vibrate, the bladder itself acting as a resonating chamber, creating a low, audible sound. These sounds are used in defense, mating, and establishing territory. Sounds produced by the swim bladder tend to be very low in frequency. The oyster toadfish, occasionally found in New York Harbor, is notable for the unusual sounds it makes.

The Five Senses . . . Plus One

When we look at the Hudson River, we see its surface and shoreline. To understand fish we must visualize the environment they inhabit below the river's surface. As a result of turbidity, light travels only a short distance, and the channel's bottom may be pitch dark. The bottom is often muddy, occasionally rocky, and littered with dead trees, old pier pilings, remains of boats, tires, refrigerators, garbage, and the like. A variety of submerged plants grow in the river's shallows. All of these things have unique smells. The interactions of water movements, living things, and human activity will create a cacophony of sound. In order to survive, a fish must sort out input from this environment. To this end, fish possess the five well-known senses. In addition, many fishes have an unusual sixth sense, an ability to feel sound and movement in their environments.

Sight. Fish vision is similar to that of humans. For some fishes, there is the complication of feeding on prey that live above the water's surface. Refraction, the bending of light which takes place when light rays pass from one substance (air in this case) to another with very different qualities (water), displaces an object in view from its actual position and requires compensation. Fishes feeding below the surface don't have to compensate for refraction; light rays travel in a straight line through a single substance.

Fish eyes differ from ours in having no eyelids. Eyelids protect eyes but also serve the function of washing them clean and keeping them moist. Living in an aquatic environment precludes this need. The iris (the ring surrounding the pupil) of the fish eye does not expand and shrink to regulate the amount of light passing into the eye. Since even the clearest of water is far less brilliantly lit than air, the pupil remains fully open to let in as much light as possible.

Fish aren't able to see farther than about 100 feet in clear water, and much less in turbid water like the Hudson's. They mostly see objects at quite close range. Those living in the water column or at the surface have more highly developed sight capabilities. Largemouth bass, for instance, depend mostly on their vision to find food. Typically, bottom dwellers like the hog-choker, a little flatfish, have small eyes. As a result of living in a light-deprived environment, the value of sight is lessened. The crew of the sloop *Clearwater* once netted near Albany a 16-inch white catfish with no eyes and no evidence that it had ever had any. Yet it was fat and otherwise healthy. This fish was able to depend on other senses to find food and avoid predators.

Touch. Fishes have a well-developed sense of touch centered in very sensitive nerve organs scattered over the skin, most prominently in the head region. In some fishes, these organs are on whiskerlike barbels, the most commonly known feature of catfish. Fish fins can also provide a sense of touch, highly developed in the searobins, for ex-

ample; these fish have evolved fingerlike feelers on their pectoral fins.

Taste. The senses of touch and taste in fish are sometimes combined in organs with multiple purposes such as catfish barbels. In addition, taste sensations experienced by fish are highly variable, as are the locations of receptor cells or taste buds. A catfish's taste buds are concentrated on the barbels, but are also randomly placed throughout the fish's skin. Other fishes' taste buds are located on the gill rakers. In yet others, taste buds have been located in pads on the roof of the mouth, on the paired fins, and around the lips.

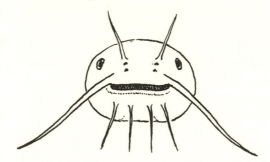

Smell. The sense of smell in fish is highly developed, as much so as in terrestrial animals. It is centered in the fish equivalent of the nose—the nares. Nares are two sets of openings found on the snout. Each set has an incurrent and an excurrent opening. Water passing between the two flows through a chamber filled with many special folds of tissue, increasing the surface area on which smells can be sensed. The water is processed by special chemical receptors that pass information on to the brain.

The sense of smell is primarily associated with feeding, specifically in locating and discriminating among food items. The feeding habits of bottom dwellers tend to depend on smell; it is highly developed in catfish, bullheads, and American eels. Fish also use smell to detect predators, differen-

Searobins, common in New York Harbor, have fingerlike feelers evolved from the rays of their pectoral fins.

Not only do the barbels (whiskers) of catfish serve as an organ of touch, they also contain taste buds that allow the fish to taste-test its food before snapping it up.

tiate between types of aquatic plants (which may be significant in choice of habitat and location of appropriate cover) and in the case of many migratory species, locate parent streams.[6]

Hearing. Many people think fish don't hear due to the absence of any obvious ears. But think again about fishing experiences and the heavy emphasis on quiet. Fish do hear; they have a sophisticated closed ear with no opening on the body. In some fishes, the ear structure is connected to the swim bladder through a chain of bones. In this fashion, the swim bladder becomes a resonator, amplifying the sound produced by vibrations or sound waves traveling through the water. The sounds perceived by the ear tend to be those at higher frequencies, perhaps those made by other fish. Lower frequency sounds are picked up by the unique *lateral line* system, the seat of a fish's unique sixth sense.

Sense Number Six. Along the side of the body in most bony fishes is a distinct line—the lateral line—consisting of special nerve-receptor cells. Each cell has hairlike extensions reaching out of the skin. These hairs are surrounded with a gelatinous substance.[7]

Any movements in the water cause the thin jelly-covered hairs to bend, a movement then perceived by the fish. This sensory system is extremely important to fish, helping as they travel in schools, maneuver to avoid obstacles, or respond to water currents. The sensitivity of the lateral line and the information it provides a fish about even the slightest motion in its environment is one reason fish move so gracefully.

Movement in Water

Using the information processed by all of these sensory organs, a fish works its fins in varying combinations to propel itself through the water. Most fishes have two sets of paired fins (pectoral and pelvic), and three median fins (dorsal, anal, and caudal) located on the midline of the back and of the belly. In many species, two dorsal fins are arranged in a line, and the Atlantic tomcod has three. Some, like catfish and bullheads, have an additional fin—the adipose fin—which serves no function in locomotion; rather, it is a fat store, used during times when the fish isn't feeding much.

Fish can swim without their fins; the movement is mainly a result of side to side undulations of the fish's body. The fins, however, make swimming on an even keel much easier and more efficient. The caudal or tail fin can act as a propeller, moving the fish forward. The dorsal and anal fins function as keels, keeping the fish's travels in a relatively straight line. The paired fins can assist in steering and act as a balancing mechanism, stemming the tendency to roll unmanageably in the water. In some fishes, the pectoral fins act as brakes.

Some fish have fins supported by spiny rays that may also assist in defense. Most notorious are catfish and bullheads, which have a spiny ray in their dorsal and in each pectoral fin that can lock into an erect position. From this arises the assumption that

This drawing shows the fins on a white perch. The pectoral fins and pelvic fins are arranged in pairs. The perch has two dorsal fins, the leading one supported by strong spiny rays, the rear one by soft rays.

spiny dorsal

soft dorsal

caudal

anal

pectoral

pelvic
(ventral)

catfish can sting. They do not sting, but a person who handles a catfish carelessly could be stuck by a spine. Bacteria on the spine can infect the wound, causing lingering pain.

Common Hudson River Fishes

Communities of fishes are not defined in as clear-cut a fashion as plant communities because fish are mobile. Nonetheless, they can be roughly grouped according to habitats they most commonly frequent. Some fishes are benthic residents, living on or near the bottom. Others are nektonic, swimming freely in open water or inhabiting shallow waters and wetlands where vegetation provides cover as well as habitat for prey. In many species, the adults tend to prefer open water while their young reside in protected areas near the river's shore and in its associated marshlands.

Benthic Fishes

Fishes that live at the river bottom have distinct differences from the more free-swimming species. They tend to be comparatively slow-moving and are often solitary. A few are omnivorous, some scavenge the river bottom, and many feed on benthic invertebrates—habits that do not require a great deal of mobility.

Sturgeon. Sturgeon, of which there are two species in the Hudson, are very primitive fishes and in evolution fit somewhere between sharks and bony fishes. Though classified as bony fishes, their skeleton is almost wholly cartilaginous. They do have jaws and covered gills. Five rows of armor plates make sturgeon look like a cross between a shark and a stegosaurus. These plates are most functional as a form of protection when the animal is small and vulnerable. As it grows the fish needs less protection due to its rather ominous presence and size.

Sturgeon are long-lived and reach sexual maturity relatively late in life. Male Atlantic sturgeon, an anadromous species, will not return to the Hudson to spawn until they are at least twelve years old, females not until they are eighteen or nineteen. Subsequently they do not return to spawn every year. When impacted by pollution or overfishing, sturgeon populations take a long time to recover.

There are several sensitive barbels immediately in front of a sturgeon's mouth. When they detect food, the mouth protrudes to form a vacuum-cleaner-like tube that sucks up the tasty morsel. Sturgeon feed on detritus, amphipods, worms, insect larvae, and the like.

Representative Species of Sturgeons

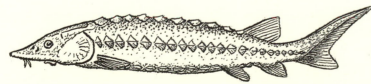

Atlantic sturgeon (*Acipenser oxyrhynchus*) is the largest fish of the Hudson estuary, sometimes achieving a length of 14 feet and a weight of 800 pounds. Mature adults enter the river in April or May, spawn chiefly between Hyde Park and Catskill, and leave by fall. Young remain from 2 to 6 years, wintering in deep water between the George Washington and Bear Mountain Bridges.

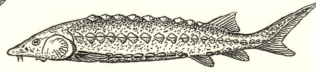

Shortnose sturgeon (*Acipenser brevirostrum*) is not rare in the Hudson, though classified as an endangered species by the federal government. It reaches a maximum size of 3.5 feet and 20–25 pounds. As is true with many fishes, females grow larger than males. Most shortnose sturgeon stay within the estuary. Ninety percent of the river's population may winter near the Esopus Meadows, south of the Kingston-Rhinecliff Bridge. Spawning takes place from Coeymans to Troy.

Representative Species of Catfish and Bullheads

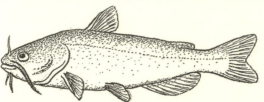
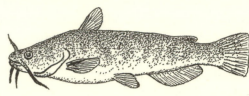

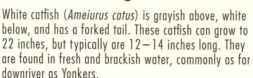

White catfish (*Ameiurus catus*) is grayish above, white below, and has a forked tail. These catfish can grow to 22 inches, but typically are 12—14 inches long. They are found in fresh and brackish water, commonly as far downriver as Yonkers.

Brown bullhead (*Ameiurus nebulosus*) is olive-green to brown above, pale white or yellow below, with a rounded or square tail. The bullhead, generally 8—12 inches long, is usually found in fresh water.

Catfish and Bullheads. Catfish are a favorite catch of many Hudson River anglers interested in putting food on the table. Unfortunately, they are also among the species most heavily contaminated with toxic pollutants. Catfish have four pairs of whiskerlike barbels around their mouths, giving rise to their name. Their skin is scaleless and covered with large quantities of mucus. They have a distinct adipose fin and sharp, serrated spines in the front of their dorsal and pectoral fins.

Flatfishes. Flounder, fluke, dab, plaice, sole . . . all are flatfishes, a group well represented in the Hudson estuary. With one exception,

Representative Species of Flatfishes

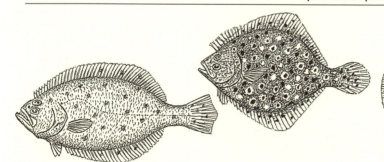

Summer flounder or fluke (*Paralichthys dentatus*) are the largest left-eyed flatfish of the Hudson; big ones, 30 inches long or more, are often called doormats. The fish's brown body is dotted with white spots surrounded by black rings. This is the only flatfish in the Hudson area that has conspicuous teeth. Active predators, fluke range from bottom to top in search of prey; fish form a major part of their diet. They are called summer flounder because, after spawning deep in the ocean, they enter the estuary during the warmer months, when they are a major quarry of anglers.

Windowpane (*Scophthalmus aquosus*) are also left-eyed. They are commonly called sundials. The name windowpane comes from its thin body; its underside is nearly transparent. This flatfish can be up to 18 inches long.

Winter flounder (*Pleuronectes americanus*) are right-eyed, solid brown above, and rarely over 16—18 inches long. This flounder lacks visible teeth but has prominent lips. Adults enter the estuary to spawn in late winter/early spring (hence their name) and move into deeper, cooler water in summer. Young-of-the-year and year-old fish are common residents of the estuary. When New York anglers say "flounder," they are usually referring to this species, a very popular catch.

Hogchoker (*Trinectes maculatus*), another right-eyed flatfish, is typically 3—4 inches long, solid or mottled brown, and nearly oval in shape, with a narrow tail and tiny, beadlike black eyes. The body is covered with small rough scales and thick, viscous slime. Its name reputedly comes from a historic practice of feeding river fish to livestock, whereupon many pigs, which swallow food whole, met their demise as the hogchoker's rough scales caused the fish to stick in their throats.

our species are most common in the saltier waters of New York Harbor, occasionally moving upriver to the Tappan Zee. The exception is the ubiquitous hogchoker, which tolerates both fresh and salty water and is regularly found north to Albany. It is most common from Haverstraw Bay to the New Jersey Palisades.

All flatfish are either right-eyed or left-eyed, depending on which side of their body the eyes are located. At birth, they look like "normal" fish larva, but within weeks the body flattens out and one eye migrates to join the other on what becomes the upward-facing side. This side is colored, typically in a brown or olive shade that blends in with the bottom. The downward-facing side is white.

Eels. Their snakelike shape and writhing behavior when reeled out of the river engenders distaste among anglers, but eels are true fish. The American eel so abundant in the Hudson is a *catadromous* fish: one that is born in salt water, spends the majority (five to twenty years) of its life in fresh or brackish water, and returns to the sea where it spawns and dies. All American eels breed in the Sargasso Sea, a region of the Atlantic Ocean southeast of Bermuda. No one has caught adult eels in the Sargasso, but it is there that the smallest larvae have been found. These larvae are transparent and shaped like willow leaves. In their first year they grow little but manage to drift about one thousand miles on ocean currents to reach the Hudson. As they approach coastal areas they transform into small "glass eels." Moving into estuaries and inland, they gain pigment and are called *elvers*. Eels are very hardy, able to take in a large percentage of their oxygen needs through their skin; they can travel overland when conditions are wet.

American Eel (*Anguilla rostrata*) This eel, up to 3.5 feet long, is grayish green above, white below, becoming more yellow-brown with age, and metallic silver or bronze immediately prior to the spawning migration. Eels have distinct nares on the head and are on a par with dogs in their acute sense of smell. They feed on invertebrates, small fish, and carrion, and are generally most active at night.

Other Common Bottom Dwellers

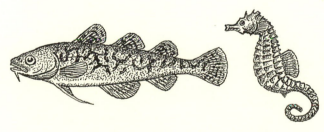

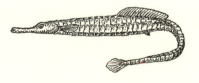

Atlantic tomcod (*Microgadus tomcod*) has three dorsal fins. The body is rarely more than 12 inches long, olive-green to brown with darker mottling and a distinctly white belly. Sometimes called frostfish, tomcod enter fresh water to spawn in late fall and winter; the eggs hatch at a chilly 40 degrees, sometimes while ice covers the Hudson. Tomcod grow fast, feeding first on zooplankton and later on small benthic organisms. Nearly all mature in one year.

Lined seahorse (*Hippocampus erectus*), a fish people are surprised to see here, is quite common from the George Washington Bridge south. Seahorses cling to plants and other objects with prehensile tails and suck up small invertebrates with their tube snouts. They swim by fluttering their pectoral and dorsal fins. The male gives birth; the young hatch from eggs that a female deposits in his abdominal pouch.

Northern pipefish (*Syngnathus fuscus*) is a close relative of the seahorse, and similarly adapted. Its body looks very much like a twig or piece of grass. It is fairly common from Peekskill south into more marine waters. An average pipefish is 6 inches long; a big one may reach 12 inches.

Tesselated darter (*Etheostoma olmstedi*) is an odd little fish (3–4 inches long) of freshwater habitats. Its name comes from its staccato, darting movements. It is a mottled brown color, with two large dorsal fins and a pair of very large pectoral fins. Darters feed mostly on insects.

Nektonic Fishes

Of the Hudson's common nektonic fishes, those that inhabit the open water of the channel are mainly plankton feeders or predators that eat the plankton feeders. Both tend to travel in schools. Nektonic species of the shallows may eat plankton, benthic invertebrates, or other fish. All have swim bladders and are able swimmers, the open water species particularly so.

River Herring. Millions of herring swim in the Hudson. Writers of bygone years describe schools of young shad headed downriver in fall as ruffling the water like a breeze, though the air was calm. The herring are generally slender fish with a very deep body, a single dorsal fin, a deeply forked tail, and a saw-toothed belly. They lack a lateral line but have the same sense organs located in canals in the head region. Most are olive green to blue above, bright silvery white on the sides. Several species have one or more rows of dark spots behind

the upper end of the gill opening. Most herring swim in large schools and feed on plankton; in turn, they are a major food for striped bass, osprey, and other predators. Eight species have been recorded in the Hudson.

Temperate Basses. Of the three species found in the Hudson, the most abundant are striped bass and white perch, familiar as sportfish, as environmental icons, and as the generic fish diagrammed in many biology texts and field guides. These fish have two dorsal fins; one has spiny rays, the other soft rays. They also have strong spines in the anal and pelvic fins.

Bluefish and Weakfish. Along with striped bass, bluefish and weakfish are the premier gamefishes of the region's coastal waters. The two are not related taxonomically but are grouped together here because of similarities in life histories and habits. Both are fierce predators; their young, born in ma-

---

Representative Species of River Herring

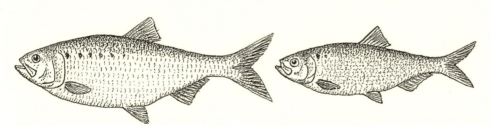
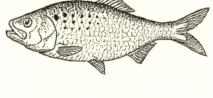

American shad (*Alosa sapidissima*) is the Hudson's largest river herring, reaching a length of 30 inches and a weight of more than 10 pounds. Adults appear in late March, spawning mostly between Hyde Park and Catskill. The young grow to 4.5 inches long before migrating to sea in fall. Maturing females return after 5–7 years, males after 4 years. Many Hudson shad survive the spawning migration, and may live 10 or 11 years, spawning each year after maturity.

Alewife (*Alosa pseudoharengus*) and blueback herring (*Alosa aestivalis*) look much alike, and both resemble shad in looks and anadromous habit. However, they seldom grow to more than one foot long. Both migrate up the Hudson in spring, spawning in freshwater shallows and tributaries, where they are avidly pursued by people with all manner of nets. The catch is typically pickled for food or used as bait for striped bass and blue crab.

Menhaden (*Brevoortia tyrannus*), also called mossbunker or simply bunker, are usually less than a foot long. Their silvery sides may have a golden or brassy cast. This coastal fish spawns offshore in late spring, after which both adults and juveniles enter the estuary, moving upriver as far as Newburgh Bay. They are the major bait used by commercial crabbers from Peekskill to the Tappan Zee.

Representative Species of Temperate Basses

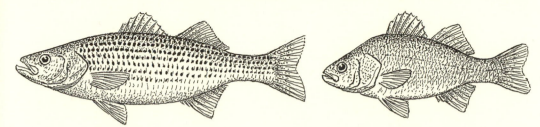

Striped bass (*Morone saxatilis*), sleek and silver with dark horizontal stripes, commonly reach a weight of 30 pounds and a length of 3 feet; a 125-pounder was caught in North Carolina in 1891. The species is anadromous; adults enter the river in April to spawn, chiefly between the Highlands and Kingston. Young remain for at least two years, many wintering among the piers on Manhattan's West Side. Stripers feed primarily on silversides, anchovies, herring, and shrimp.

White perch (*Morone americana*) rarely exceeds 10 inches in length and is a uniform silver color, slightly darker above, with no striping. The body is deeper than that of the striped bass, the back having a distinct arch. This fish, common throughout the river, is most abundant in brackish water. There is a slight upstream migration during spawning in May and June. Young perch feed primarily on small invertebrates, older ones mostly on small fish.

rine waters, enter the Hudson in their first summer to feed on its abundant small fish.

Sunfishes. The sunfish family includes the familiar "sunnies" and the larger black bass so popular with anglers; twelve members of this group have been recorded in the Hudson and its tributaries. Many of the former are distinctively colorful as adults, though their young look quite a bit alike. The oper-

culum of many species has an earlike flap, often with a dark spot on it. Sunfishes are spiny-rayed fishes; the spiny and soft dorsal fins are usually continuous. Most inhabit slow-moving or standing fresh water, often favoring weedy shallows.

Sunfishes have interesting breeding habits. Males build nests in shallow water, often so close together as to look colonial. In some species there is an intricate court-

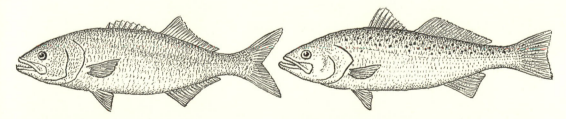

Bluefish (*Pomatomus saltatrix*)
Bluefish are shiny silver with a green or blue cast on the back and a black spot at the base of the pectoral fin. Young-of-the-year "snapper" bluefish range north to New Hamburg, feeding voraciously and reaching a length of 10 inches while in the river. Schools of adult "blues," some up to 15 pounds, sometimes enter the estuary and make the water churn and boil as they attack menhaden and other prey.

Weakfish (*Cynoscion regalis*)
Weakfish are long and slender, their body gray above, silvery below, with a yellowish cast to their pelvic and pectoral fins. Weakfish are less dramatic in their predatory behavior than bluefish, and they don't penetrate as far north, juveniles having been found upriver to Indian Point.

Representative Species of Sunfishes

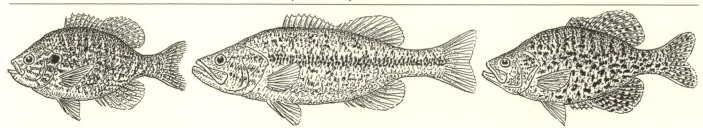

Pumpkinseed (*Lepomis gibbosus*), the Hudson's most common sunfish, is very colorful: green with dark mottling, a yellow breast, blue on the side of the head and lower jaw, and a red spot on the black opercular flap. A pumpkinseed more than 6 inches long is a big one. Other sunfish common here include the redbreast sunfish (*Lepomis auritus*) and bluegill (*Lepomis macrochirus*). Both grow a bit larger than the pumpkinseed and lack the red spot on the opercular flap.

Largemouth bass (*Micropterus salmoides*) supports a notable recreational fishery—including fishing tournaments—on the Hudson. It is the largest of the sunfishes, the New York record being close to 11 pounds. The body is greenish bronze in color with a dark horizontal band along its side. Largemouths, common residents of the river's shallows, are voracious feeders, known to eat almost anything that moves. Smallmouth bass (*Micropterus dolomieu*) have only slightly smaller mouths and generally prefer cooler, clearer, and rockier areas of the Hudson.

Black crappie (*Pomoxis nigromaculatus*) have the deep, compressed (from side to side) bodies of sunnies but grow to greater size (commonly to 12 inches) and have a larger mouth. The fish is greenish above, silvery on the sides, and covered with dark spots and mottlings which give it its alternative name, calico bass.

ship ritual, in others the male waits in the nest to be discovered by an interested female. Courting males become more intensely colored. After mating, the male will guard the nest until the eggs hatch and may herd the young around for a short time.

Minnows. In many people's minds, "minnow" is a generic term for any small fish. Indeed, many minnows are small, but size is not the scientifically determining factor: the carp, often two feet long and twenty pounds in weight, is classified as a minnow. Typically,

Representative Species of Minnows

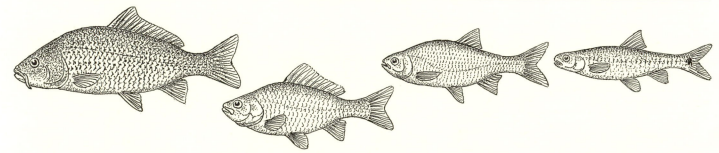

Common carp (*Cyprinus carpio*), imported from Eurasia in the 1800s, are usually yellow to metallic gold in color, with two pairs of barbels on the upper lip. They are frequently seen spawning in weedy shallows in early summer, a female attended by several males. The group moves together, thrashing wildly in water that barely covers them. Carp are omnivorous, feeding mostly on benthic life. They can tolerate polluted water with low oxygen levels.

Goldfish (*Carassius auratus*) resemble carp but are smaller, to a foot long, and lack barbels. Their coloration varies from olive-green to orange to red, often with black or white spots. They are also omnivorous. Goldfish are less tolerant of polluted conditions than are carp.

Golden shiner (*Notemigonus crysoleucas*) has a compressed, deep body, typically 4–6 inches long. Its lateral line dips low on the side. They are golden in color and have yellow or orange fins. These shiners prefer areas that are heavily vegetated while avoiding those with a lot of silt. They feed mostly on small invertebrates.

Spottail shiner (*Notropis hudsonius*) is a small, slender fish, typically 2–3 inches long. The body is olive colored above, white below. It has a distinct spot at the base of its tail. Spottail shiners feed on zooplankton and benthic organisms. The species name *hudsonius* refers to the Hudson River, in which this minnow was discovered and first described by DeWitt Clinton.

Representative Species of Killifish

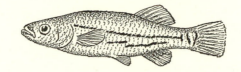

Banded killifish (*Fundulus diaphanus*) inhabits fresh water and slightly brackish reaches of the river. They are olive green above and silvery on the sides, with numerous dark vertical bars.

Striped killifish (*Fundulus majalis*) is common in the shallows around the Statue of Liberty and similar wetland areas in saltier parts of the estuary. It is pale olive or brown in color with dark stripes, vertical in the male and horizontal in the female.

Mummichog (*Fundulus heteroclitus*) is stouter than the banded killifish. Males are dark green above, their sides indistinctly striped with silver and dotted with white or yellow spots. The belly and lower fins of breeding males become intensely yellow. Females are paler, olive drab in color, sometimes with dark vertical bars. This species ranges widely in the estuary; it is found with banded killifish in fresh water and striped in salt.

minnows have soft rays in their fins, occasionally a hard, serrated ray at the front of the dorsal and anal fin. Their jaws are toothless. Some have barbels. Minnows have prominent scales, roughly round in shape, which detach easily. Many species live in the shallow, vegetated habitats of Hudson River wetlands.

Killifish. Killifish fall into the generic "minnows" category but are easily distinguished from true minnows by their rounded or squared-off tail fins; the true minnows have forked tails. "Killies" are seldom more than four to six inches long. Their mouths are aimed upward and well-adapted for feeding at the surface, but these fish also scout the bottom for their meals of small invertebrates. Killifish are abundant in the weedy shallows of the Hudson estuary, where—along with the true minnows—they are an important food source for larger predators.

Other Common Nektonic Species

Bay anchovy (*Anchoa mitchilli*)—not the fare served up with pizza or Caesar salads—is a small, slender fish, nearly transparent, with one dorsal fin and a distinct silver band along its side. The mouth is large, extending well past the eye. This anchovy feeds mostly on plankton and detritus, and its abundance makes it an important link in the estuary's food chains.

Atlantic silverside (*Menidia menidia*) is the most familiar of the Hudson's three silversides. These fishes are small, light in color or nearly transparent, and flash a bright silver stripe down the side. A very small spiny dorsal fin in front of the larger soft-rayed dorsal separates silversides from anchovies. This species is a common summer resident in the brackish water of the lower Hudson.

Fourspine stickleback (*Apeltes quadracus*) has four spines in front of its dorsal fin. Its length seldom exceeds 2.5 inches. Males develop bright red pelvic fins during courtship and breeding. At this time, a male will establish and defend a territory, build a nest of plant material, and attend the eggs laid in the nest by a female. This species is usually found in thick vegetation, where it feeds on tiny invertebrates. Primarily a fish of marine shallows, the stickleback occurs widely in freshwater portions of the Hudson and its tributaries.

Fish and Fisheries

The Hudson's fish populations have provided the river with a long history as a pantry and a playground: those who fish and sell their catch for a living have pursued shad, sturgeon, striped bass, herring, eels, and other species; recreational anglers have focused on striped bass, black bass, shad, white catfish, and other smaller panfishes.

The river's most important commercial fish has always been the American shad. A shad fishery has existed here for as long as humans have inhabited the valley. The native people living along the Hudson called shad "porcupine fish turned outside in" because of its many bones. In spite of that unpleasantry, many still consider shad to be a seasonal delight of spring; the scientific name means "savory herring," or "herring most delicious." Some liken smoked shad to a religious experience. Shad roe is considered a delicacy.

The fishery continues today in essentially the same low-technology, labor-intensive form it has had for centuries. Gill nets are commonly used; their nearly invisible nylon meshes are sized to allow a shad's head to push through, but not its body. As the fish tries to back out, its gill covers tangle in the mesh. In shallows along the Hudson's New Jersey shore, these nets are strung between hickory stakes driven into the bottom. In the Tappan Zee and Haverstraw Bay, gill nets are suspended between floats at the surface and heavy weights at the bottom. These stake nets and anchor nets are checked around slack water, when the current is about to change direction. In deeper areas from the Highlands north, gill nets are hung from floats and allowed to drift with the current for several hours.

Early accounts of the river tell of natives spearing sturgeon by torchlight. As Europeans came to dominate the valley, sturgeon were so abundant and useful that they were referred to as "Albany Beef." Overfishing and pollution were likely causes of a decline in the catch after the 1800s. In recent decades, most Atlantic sturgeon were taken as an incidental catch in the shad fishery. However, in the past few years this species—its roe valuable as caviar and its meat fetching a pretty price—has come under increasing fishing pressure in the Hudson and in coastal waters off New Jersey. Fisheries managers have become concerned about a decline in numbers of young Atlantic sturgeon in the Hudson.

Though many economically valuable species spend the early parts of their lives in the Hudson nursery, while here they are too small to be of great interest to humans. Bluefish and menhaden are examples. Neither is intensively pursued in the Hudson itself, but the estuary is a support system for coastal fisheries. Bluefish are one of the most important recreational species on our coast; anglers spend millions of dollars on bait, tackle, fuel, charter boats, motel rooms, and food during their trips to catch this species. Bluefish also are pursued by commercial fishing interests. Menhaden don't appear on dinner tables, but they are an important source of fish meal and oil and of animal feeds. By volume of catch and its dollar value, menhaden are a major commercial species on the East Coast.

Before 1976, the Hudson had also hosted active fisheries for American eel and striped bass. Eels are considered to be a delicacy in some Asian and European cultures. Striped bass rank high on lists of culinary delights along the eastern seaboard of the United States. But in 1976, New York State closed the Hudson's commercial fisheries for these species and advised the public to eat neither. The reason: contamination of the Hudson and its fish by toxic polychlorinated biphenyls—PCBs.

Is It Safe to Eat the Fish?

Revelation of the PCB problem was a cruel blow, coming at a time when sewage treatment efforts were gearing up and public hopes for river cleanup were high. PCBs are a suspected human carcinogen. Their stability and tendency to bioaccumulate in fatty tissue results in a phenomenon known as *biological concentration:* in moving up a food chain, one finds increasing levels of toxic contaminants. A predator near the top of a food chain, striped bass for example, can have as much as one million times the PCBs found in its watery environment. Stripers typically contain more than the federal government's current limit of two parts per million of PCBs in fish intended for human consumption.

As of 1994, New York State's Department of Health advises that women of child-bearing age, infants, and children under age fifteen eat no fish from the Hudson estuary, including New York Harbor. The Department recommends that other individuals should restrict consumption based on location and species of fish as follows: eat no fish except American shad taken between the Troy Dam and the Rip Van Winkle Bridge in Catskill; eat no more than one meal (one half pound) per week of shad taken anywhere below the Troy Dam and of Atlantic sturgeon, blueback herring, blue crab, bluegill, pumpkinseed, and yellow perch taken south of the Rip Van Winkle Bridge; and eat no more than one meal per month of any other species taken south of that bridge.[8]

While covered by these advisories, shad and sturgeon are sold commercially since their PCB levels fall below the federal limit.

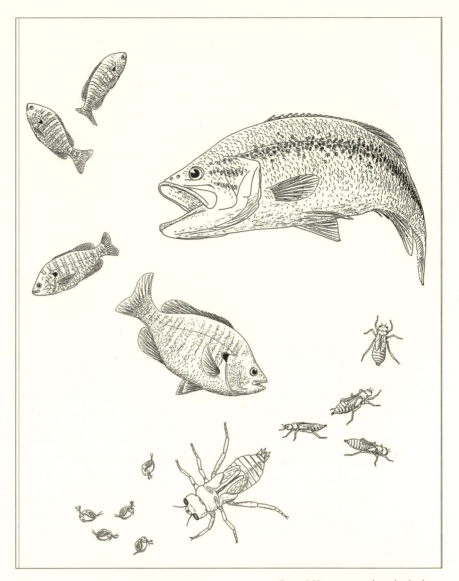

Being in the river only briefly limits their exposure to contaminants, as do their feeding habits; both eat low on the food chain. Shad in particular avoid contamination since they eat little or nothing on their spawning run and consume plankton when they are eating.

While striped bass have historically been pursued for sport and food in the Hudson, the coastal fisheries for this species have been much more extensive. To a greater degree than with bluefish and menhaden, the Hudson's nursery is vital to these

Toxic PCBs are stored in the bodies of animals that ingest them. The dragonfly nymph feeding on water fleas accumulates small doses of PCBs ingested with its prey. The sunfish that eats the dragonfly nymph thus gets a stronger dose; as the fish eats more nymphs, its PCB burden reaches higher levels. A largemouth bass at the top of this food chain, accumulating the concentrated doses in the sunfish it eats, builds up even greater concentrations of PCBs, which may pose a threat to humans who eat bass.

fisheries; unfortunately, the Hudson's PCBs, traveling with the migrating bass, have had major negative consequences for the fisheries. Since a large percentage of the stripers caught as far away as the east end of Long Island come from the Hudson, New York State has severely limited the commercial fishery there, where bass had been the mainstay of fishing families for generations, and restricted anglers to a limit of one fish per day.

As with so many other environmental problems, PCB contamination of striped bass reminds us of the interconnectedness of systems or geographic areas that we usually consider to be discrete entities. Many people tend to view the river as a closed system with a clear boundary, but, as we've seen, life in the watershed fuels life in the river through contributions of detritus, and the resources of the estuary support organisms in coastal waters beyond the Hudson. In the next chapter, we will explore the ways in which the reptiles, amphibians, birds, and mammals of the river cross the boundary between water and air and depend on the Hudson's resources.

Chapter 6

The Hudson's Birds and Beasts

The Chapter in Brief

As classes of animals, the amphibians, reptiles, birds, and mammals evolved to inhabit terrestrial environments, yet many species exploit and depend upon aquatic habitats like those found along the Hudson. Amphibians are uncommon in the estuary for reasons including tidal fluctuation, pollution, and predation. Reptile diversity in the river's wetlands is fairly low, a few turtles and snakes being the most common representatives of the class. Birds, however, are abundant and diverse: waterfowl, shorebirds, herons, gulls, raptors, and many other families use these habitats extensively. Their visibility and the high degree of human interest in birds makes them important indicators of environmental problems. Muskrats and a few other mammals are common residents of tidal wetlands; many other species opportunistically roam such habitats in search of food.

Living on the Edge

To most humans, crossing the boundary between the watery world of the Hudson and the realm of air and dry land is a big deal. We post lifeguards, or at least make sure we are with companions, before entering the water. We may hesitate a bit, worried about the dangers of pollution. Toes or fingers go in first, testing the temperature, then there is a last delay for a couple of deep breaths before we finally take the plunge.

For many of the Hudson's amphibians, reptiles, birds, and mammals, moving between water and air is a matter of course—an act performed as easily as we walk through doors to enter or leave a building. Many of them live on the edge—ducks floating on the river's surface, for example, or muskrats slipping in and out of the water as they forage busily in a marsh. Except for the amphibians, they do not breathe under water but are quite at home there. These animals depend on the Hudson for food and shelter just as the fish and invertebrates do, and are likewise exposed to the river's pollutants.

Many terrestrial animals make use of the Hudson's habitats, particularly its marshes and tidal swamps, on an occasional basis. On late summer evenings, for instance, tremendous flocks of migrating swallows swirl into the marshes to roost. This chapter, however, will focus on those animals and birds that call such habitats home, substantially depending on these environments for food, shelter, and breeding sites.

Amphibians

Amphibians lead double lives. Almost all of our amphibians hatch from eggs laid in water and live for a time as aquatic larvae—frog tadpoles being familiar examples. They then metamorphose—change form—into air-breathing terrestrial creatures.

Even as adults, amphibians require moist conditions for survival. Though most have lungs, they also "breathe" through their skin. Oxygen passes directly into tiny blood vessels concentrated under the skin. For this to happen efficiently, their skin must be moist.

Amphibians found in the Hudson Valley include frogs, toads, and salamanders. During a walk through woods bordering the river's marshes, or along streams flowing into the river, one might find good numbers of any of these animals. It might be reasonable to assume that the Hudson's wetlands would provide fine habitats for such water-dependent creatures, but in actuality, few are found there in any numbers. Five factors may account for this scarcity.

1. Amphibians are chiefly shallow-water creatures, and the shallows of the Hudson are subject to tides. The regular cycles of exposure and flooding in the intertidal zone may pose difficulties for adult amphibians, and certainly are problematic for their eggs, which must stay wet.
2. Though sometimes found in slightly brackish water, amphibians avoid salt water and are absent from the lower portions of the Hudson estuary.
3. Intertidal waters are subjected to high temperatures in summer and ice scour in winter, conditions which threaten any animals that cannot leave or burrow deep in the mud.
4. Many predators—large fish, herons, and snapping turtles, for instance—prowl these areas and may limit amphibian populations.
5. Some amphibians are very sensitive to pollution, a problem in the Hudson.

Frogs and Toads

Protuberant eyes, long hind legs, and a hopping style of locomotion characterize these familiar amphibians. Even when the animals are not visible, their calls are distinctive enough to allow a naturalist to distinguish them by ear.

The green frog is the most common amphibian of the river's tidal wetlands, though given the paucity of amphibians, that is not to say it is abundant. This frog breeds here in limited numbers. Bullfrogs appear more rarely. Two treefrogs—the

gray treefrog and the spring peeper—and the pickerel frog occasionally are heard in these habitats but it is doubtful that they breed here. The American toad has been observed breeding in the Iona Island marsh, but this does not seem to be a common occurrence in the Hudson.

Salamanders

Salamanders are often confused with lizards; both have long, relatively slender bodies with distinct heads, four legs of roughly equal size, and long tails. However, salamanders lack the scaly skin and clawed toes of lizards, which are reptiles. In the Hudson Valley, salamanders are very common, lizards rare.

Though salamanders can often be found within a few frog leaps of the river, they are uncommon in the Hudson's wetlands. An aquatic salamander once known to occur in the river—the mudpuppy—may have beeen wiped out here. One or two other salamanders common in tributary streams occasionally appear in river wetlands near the mouths of these streams.

Mudpuppy (*Necturus maculosus*)
This large (up to a foot long) salamander sports gills in plumes on each side of its neck. In the past, this benthic animal was caught rarely by anglers in freshwater reaches of the Hudson.

Reptiles

In evolution, amphibians link the fishes to the reptiles. All are vertebrates, and all are cold-blooded. The fishes, which lead completely aquatic lives, gave rise to amphibians adapted to air and land. The amphib-

green frog   *bullfrog*

Representative Species of Frogs and Toads

Green frog (*Rana clamitans*) is usually greenest around the face and browner on the back and toward the rear, where there is often darker mottling. Large individuals may be 3.5 inches long (excluding the legs). Green frogs differ from the similar bullfrog (*Rana catesbeiana*) in having two ridges of skin extending rearward along the back, one from each eye. In the bullfrog, these ridges do not extend along the back but instead curve downward around the animal's ear.

ians, still dependent on moist conditions and on water for their eggs and larval stages, gave rise to the reptiles, which severed those ties to the ancestral watery home. Reptiles have evolved well-developed lungs, for the most part eliminating the need for skin breathing with its attendant requirement for moisture.[1] Their embryos develop in an egg surrounded by protective membranes and a shell. These maintain fluid conditions around the reptile embryo, preventing it from drying out; thus the egg does not have to be laid in water.

While holding onto these evolutionary adaptations for terrestrial life, some reptiles nonetheless inhabit watery environments. As is the case with amphibians, many reptiles common in wetland habitats elsewhere in the Hudson Valley are much less so in the river's tidal wetlands. However, a few turtles and snakes can be seen regularly.

Turtles

Several species of turtles lead almost completely aquatic lives, venturing onto dry land only to lay their eggs or when forced away from their watery homes by drought or other extreme conditions. Some, the painted turtle for example, sunbathe on rocks or floating logs. Others, including the most common turtle of the river's tidal wetlands, the snapping turtle, seldom bask out of the water but can be seen swimming near the surface or lying half-buried in the mud flats left by a retreating tide. On calm, warm days, pools in river marshes are stippled here and there by just the tips of the noses of snapping turtles getting a breath of air.

Snakes

Start discussing snakes of aquatic habitats and quickly someone will describe the water moccasin they saw while out fishing in the Hudson Valley. Large nonpoisonous water snakes, dark and thick-bodied, may react in threatening fashion if surprised or cornered, but the venomous water moccasin, more properly called the cottonmouth, comes no nearer the Hudson than the state of Virginia.[2]

Two snakes are widespread but apparently not especially common anywhere in the Hudson's tidal wetlands. The well-

Northern Water Snake (*Nerodia sipedon*)
This able swimmer and diver preys mostly on fish. It basks on logs, branches, and rocks, quickly slipping into the water when approached. The rock riprap of railroad causeways and piers is a favored habitat within the river's tidal wetlands. Older individuals, 3–4 feet long, are heavyset and drably dark; younger ones are more slender with brown crossbands and blotches on a lighter background.

Representative Species of Turtles

Snapping turtle (*Chelydra serpentina*) is found even in the brackish Piermont Marsh; substantial populations live in some of the river's freshwater marshes. The big head and long tail are distinctive. The largest of the region's turtles, one Hudson specimen weighed 44 pounds. While snappers occasionally dine on ducklings, their reputation as fearsome carnivores is greatly overstated; most of their food is plant matter, carrion, and small or slow-moving fishes.

Painted turtle (*Chrysemys picta*) is small (shell up to 6 inches long) and ornately patterned—the head with bright yellow stripes and spots, the shell's edge with red lines. These turtles are widespread in the river's freshwater marshes, but in low numbers. They eat plants and small invertebrates.

Diamondback terrapin (*Malaclemys terrapin*) prefers brackish tidal wetlands. It has been found a few times in marshes from Iona Island to Piermont and is considered common in tidal wetlands at New Jersey's Liberty State Park. In most individuals the plates of the top shell are patterned with concentric rings or ridges.

known garter snake with its yellow stripes is nearly ubiquitous in the Hudson Valley. Fish are included in its diet, and the search for such prey may bring it into the river's wetlands. More truly aquatic is the water snake.

Birds

Be it the dog days of summer or a below-zero morning in February, there is one class of creatures almost always in evidence on the Hudson: the birds—at least a few gulls, maybe a flock of migrating waterfowl, or perhaps an osprey wheeling overhead in its hunt for fish. Among the Hudson's vertebrates, birds are second only to fish in overall numbers; they rival fish in their diversity.

There are many reasons for this abundance. Like other creatures of the estuary, birds benefit from its productivity, finding large supplies of food here. The Hudson Valley serves as a flyway, a route followed by birds as they migrate north in spring and south in fall. During these travels, many species settle on the river and its wetlands to rest and feed.

As a class, birds exploit all of the habitats available in the Hudson ecosystem, and are active in all seasons. Their warm-blooded nature and feathery insulation allows some species to survive even the coldest months, when sparrows flit through frozen marshes hunting seeds, and ducks dodge ice cakes on the river's surface and dive beneath them to catch fish and invertebrates. Each species has particular adaptations of anatomy and behavior which suit the requirements of its diet and life in the chosen habitat.

The Hudson's birds are too numerous to allow description here of all the varieties one might see. Only a few common species from the families of birds that use the river are included. The descriptions are orga-

nized in four major groups based on habits and habitats, but keep in mind that birds cannot read and will not always place themselves in such neat pigeonholes. Also remember that their presence follows seasonal patterns; these will be noted in the species descriptions.

Swimming Birds

The most familiar swimming birds are waterfowl—ducks, geese, and swans—but gulls, cormorants, coots, and an occasional loon or grebe can also be seen on the Hudson's surface. Many are social, associating with one another in flocks ranging from loose collections of a few birds to huge rafts—groups of hundreds.

Most of these birds have webbed feet which serve as efficient paddles. Some are excellent divers; they can reach the bottom to find fish and benthic invertebrates. Others feed in the shallow water of the river's wetlands by tipping up: pointing their tails skyward and submerging the front half of their bodies. Except for cormorants, these birds can oil their outer feathers to waterproof them. The underlying downy plumage stays dry, retaining its insulating ability and keeping the birds warm even in frigid winter weather.

Duck hunting has a long history on the Hudson. In fall, duck-hunting blinds sprout on the river's flats and in its marshes. These are rafts or platforms covered with cattail or reed to hide hunters within. Occupied blinds are usually surrounded with waterfowl decoys. A few gunners employ a method of hunting called *creeping:* lying low in a camouflaged boat and very patiently paddling or drifting toward their quarry.

Geese and Swans. The largest of the waterfowl, geese and swans have especially long necks which enable them to reach submerged aquatic plants in deeper water than smaller ducks. Geese also graze on land and will leave their aquatic habitats to find fresh young plant shoots in lawns and fields.

Surface-feeding Ducks. These ducks are birds of shallow wetlands. They rarely dive, but more often tip up to reach underwater vegetation and invertebrate animals. They also feed by dabbling—scooping up water and food items and, like draining pasta in a colander, allowing the water to dribble out through comblike structures on the sides of their bills. Surface-feeding ducks take flight by leaping directly into the air.

These ducks are numerous in spring and fall, when a great variety drop in on the Hudson during migration. They are less common in winter, when many of the shallows on which they depend are locked up in ice. Only the large, hardy mallard and black ducks winter in any significant numbers. Ducks are also not all that common in the summer breeding season. Fluctuating water levels in the river's tidal marshes limit available nest sites. The species described here occasionally breed in association with these wetlands, but mostly nest on land and then raise their hatchlings on the marshes.

Representative Species of Geese and Swans

Canada goose (*Branta canadensis*) is the familiar honker with its long black neck and white cheek patch. A few nest in the Hudson's marshes, but they are more commonly seen in large flocks during migration and in winter. The somewhat similar but smaller brant (*Branta bernicla*) migrates through the Hudson Valley and winters on saltier portions of the estuary. Large flocks can be seen in early spring near the Statue of Liberty.

Mute swan (*Cygnus olor*) is the biggest of the Hudson's waterfowl. Adults are pure white with a graceful curved neck and an orange bill. Not native to the U.S., it was brought here by European settlers.

Diving Ducks. When traveling the railroad along the Hudson's shore, one can quickly separate the diving ducks from the surface feeders. Frightened by the onrushing train, the former take to the air only after getting a running start over the river's surface, while the latter can spring up into the air.[3] Generally found on the open Hudson, these ducks are adapted for swimming underwater. Compared to surface-feeding waterfowl, their legs are placed farther back on their bodies, making them better propellers.

Representative Species of Surface-Feeding Ducks

Mallard (*Anas platyrhynchos*) males have a green head, white ring around the neck, and dark brown chest. As with most ducks, the females are much duller in color but share with the males a blue patch in the inner portion of the wing.

Black duck (*Anas rubripes*) is a very dark mottled brown in color. When it flies, the silvery white undersides of the wings contrast sharply with the dark body.

Wood duck (*Aix sponsa*) nests in cavities in large trees and sometimes feeds in forests adjacent to wetlands. They commonly use large nesting boxes put out in and around marshes. The male is generally acknowledged to be the most beautiful of North American ducks, colored in brilliant and varied hues.

Representative Species of Diving Ducks

bufflehead

common goldeneye

common merganser

red-breasted merganser

Greater scaup (*Aythya marila*) and lesser scaup (*Aythya affinis*) males have a dark (black at a distance) head, chest, and tail; the body is light gray to white. The two species look so similar that, unless conditions are ideal, many birders and hunters do not distinguish between them. Both occur in large rafts and feed on mollusks and other invertebrates.

Bufflehead (*Bucephala albeola*) males are distinctive, little ducks with white sides and a big patch of white toward the rear of the head. They appear regularly in migration and winter (though not in big flocks), often with the larger common goldeneye (*Bucephala clangula*), also black with white sides and white on the head—a small oval between the bill and the eye. These two species eat benthic invertebrates and plants.

Canvasback (*Aythya valisineria*) eats more plants than other diving ducks; as suggested by its scientific name, *Vallisneria* (wild celery) is a favorite food. The male has a white body, black chest, and a reddish head with a distinctive sloping profile.

Common merganser (*Mergus merganser*), a fish-eating duck, frequents fresh and somewhat brackish waters. Small groups of mergansers are often seen swimming among ice floes. The long white body, dark head (glossy green in good light), and long red bill identify the male. On saltier water around New York Harbor, the red-breasted merganser (*Mergus serrator*) takes the place of the common.

These ducks often are seen in huge rafts during spring and fall migrations, and many winter on the lower Hudson, staying south of the ice cover or using openings in the ice to enter their underwater feeding grounds. None breed along the tidewater Hudson; a few do nest in the Adirondacks.

From a distance, the males of most of the diving ducks are patterned in black and white; the arrangement and shape of the white areas is very helpful in identification. Females are generally brown, with less obvious identification clues.

Cormorants. If it swims like a duck and quacks like a duck, it must be a duck. Cormorants swim like ducks but do not quack, and they are not related to ducks. They lack the ability to waterproof their plumage, so after spending time diving underwater in pursuit of fish these birds must climb out on a rock, log, or buoy and dry out, striking a distinctive erect pose with wings spread. Swimming, they ride low in the water, their long, snaky necks characteristically holding the head and bill tilted upward.

Coots. Though they swim and dive in ducklike fashion, coots belong to the family of birds called rails. They lack webbed feet, but each toe has wide lobes of skin which serve as workable paddles. Coots bob their heads back and forth in pigeonlike fashion as they swim.

Double-crested Cormorant (*Phalacrocorax auritus*)
The only cormorant regularly found on the river, this large, dark bird can be seen on both fresh and salt water. Upriver it is a common migrant and a summer straggler. There are nesting colonies in New York Harbor. It is absent in winter.

American Coot (*Fulica americana*)
Among ducks, the coot is set apart by its evenly slate-gray body, black head, and white chickenlike bill. It is a common river migrant (most numerous in fall) and an occasional winterer. Coots eat plants and small invertebrates.

Wading Birds

These birds haunt the river's margins, following the tide in and out over the shoreline, tidal flats, and marshes. Shorebirds, herons, and rails are not adapted for swimming; instead, they have long legs which allow them to wade out into the water.

Since their preferred habitat is covered with ice in the winter, at least in the Hudson's more northerly reaches, wading birds use the Hudson mainly in summer and during spring and fall migration. A few individuals may try to make it through the winter in more sheltered sites along the lower river.

Shorebirds. A typical image of shorebirds is a flock of little brown birds scurrying along a surf-pounded beach, darting after a retreating wave to glean delicacies from the wet sand in front of the next breaker. But a far greater number of these birds can be seen on mudflats or in shallow pools left in marshes by the falling tide.

In such habitats along the Hudson one might find an array of sandpipers, plovers, yellowlegs, and other shorebirds during migration, especially in the fall. Their number and diversity peaks around the Hudson's mouth, where shorebirds traveling down the river meet a larger contingent moving along the Atlantic coast. The breeding grounds for most shorebirds lie far to the north. Few nest in the Hudson Valley, and of these, even fewer nest along the river itself.

Shorebirds feed mainly on invertebrates—worms, crustaceans, insects, and mollusks. Many have long bills for probing in water and mud.

Representative Species of Shorebirds

killdeer

semipalmated plover

Killdeer (*Charadrius vociferus*), a noisy shorebird of the group known as plovers, often forages along the Hudson. It nests in open spaces, including railroad rights of way, athletic fields, and the flat roofs of modern school buildings. Robin-sized, the killdeer is brown above, white below, with two black bands across its chest. During migration, the semipalmated plover (*Charadrius semipalmatus*) appears along the river. It resembles a small killdeer with one black band across its chest.

Spotted sandpiper (*Actitis macularia*) breeds along the river. In summer it indeed has black spots scattered across its white underparts; but before seeing those, you might notice that this small sandpiper constantly bobs its rear end up and down—a behavior called *teetering*. It takes to the air in a distinctive manner, holding its wings stiffly bowed and flying with shallow, quivering wingbeats.

Least sandpiper (*Calidris minutilla*) is the smallest of a group of look-alike shorebirds called "peeps" by birdwatchers. Most are sparrow-sized and sparrow-colored. Flocks of least sandpipers are common along the Hudson in migration, particularly in marshes and freshwater habitats. The similar semipalmated sandpiper (*Calidris pusilla*) prefers more open flats and is more common near the coast.

Greater yellowlegs (*Tringa melanoleuca*) is pigeon-sized, grayish brown above, white below, with a white rump and tail and long, bright yellow legs. It is common in migration along the estuary. Yes, there is a lesser yellowlegs (*Tringa flavipes*), also seen occasionally during migration.

Representative Species of Herons, Egrets, and Bitterns

Snowy egret (*Egretta thula*) is most common in the lower estuary but wanders upriver, particularly in late summer. Somewhat larger than a crow, this all-white heron has a black bill, black legs, and golden-yellow feet. The larger great egret (*Casmerodius albus*) has a yellow bill and black legs and feet. Both species nest in the New York Harbor area.

Least bittern (*Ixobrychus exilis*) is the smallest (the size of a pigeon) and least apparent of the Hudson's herons, though it regularly breeds in tidal marshes, hanging its nest in cattails and other emergent vegetation above the reach of the tides. The large buff-colored patch in each wing identifies this heron.

Green heron (*Butorides virescens*) has a dark green back, but it often appears black unless seen in good light or at close range. This crow-sized heron is widely distributed along the Hudson, nesting in tidal swamps and woodlands adjacent to tidal marshes.

Great blue heron (*Ardea herodias*) is the largest wading bird found along the Hudson, 4 feet tall with a 6–7 foot wingspread. The body and wings are as much gray as blue; the head is lighter, almost white. Breeding colonies are scattered throughout the valley, but none is currently known to exist right along the river.

Herons, Egrets, and Bitterns. Some of the Hudson's showiest and most impressive birds, recognizable even from an Amtrak train speeding along the Hudson at 80 miles per hour, are the herons and their relatives. They have long, daggerlike bills adapted for catching fish and other small animals. Most people are familiar with the unmoving but alert posture of herons waiting for such prey. A few species, the snowy egret among them, more actively pursue their quarry, dancing around in shallow water to stir up food.

The least bittern and green heron regularly nest in the Hudson's wetlands. Other species nest in trees and shrubs away from the river but hunt for food here during the breeding season or in migration. In recent years, a noteworthy nesting population of herons and egrets, New York State's largest such congregation, has built up around New York Harbor. In 1991, New York City established the Harbor Herons Wildlife Refuge to protect important nesting sites on islands in the Arthur Kill and Kill van

Kull, the waterways that separate Staten Island from New Jersey. Somewhat incongruously, the industrial development surrounding these islands has created a no-man's-land where the birds have found the isolation they require for nesting.

Rails. The expression "thin as a rail" refers not to railroad tracks or to fencing but to birds of this family, which compress them-

Virginia Rail (*Rallus limicola*)
This most common member of the rail family along the Hudson (except for the ducklike coot) nests in its marshes. A long bill allows it to pick invertebrates from shallow water, mud, and marsh vegetation. A rich reddish brown color covers its breast and is streaked through the feathers of its upperparts. The clapper rail (*Rallus longirostris*) is larger, grayer, and restricted to the saltier marshes around New York Harbor.

selves from side to side in order to slip through the dense growth of plant stems in marshes. Rails have very long toes, the better to distribute their weight over the uncertain support provided by soft mud and mats of vegetation. If you see one, it might remind you of a small chicken, but catching sight of them is difficult due to their secretiveness and the thick vegetation of their marsh habitats.

Perching Birds of Wetland Habitats

Thrushes, blackbirds, wrens, finches, sparrows, flycatchers, swallows, jays—these and most of the familiar birds of our yards, woodlands, and fields all belong to the largest order of birds, the perching birds. Very few of these have actually become adapted to an aquatic life, so you won't see them out on open water or bare tidal flats. But in the high marsh and tidal swamps of the Hudson, perching birds are abundant. Most feed on insects and other small invertebrates; the blackbirds, finches, and sparrows also eat large quantities of seeds.

Of the many perching birds that you might see in these habitats, most are visitors in search of food and shelter. Fewer actually live the larger part of their lives there. The species described here do breed in the Hudson's marshes and swamps. Excepting the goldfinch, a year-round resident, they are migratory, with only the rare straggler hanging around into the winter. The marsh wren, red-winged blackbird, and swamp sparrow rank one, two, and three, respectively, in abundance among summer birds of the river's freshwater marshes, and are also common in brackish marshes.

Representative Perching Birds of Wetland Habitats

American goldfinch

yellow warbler

Marsh wren (*Cistothorus palustris*) populations are greatest in dense stands of cattail, where their bubbly trills are more evident than the birds themselves. Wait patiently to sight this tiny brown bird, stubby tail cocked over its back, clinging to a cattail stem. Marsh wren nests are a woven ball of cattail leaves the size and shape of a coconut, hanging on cattail stems a few feet over the water.

Red-winged blackbird (*Agelaius phoeniceus*) males are unmistakable, though the red wing patches are often hidden unless the bird is singing. The females resemble large striped sparrows. Of the marshes' migrant perching birds, the male redwings are the first to return in spring.

Swamp sparrow (*Melospiza georgiana*) is common but often overlooked given its retiring nature and relatively dull color. One cannot miss its song, however—a rattling series of chips reminiscent of a sewing machine in action. A reddish brown cap and unstreaked breast distinguish adult swamp sparrows.

Yellow warbler (*Dendroica petechia*) is not restricted to marsh habitats but is abundant there, particularly at the edges. It nests in shrubs or small trees scattered around the marsh on higher ground. This tiny bird is all yellow; males have a few reddish streaks on their breasts. Another small yellow bird common in marshes is the American goldfinch (*Carpodacus tristis*); its wings and tail are black. It nests in shrubs and in purple loosestrife.

Wide-ranging River Birds

The birds grouped here can't be assigned to one particular river habitat; they may be seen over, or in, different ones. Most typically hunt over open water, be it the channel or shallow water covering flats or submerged vegetation.

Gulls. "Sea" gulls are familiar to everyone, even people who live far from the sea. Virtually every shopping mall near the Hudson has its complement of gulls patrolling for garbage. Their catholic tastes have allowed gulls to prosper in direct response to the increasing amounts of wastes tossed out by humans. Garbage dumps and sewage outfalls have been considered hotspots by birdwatchers interested in finding rare gulls.

Gulls are strong fliers; they also have webbed feet and can swim well. Their bills are hooked and powerful; in addition to scavenging, the larger species will prey on other birds and small mammals as well as more typical gull fare: fish, mollusks, crustaceans, and human food scraps. Most adult gulls are gray on their backs and wings and white below. Young birds, however, go through two to four years of brownish plumages before gaining the adult coloration.

Gulls can be seen in all seasons along the Hudson. Herring, great black-backed, and laughing gulls nest in scattered colonies

Representative Species of Gulls

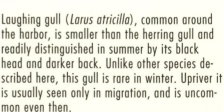

Herring gull (*Larus argentatus*) is the "standard" gull, about 2 feet long with a wingspread of 4–5 feet. It is found all along the Hudson. The smaller ring-billed gull (*Larus delawarensis*) differs in having a dark ring around its bill and yellowish or greenish legs (herring gulls' legs are pinkish). Ring-billed gulls do not nest along the estuary. They are common in migration, and in winter, upriver observers often see more ring-billed than herring gulls.

Great black-backed gull (*Larus marinus*) is larger than the herring gull and has a very dark gray (almost black) back and upper wing surface. It regularly wanders upriver, but is most common in New York Harbor.

Laughing gull (*Larus atricilla*), common around the harbor, is smaller than the herring gull and readily distinguished in summer by its black head and darker back. Unlike other species described here, this gull is rare in winter. Upriver it is usually seen only in migration, and is uncommon even then.

around New York Harbor, but not along the Hudson itself. Those seen in summer upriver are young birds, nonbreeding adults, or stragglers from breeding grounds elsewhere.

Kingfishers. Kingfishers plunge headlong into the water to catch small fish with their strong, daggerlike bills. They may fish from a perch or hover over a likely spot. Since their style of fishing requires shallow, ice-free water, only a few hardy individuals hang around the Hudson in winter. Of eighty-six species of kingfishers found worldwide, only one occurs on the Hudson, or in most of the U.S. for that matter.

Belted Kingfisher
(*Ceryle alcyon*)
Our kingfisher is shaggy-headed, pigeon-sized, and slate blue in color, with a distinct white collar. Its harsh rattling cry is a familiar sound along the Hudson. Kingfishers nest in burrows excavated into embankments.

Raptors. Raptors are the birds of prey: eagles, hawks, falcons, and owls. All have hooked beaks for tearing the flesh of their prey, which is captured with taloned feet. While a variety of species may hunt along the river and over its marshes, the bald eagle and osprey depend on water, for fish is their preferred food. As top predators in food chains that concentrate toxic pesticides, both these species declined in numbers through the 1950s and 1960s, but their numbers along the Hudson are now apparently rebounding.

The Miner's Canary

In the days before sophisticated electronic detection equipment, coal miners took canaries underground to warn them of low oxygen levels in deep shafts. The birds would succumb as oxygen levels dropped, warning miners of the hazard to their lives.

Even with today's sophisticated analytical instruments, birds still warn us of environmental problems. Birds' visibility and the number of people interested in them makes fluctuations in their populations more apparent than might be the case with other creatures. An example was the decline

Bald Eagle (*Haliaeetus leucocephalus*)
Adults are huge and easily identifiable; eagles less than four years old lack the white head and tail. They feed on fish, usually dead or dying, snatched from the surface of the river. A half dozen or so roost on Iona Island in winter, and the bird is being seen more widely along the Hudson in all seasons. In 1992 and 1994, pairs nested along the river but did not successfully raise young.

Osprey (*Pandion haliaetus*)
Ospreys soar or hover over the river till prey is sighted, then plunge in feet first to catch fish, most often goldfish, catfish, and herring. They are somewhat smaller than eagles, brown above, and white below. The fish hawk is a common migrant over the Hudson. A few stragglers might be seen in summer, but the species is not known to nest along the tide-water Hudson. Ospreys do breed in the Adirondacks and on Long Island.

of bald eagles, ospreys, and peregrine falcons here in the Hudson Valley and throughout the eastern United States due mainly to poisoning by chlorinated hydrocarbons, most notably the pesticide DDT.

Such predators exist at the end of long food chains that concentrate toxic chemicals. In the 1960s, ring-billed gulls in a Long Island salt marsh were found to have levels of DDT a million times higher than levels in the water. Similar concentrations in raptors interfered with their calcium metabolism, resulting in thinner eggshells (which broke during incubation) and other reproductive problems.

A well-studied example along the Hudson is the peregrine falcon. This speedy raptor once commanded the air over the river from long-established nest sites between the Highlands and New York City. The falcons survived turn-of-the-century egg collectors, nest-robbing by falconers, the ill will of people who shot at them out of hatred for predators, and the disturbances of road construction along the Palisades. As of the early 1940s, eight pairs nested at the historic sites, but with increasing pesticide use following World War II, their nesting success declined. After 1951, when two peregrine chicks hatched opposite Yonkers, thirty-seven years went by before another successful nesting occurred on the Hudson—three young raised on a tower of the Tappan Zee Bridge in 1988. Now as many as ten pairs may nest around New York City.

In the intervening years the dangers of DDT and other pesticides had been recognized, its use in the United States was banned, and a strategy for reestablishing nesting peregrines was devised. As noted above, bald eagle and osprey populations in the Northeast have likewise benefited from those developments.[4] We must hope that a similar process of research followed by appropriate action will have positive results in halting other recent population declines—those among waterfowl and some songbirds, for instance. Destruction of wetlands and acid rain are among the suspected reasons for the decline of waterfowl; the cutting of forests both in the United States and in the tropics might be a factor in the dwindling numbers of some migrant songbirds.

Of course, the miners weren't all that concerned with the death of their canaries per se; they were worried about their own welfare. We should be concerned about both; maintaining the abundance and diversity of native species in the Hudson and other ecosystems, and protecting ourselves from the deleterious effects of toxic pollutants, acid rain, and habitat destruction in the forests and elsewhere. We should appreciate the Hudson's birdlife both for itself and for the warnings it might provide.[5]

Mammals

Like the reptiles from which they evolved, mammals are primarily terrestrial creatures, some of which have become adapted for watery environments. And given the opportunistic natures of many mammals, even those not especially adapted for life in water have learned to take advantage of resources offered by the Hudson and its wetlands—white-tailed deer, for example, which relish some marsh plants. A 1978 study of natural areas along the river in Columbia and Dutchess Counties listed thirty-five mammals as occurring there, of which seventeen were known to use tidal wetland habitats. However, only a handful of these reside and reproduce in such environments.

Representative Mouselike Mammals

White-footed mouse (*Peromyscus leucopus*) is brown above, white below, with large ears, big eyes, and a tail almost equal to the body in length. This 7-inch long rodent is generally a woodland creature, found along the edges of marshes, but it does inhabit tidal swamps and brushy sections of marsh, commonly occurring in purple loosestrife. On occasion it will nest in duck blinds out in marshes.

Meadow vole (*Microtus pennsylvanicus*) is the so-called meadow mouse. It has smaller eyes and ears and a shorter tail than the white-footed mouse. The 1978 study cited in the text did not list this animal as using freshwater tidal wetlands; however, it is abundant in the *Spartina* meadows of brackish and saltwater marshes.

Norway rat (*Rattus norvegicus*), perhaps the most familiar of the Hudson's rodents, is larger than a mouse and has a long tail only sparsely covered by hair. Common in both urban and rural settings, rats frequent old docks, duck blinds, and rock riprap. They can swim when the occasion calls for it. This rodent is not native to the U.S.; it arrived here on ships from the Old World.

Short-tailed shrew (*Blarina brevicauda*), about 5 inches long at most, is an insectivore. A leaden gray in color, this energetic mammal has no visible ears and tiny eyes. It mostly eats insects and other tiny invertebrates; larger prey creatures may be disabled by the shrew's poisonous saliva.

Mice and Mouselike Mammals

To most people, the tiny furry animal that scurries away from underfoot is a mouse. To the naturalist, it could be any of a number of small mammals: perhaps one of the rodents—mammals with strong front teeth used to gnaw food (primarily seeds and plants, with the occasional smaller creature tossed in)—or one of the insectivores, voracious little bundles of carnivorous energy. These tiny animals are important links in the food chain, eaten by larger mammals, hawks, herons, and a wealth of other predators.

Muskrat

Muskrats are common inhabitants of the Hudson's marshes, both brackish and fresh. These rodents build houses out of plant stems and mud; though these structures project above the water, the entrances are below the surface. They also live in burrows excavated into the river's shore. Muskrats are active all year round, their thick brown fur providing warmth in winter and making them the object of extensive trapping efforts. They feed chiefly on plants; cattails are particularly favored. The somewhat similar beaver is not common in tidal habitats.

Large Predatory Mammals

Dogs, cats, foxes, and raccoons are among the familiar predatory mammals that include the Hudson's tidal wetlands on their hunting rounds. However, they are not dependent on such habitats. Otter and mink do depend on wetland habitats such as those found along the Hudson. These members of the weasel family generally stick close to water, denning along the shoreline, and feeding largely on fish. These animals and the other large wild carnivores, often most active at night, are elusive and seldom seen. Clues to their presence are scat—fecal

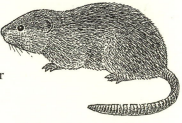

Muskrat (*Ondatra zibethica*) Muskrats may reach a length of about 2 feet, including a long, naked tail that is flattened from side to side, perhaps for use as a rudder. They are excellent swimmers and divers.

River Otter (*Lutra canadensis*)
This large predator (adults 3–4 feet long), unlike its relative the mink, has webbed feet and a furry tail which tapers to a point. Otters range widely; their home territories may be 15 miles in extent. Sighting one along the Hudson is thus a very lucky occurrence, especially since their numbers have apparently declined, perhaps due to PCB poisoning.

Mink (*Mustela vison*)
Smaller than otters (usually less than 2 feet long), mink are covered in rich brown fur of value to the fashion industry. Few are found along the Hudson these days, however. Mink are known to be very sensitive to PCBs; it is suspected that PCB pollution has led to a decline in their populations there.

droppings, the shape, size, and contents of which often distinguish the species which left them behind—or tracks in wet sand or mud along the river's shore.

Marine Mammals—Whales, Dolphins, and Seals

Whales and dolphins have become so thoroughly adapted for life in water that many people consider them to be fish. But like all other mammals, they are warm-blooded, breathe air, have at least a little hair, and produce milk to feed their young.

A whaling industry was based on the Hudson for some fifty years starting in the late 1700s. The main port was the city of Hudson, which in 1785 had twenty-five sailing vessels out on the oceans. In the early 1830s, another peak period for the river's whalers, four companies in Hudson, Poughkeepsie, and Newburgh sailed about thirty ships.

The whalers' catch came from the high seas, not the river. Large whales are very

unusual visitors in the Hudson. Historians tell of two which made it past Albany to Cohoes in 1647, one of which beached itself and died. Practical settlers rendered the remains to produce a great deal of oil, yet enough was left in the rotting carcass to coat the surface of the river for three weeks. There are other records of whales off New York City, including a humpback whale that made a brief tour up the Hudson in 1988.

Harbor porpoises were regular summer visitors through the mid-1800s, following the salt front north as far as Peekskill. In autumn 1936, common dolphins swam upriver; individuals were found dead in Albany and in Highland (across from Poughkeepsie).

Historically, harbor seals were regular visitors to the estuary. While not observed here in any significant numbers today, seals are occasionally reported from Liberty State Park behind the Statue of Liberty, and sightings farther upriver have increased in recent years.

The Most Commonly Seen Mammal

Of all the mammals found along the Hudson, none is more commonly seen than *Homo sapiens*, the human being. Like the white-tailed deer, raccoon, and other animals, we humans do not make our permanent residences in the Hudson or its wetlands, but we do capture food from the river, travel on its waters, and find recreational pleasure and aesthetic inspiration there. However, our power to alter the physical nature and the ecological functioning of the Hudson far exceeds that of the creatures discussed so far. The next few chapters will survey our interactions with the river, first in historical narrative, and then in terms of impacts on the Hudson ecosystem.

Chapter 7

Exploration, Colonization, and Revolution

The Chapter in Brief

Belief in a northwest passage to the Indies shaped the European conception of the New World and lured explorers to the Americas. Rivers were central to early exploration and settlement and became the basis for community building and trade. Native peoples, with a ten-thousand-year history and an ancient culture, were quickly displaced following the European invasion. The Hudson, so central to the growth of colonial New York, was also a strategic key to the Revolution, and as a result was memorialized as our first national river.

The World Turned Upside Down

The history of the Hudson River is often said to begin with its discovery by Henry Hudson in 1609. This Eurocentric view of events has neglected the ancient history of the native peoples who lived along the Hudson and in the valley for ten thousand years and first named the river "Muhheakantuck" sometime in the Woodland period (1500 B.C. to A.D. 1600).[1] The loss of this ancient name is symptomatic of the loss of the region's native history. Even in those instances where native names have survived, such as Esopus, Neperhan, Nyack, Ossining, Pocantico, Poughkeepsie, Tappan, Wappinger, and Weehawken, we tend not to identify them with the pre-European history of the river.

The Euro-American history of the Hudson is but a moment in the great sweep of geological and native time in the Hudson Valley. While literacy and technology have convinced many that what happened before the European invasion was prologue, recalling the native Muhheakantuck should serve

as a counter to this ethnocentric view of our history in general and the Hudson River in particular. If European explorers laid claim to the lands of the New World by the act of naming, then we must recognize the prior claim of native peoples inherent in Muhheakantuck and examine the disposition of that claim by the Europeans.

The difficulty in reconstructing the native history of the Hudson River is tied to the nature of the surviving record, much of it found in archaeological sites and oral traditions. The early record begins with the work of archaelogists and the discovery and classification of projectile points found in Orange County, dated from about 10,600 B.C., and shell heaps at Haverstraw Bay and Croton Point, dated from 6000 B.C. The historical record is more abundant as we move to the Woodland period from 1500 B.C. to the European invasion in the seventeenth century.

Shatamuc

In the Late Woodland period the native population along the Hudson consisted of

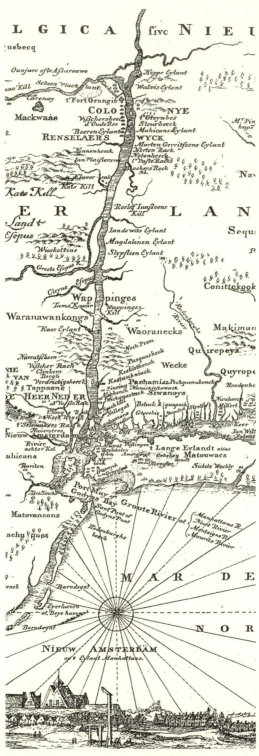

The 1650 Janssonius-Visscher map of New Netherlands included names and locations of river-based native tribes. The depiction of the Hudson and its tributaries is generalized. The map includes an outline of New Amsterdam's seventeenth-century skyline.
(Courtesy of Clearwater.)

tribes or bands of the Algonquin Eastern Linguistic group: the Munsee, who settled along the Hudson south of Albany, and the Mahicans, speaking a different dialect, to the north. The Mahicans, often referred to as the River Indians, called the Hudson "Shatamuc." The Munsee speakers formed bands known as Highlanders or Wappingers, and were further identified by their locale—Wappinger (Dutchess and Putnam), Kichtawank (Northern Westchester), Sinsink (Ossining), Wiechquaeskeck (Tarrytown–Dobbs Ferry) and Rechgawank (Yonkers, the Bronx, and Manhattan).

Population estimates for the valley are hard to come by, ranging anywhere from six thousand to twelve thousand natives in the seventeenth century. Settlements—those at Wicker's Creek in Dobbs Ferry or on Croton Point, for example—were located along the Hudson or its tributaries, insuring ease of transportation, abundant food, and fertile land, and establishing a pattern soon to be duplicated by the Europeans.

From Manhattan to Albany, on both sides of the river, native groups of a few hundred members burned, cleared, and planted the land. They built clusters of wigwams, sometimes protected by a palisaded wall. Fall was the principal hunting season; game included deer (the most important), bear, wolf, raccoon, weasel, and other small animals along with turkeys, passenger pigeons, and other birds. Spring and summer were the principal times for fishing the Hudson and its tributaries, filled with shad, striped bass, sturgeon, eels, and oysters. Fish were caught with stone-weighted seines, weirs, nets set on poles, hooks, and even bow and arrow. Fish and shellfish were sun-dried on racks, their discarded remains providing archaeological clues for future historians. Fishing and river transportation were accomplished by use of the dugout canoe, hollowed out with the aid of scrapers and fire from the trunk of the tulip tree.

Daily meals, boiled in conical clay pots or baked in corn husks, consisted of cornmeal mush and fish or meat. The evolution of these cooking utensils offers additional clues to the river natives' way of life. For ills encountered in their daily lives the natives sought out the curative powers of the sweat bath and the spiritual powers of the *shaman* who prescribed local herbs and plants.

Native bands were led by a chief or *sachem*, who served as mediator and religious leader. Family organization, birth and death rituals, political organization, and a symbiotic relationship with nature were all informed by a rich mythological tradition. This mythology included the manitous, lesser gods or spirits who dwelt in all aspects of the earth, water, and sky, and the great god Manitou who in ancient times,

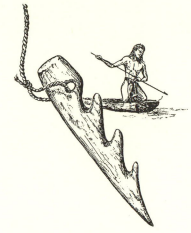

Bone harpoons, made from antlers or leg bones of deer or moose, were used to take large fish such as sturgeon. After being split lengthwise, the bone was ground into the appropriate shape.

Without salt, smoking and drying were the principal means of preserving fish for food. Fish were cut into chunks; crabs were roasted in their shells.

it is said, confined rebellious spirits in the Highlands until the Hudson broke through this "prison." There can be little doubt that at the time of European exploration native peoples had a substantial culture.

Natives felled trees by using dried moss and wood chips to fire trees close to the roots. Limbs were burned off, the bark stripped, and the raised log burned and chipped into shape to make a dugout canoe.

This print, titled *Sa Ga Yeath Qua Pieth Tow, King of the Maquas*, was redrawn by John Simon from a 1710 print by John Verelst. The latter, titled *Etoh oh Koam, King of the River Nation*, is the only known detailed depiction of a Mahican chief.
(Print Collection, Miriam and Ira D. Wallach Division of Art, Prints and Photographs, The New York Public Library, Astor, Lenox and Tilden Foundations.)

The Hudson River and its valley had a long native history which predated Hudson's arrival—a history closely linked to the river and the natural resources it provided. Its reconstruction remains a challenge to students of our past.[2]

Exploration and Settlement . . . or Invasion?

To understand the history of the native peoples after 1609 we need to examine their seventeenth-century contacts with Europeans from the native perspective. At first, natives in the region greeted the Europeans with friendly curiosity, but this soon turned to suspicion and hostility. Both responses are evident in the journals of Hudson's 1609 visit.

Revisionist historians have begun to use the term invasion to describe the first phase of European exploration and settlement of the New World. Invasion, they argue, is the proper term to describe the rapid displacement of the natives from the river valley and the destruction of their culture by technology and European civilization. But the term is most appropriate when applied to the traumatic introduction of European diseases such as measles, smallpox, and typhus, to which the natives had no immunity. According to a 1640 statement attributed by the Dutch to river natives, disease reduced the native population to one tenth of its original size. Venereal disease, spread by promiscuous fishermen and fur traders, also contributed to the rapid decline.

Trade with the native peoples not only introduced European technology but profoundly changed the equilibrium between the Munsee, the Mahicans, and the natural world. Trapping for profit, which drove natives to maximize their yield, brought destructive pressures on the beaver population and altered village and family work habits. Interdependence slowly gave way to exploitation, and the ensuing tribal rivalries over territorial claims led to wars and further population displacement.

Native civilization, which had been slowly evolving for ten thousand years in the valley and along the Hudson, came to a sudden and quick end within the first century of European settlement. The river natives who survived the encounter migrated westward into New Jersey in small bands, or were absorbed into larger regional groups.

The Northwest Passage

At the center of European *cartography* of the New World was the enduring myth of a northwest water passage to India. When specific geographic information was in short supply cartographers did not hesitate to add a Northwest Passage to their maps of the New World. This idea, so fixed in the imagination of every European explorer, shaped their views of the New World and fueled many an obsessive, unsuccessful, and even tragic search.[3]

The belief in a westward-leading water route focussed the energy and planning of the explorers of the 1600–1700s and their underwriters on the rivers of the New World. Dreams and expectations, indeed the future itself, were tied to America's rivers, which not only served as avenues of exploration but contained the promise of a new history.

European expansion took place in atmosphere of fierce economic and religious rivalry. It is not surprising that the rivalry would extend to exploration and colonization. The Hudson of the 1600s and 1700s is not only integral to our colonial history but a key element in Europe's global history as well.

Knocking at the Door

The passion for exploration was so intense that it monopolized the European's adventurous spirit and created a generation of men eager to journey to the New World. In 1524 the Italian Giovanni da Verrazano, under the sponsorship of King Francis I of France, crossed the Atlantic in search of the westward passage, sailed up the northeast coast, and entered New York Bay. Verrazano recorded the first impressions of the harbor and the native peoples and described the lower Hudson as the "River of the Steep Hills" and the "Grand River."

Estevan Gomez, a Portuguese in the employ of the Spanish, followed Verrazano in 1525 and may have explored the lower Hudson. Spanish maps accept this as fact by naming the Hudson "Rio de Gomez,"

and "Rio de Guamas." The French followed the Spanish and, based on evidence of their trading with the natives, may have ascended the Hudson. But none of these claims stuck.

Enter Henry Hudson

In the early 1600s, the Dutch, locked in a struggle with Spain and Portugal and eager to compete with their English rivals, established the East India Company, which financed the Englishman Henry Hudson's third trip to the New World. The *yaagt* or pursuit ship *Half Moon*—84 feet long, 20 feet wide, and displacing 122 tons—sailed on April 16, 1609, with an Anglo-Dutch crew of sixteen to eighteen men. Hudson, newly inspired by maps from the Virginia explorer Captain John Smith, remained convinced that he was on the brink of discovering the Northwest Passage.

Ice forced Hudson to revise his charted course for the Arctic and turn south and west on the 14th of May, yet he remained confident that the passage to the East would be found at forty degrees latitude. The *Half Moon* arrived in New York Harbor on September 4, 1609, and remained there for nine days, exploring the Upper Bay and trading with the natives. Hudson then began a slow, methodical exploration of the river which, based on initial indications of breadth, depth, and salinity, seemed promising. The only known surviving record of this journey is the journal of Robert Juet, the *Half Moon*'s mate.

On September 11, the *Half Moon* passed the Narrows and anchored off the upper west side of Manhattan. From this point Hudson moved farther northward, continuing to test the river's salinity and depth. On the 13th of September he reached the site of present-day Yonkers, on the 14th the Highlands and West Point, on the 16th what is now Hudson, and on the

Arrival of Henry Hudson, September 4, 1609 (Asher B. Durand). Local natives had prior knowledge of Europeans, but their expectations about the encounter are only partially known. (Collection of The New-York Historical Society.)

17th he anchored at Castleton. The crew explored farther northward and confirmed what Hudson had begun to suspect: that this river was not the Northwest Passage but an estuary with a freshwater source. A continent, not an ocean, lay before him.

Robert Juet's logbooks record the first European response to the river and the adjacent landscape. Juet noted that the land was "pleasant, high and bold" and the Hudson "as fine a river as can be found." Hudson and his crew were intoxicated with the river's sweet smell—the perfumes of grasses, wildflowers, and trees, a smell so sweet "that we stood still."

But in addition to this sensual and *aesthetic* response Juet also noted the economic possibilities: "The land is the finest for cultivation that I have ever in my life set foot upon," a place to appreciate and to develop, a garden of the new world but one which could profitably be cultivated. The European's dual response at the moment of dis-

covery foreshadows the later history of the Hudson River as a source of aesthetic enrichment and economic opportunity.

In the 1600s the Hudson was a river abundant in natural resources: a river valley of oak, chestnut, and hickory forest, with fall leaves rich in color; game and fish so abundant that people "imagine that animals of the country will be destroyed in time, but this is an unnecessary anxiety." The river seemed like a limitless resource. Even Manhattan Island, cut through with bays, coves, marshes, and streams, had fresh water and trout.

Hudson had several encounters with the native population, and following one exchange he concluded that "they were a very good people." However, curiosity, gift-giving, and trading quickly deteriorated within the first days of discovery into petty thievery and mutual suspicion, culminating in open hostility and loss of life. This first encounter with the natives left the Europeans wondering about the nobility of the "savage."

While Hudson never returned to Holland (he was detained and removed from the *Half Moon* by the English at Dartmouth on the return journey), the Dutch would quickly seize the initiative and lay claim to the river and the valley. Though Hudson had not discovered the Northwest Passage, he had come upon a major river, the "Manhatees" as he styled it, an avenue to the north and to the North American wilderness.

Of Beavers and Bouweries

The Dutch wasted no time acting upon Hudson's discovery. In 1610 Amsterdam merchants sent a ship out to "the Groote Rivier" to trade with the natives for beaver pelts, the Hudson's cash crop. This first response reflected the Dutch commercial view of the Hudson as the source of a valuable commodity and a highway for trade.

The Dutch organized the West India Company in 1621 to monopolize the river trade. In 1624 thirty families of Walloons set sail for the "River of the Prince Mauritius," an official designation chosen to honor the Dutch soldier Maurice of Orange.[4] While Walloon communities in Manhattan and Fort Orange (the site of present-day Albany) provided the seed for the establishment of permanent settlements, the Dutch needed to expand the number and size of agricultural settlements to support both their territorial claims and the growing fur trade. They failed to attract sufficient numbers of colonists, and those who came tended to move inland, secure from the threats of hostile natives and their French allies. Their long-term inability to create a population base in New Netherlands would inhibit Dutch colonization of the valley and by midcentury undermine their control of the river.

Desperate to attract colonists to New Netherlands, the Dutch tried innovative land schemes like the patroon system,

The Stadthuys of New York in 1679, Corner of Pearl St. and Coentijs Slip (G. Hayward & Co., issued 1867). The commercial nature and architectural fashion of New Amsterdam is visible in this print of the seventeenth-century waterfront. Sloops are tied up at a wharf constructed with landfill, a practice which the Dutch initiated in New York. The large building is the Stadt Huys, the administration center for the company governing the colony. (Eno Collection, Miriam and Ira D. Wallach Division of Art, Prints and Photographs, The New York Public Library, Astor, Lenox and Tilden Foundations.)

Establishing Hudson Valley farms like this one, complete with windmill, Dutch farmers cultivated corn, oats, and wheat. However, the more lucrative beaver trade retarded Dutch agricultural development here.

which promised a sixteen-mile land grant along one shore (or eight on both sides) of the Hudson, provided the grantee plant a colony of fifty people. Two patroonships were established on the Hudson; one at Rensselaerwyck took hold. The centrality of rivers—the Connecticut, Delaware, and Hudson—to such land schemes underscored the importance of rivers to development of New World colonies.

It was understandable that the first Dutch towns and the adjacent farms or *bouweries*, including New Amsterdam, Beverwyck, and Esopus, would be located along the river, where economic function joined with communication. The Dutch bouweries produced corn, peas, oats, and wheat; because of the Dutch taste for beer, hops were cultivated as well. The standard Dutch fertilizer was oyster shell, found in great heaps along the Hudson's banks. Their diet depended heavily on the river's oysters, perch, sturgeon, bass, smelt, shad, alewives, eels, and tomcod.

The fur trade depended on ships not only to transport furs to Europe but also to supply traders with the necessary items for barter. Ships from Holland, anchored in New Amsterdam Harbor, would exchange cloth, clothes, implements, blankets, liquor glasses, liquor, candles, and even cattle for pelts brought downriver by fly boats. These

boats would then return upriver loaded with imported goods to trade for more pelts.

Trade between Holland and New Netherlands quickly established the protected New Amsterdam harbor at the mouth of the Hudson as the fulcrum of an international trade linking Europe with the New World. New Amsterdam became the commercial center of the Dutch colonial enterprise in the New World and fixed the Dutch view of the Hudson as a highway for trade. The Hudson of the 1600s was as closely linked to the European market as to the interior of colonial America. For transplanted Europeans it represented not only the promise of a new future but the link to a known past as well.

The Hudson River Sloops

River trade was dependent on Dutch boats and seamanship. One of the lasting contributions of the Dutch was the Hudson River sloop, which came to dominate river trade for two centuries. Sloops measured 65 to 75 feet in length, in a few cases 90 feet. They had a single mast with a mainsail, a jib, and often a topsail. At first the Dutch used leeboards but these soon were replaced by a centerboard or keel. They were steered by a long tiller. The generous holds and deck space could accommodate up to a hundred tons of cargo. Their maneuverability and shallow draft equipped them to serve a river trade that extended into tributaries of varying depths and widths, linking the Hudson to interior settlements.

The sloops' dependence on winds and tides placed river travel at the mercy of nature. A trip from New Amsterdam to Fort Orange could take twenty-four hours under optimum conditions, or stretch out over several days. Though good seamanship could reduce the time of the journey, all captains waited on the river and its natural uncertainties. Dutch sloop captains, with their skill and knowledge of the Hudson's topography, survived into the English period; Dutch remained the language of some river captains well into the nineteenth century. In the 1600s many of the sloop crews were black and, according to some observers, took their orders in Dutch. African Americans would play key roles in the maritime activities of the Hudson well into the nineteenth century, captaining vessels and running shipping companies.

Sloop captains measured the Hudson in *reaches* stretching from the Palisades up to Albany.[5] Measurement of distances by reaches rather than miles is another indication of the river's significance in the conceptualization of space. Expanding river trade and passenger traffic inevitably led to the development of a shipbuilding capacity on the Hudson in Manhattan and, later, upriver in Nyack, the latter famous for its brightly marked sloops.

The Lasting Dutch Imprint

Historical assessment of the Dutch colonial experience in the valley has been complicated by Washington Irving's mythical Dutch in *Diedrich Knickerbocker's History of New York* (1809). These folk characters, filled with fear of the New World and grounded in the superstitions of the Old, would come to overwhelm the historical Dutch who were practical, profit-seeking, and fully engaged with the pleasures of the river and the valley.

While Irving's stereotyping distorted our impression of the valley Dutch, it did contribute a sense of mystery to the romantic image of the Hudson which blossomed in the second quarter of the nineteenth century. In addition to correcting the distortion, we may need to explore the way in which Irving's Dutch were used to create a different river, not an economic highway but a mysterious and romantic river.

The sloop *Clearwater* reminds us of the Dutch sloops, which were the workhorses of Hudson River trade well into the nineteenth century. Sloop captains were close observers of the river, dependent as they were on personal knowledge to safely navigate its waters. *(Photo by Charles Porter. Sloop schematic courtesy of Clearwater.)*

Nevertheless, the historic Dutch imprint on the Hudson is clearly commercial. They saw the river as an economic artery connecting the American hinterland to Europe, and New Amsterdam at the mouth of the river as a center of New World trade. Though they failed to attract a sufficient number of Dutch settlers, they introduced other groups to New Netherlands, creating a polyglot population that has marked the subsequent history of the Hudson.

English Claims

In August 1664 an English fleet under Colonel Richard Nicolls landed at the Battery, raised the English flag, and ousted the Dutch governor, Peter Stuyvesant. With this surprisingly bloodless battle the English established their hegemony over New Netherlands and the Hudson River. But English claims on the Hudson went back as early as 1619 when they challenged the Dutch right to trade on the "Great River." That challenge continued unabated until 1664.

In an effort to legitimize their claim the English argued that territorial claims were based on the dominion of the monarch of the discoverer and not of his employer. Thus the river, which they renamed Hudson in 1664, constituted the historical basis of their claim to all of New Netherlands. The Dutch term "North River," used to indicate the northern boundary of Dutch territory, was now meaningless.[6]

The European battle for empire, which for fifty years had contested trading rights to the Hudson and led to a few small skirmishes, ended with the English flag-raising at the Battery, an action which initiated the ceremonial use of the Hudson. Later, in 1783, the Americans marked their newly won independence with another river celebration at the Battery, establishing the ceremonial place of the Hudson in America's history, a tradition which is still alive.

New Settlers, New Names

The renaming of the river was followed by rapid Anglicization of Dutch culture. Other name changes followed; New Amsterdam became New York, Beverwyck became Albany, and Rondout became King's Town or Kingston. But there were a few Dutch survivals. Some river-connected places kept their Dutch names: Hoboken and Harlem, Spuyten Duyvil and Peekskill, Kinderhook, Catskill, Watervliet, Yonkers, and Fishkill. Pockets of Dutch culture endured in the schools and churches; even the use of the Dutch language in the valley survived into the nineteenth century.

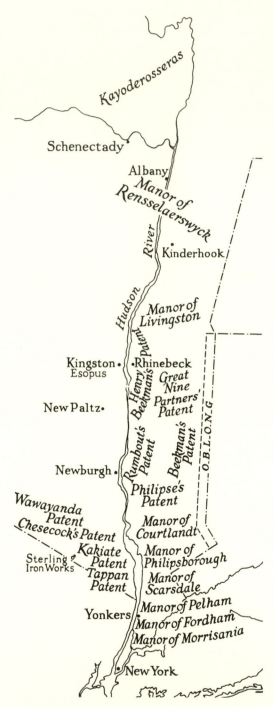

Hudson Valley manors were primarily located on the east side of the river and peopled with tenant farmers. The manors would be dismantled after the Revolution and the land sold to tenant farmers or returning Continental soldiers.
(*From Atlas of American History, edited by James Truslow Adams.*)

Land holdings were transferred to the English manorial system.[7] Four permanent river manors were established: one at the former Dutch patroonship Rensselaer-wyck, a second to Robert Livingston, a third to Frederic Philipse, and a fourth to Stephanus Van Cortlandt, the only river-born of the quartet. These English manors once again emphasize the importance of the river to colonial geography and land distribution.

The English had modest success in attracting settlers to the river valley, though, like the Dutch, their century-long struggle with hostile native bands made new settlements vulnerable. The valley population continued to be a diverse one: to the original Dutch, Huguenots, and English were added Germans, Danes, Flemish, and—after 1730—the great migration of New Englanders westward across the valley. Like those who came before, the new arrivals left their mark in the names of river communities—the Germans in Rhinebeck and New Hamburg, the Yankees in Highland Falls and Cornwall, for example.

The Yankees entering the valley at the end of the eighteenth century brought with them vestiges of their Puritan attitude toward nature, which they saw as a dangerous threat to the advance of civilization and Christianity. These emigrating New Englanders, consisting of yeomen farmers, traders, and small entrepreneurs, rejected the aesthetic and pleasurable aspects of nature. They aimed to Christianize and civilize the river and valley, transforming the landscape in the name of progress. Ironically it may not be the Dutch, in spite of Irving's efforts to the contrary, who brought fear of nature to the Hudson, but rather their Yankee cousins.

Predators of Another Sort

Trade continued to dominate the economic life of the colonial Hudson in the eighteenth century. The central trading roles of New York and Albany were strengthened under the English. But the English phase of the river's economic history had a special twist—pirates and piracy. In New York City, pirates found a harbor that served as a safe haven and a city eager to treat them as celebrities. At one point late in the seventeenth century, nine pirate ships were anchored in the harbor, all protected by English colonial officials who shared in the profits. Pirated cargoes made their way to river markets via New York merchant vessels which often bartered for such cargoes outside the port.

But the pirates were not content to remain at the mouth of the Hudson. They ventured upriver, according to *Albany*

A South Prospect of the Flourishing City of New York, by T. Bakewell, a 1746 view from Brooklyn, depicts a busy New York Harbor, the Manhattan skyline, and a newly constructed wharf on the Brooklyn side of the East River.
(Collection of The New-York Historical Society.)

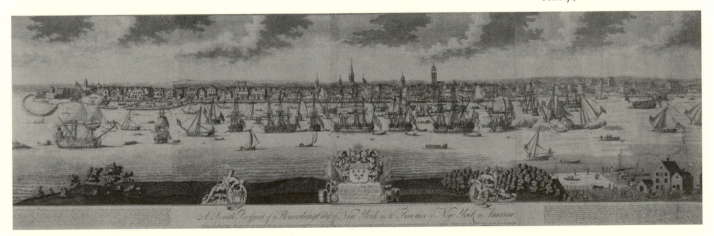

A South Prospect of Flourishing City of New York in y.e Province of New York in America

Records of 1696, to "waylay vessels on their way to Albany, speeding out from covers and from behind islands and again returning to the rocky shores, or ascending the mountains along the river to conceal their plunder." The situation became so desperate that the Earl of Belmont, with the support of Robert Livingston, formed a company, procured the thirty-six gun ship *Adventure*, and hired Captain William Kidd to break up the pirate trade. A reversal of fortune found Kidd, at sea with a mutinous crew, turning to piracy to survive. Upon his return Kidd was arrested and sent to England, where he was tried and hung as a pirate. The Hudson's pirate history illustrates how open and contested were the seas and rivers of the world in the battle for new trade and more profits.

The African-American Presence

The African-American population, brought to the valley as slaves by the Dutch, grew under the English. By 1750 the ratio of blacks to whites was one to nine; in New York City it was one to four. Many worked the ships of the river, serving as crews for sloops and as cargo handlers for larger transatlantic vessels. But throughout the Hudson Valley, African Americans also worked as slaves on farms and in domestic service, and as soldiers battling the French and the natives.

Along the Hudson, African Americans may have been concentrated not only in New York City but in Newburgh, Poughkeepsie, Hudson-Claverack, and Albany. It is difficult to ascertain the exact mix of free blacks and slaves in these communities during the early days of settlement, but it is known that the number of free African Americans increased after the Revolution and continued to do so throughout the nineteenth century.[8]

By the middle of the eighteenth century the Hudson Valley constituted one of the major regional societies on the continent, marked by a firm sense of place, and "distinct in peoples, economies, and cultural landscapes."[9] The region would be increasingly shaped by internal dynamics as it matured and became more conscious of its local, if not its American, identity. The confrontation between this sense of identity and England's attempted imperial reorganization following the French and Indian War led to political disintegration and hastened the coming of revolution.

Revolt along the Hudson

One of the central objectives of the British revolutionary war plan of 1776 was to seize, hold, and use the Hudson as a wedge to separate the New England colonies from the Middle Atlantic and Southern colonies. The British understood that the Hudson was a strategic key to the unification of the colonies and a central artery for intracolonial trade. George Washington and his commanders also recognized its importance; they chose to stand and fight important battles here early in the war, and later to commit part of the Continental Army to its defense.

The British plan of attack required that they gain control of New York City and Albany and establish posts along the Hudson. General William Howe would initiate this plan with the capture of New York City, and then move up the river toward Albany to meet a second British Army coming from the north under the command of General John Burgoyne.

In anticipation Washington assembled an army of twenty-five thousand men in Manhattan to defend the city. Hulks were sunk in the harbor and *chevaux-de-frise* placed on the East River. Additional forts were established along the river: Fort Washington near Manhattan's northern tip, Fort Lee across the Hudson, posts overlooking Haverstraw Bay at Stony Point and Verplanck's Point, Fort Independence near Peekskill, and—in the Highlands—Forts Clinton and Montgomery at Popolopen Creek, Fort Arnold, Fort Putnam, Constitution Island, and West Point. Their placement was determined by the course of the river. Those in the Highlands offered particular advantages; there, the difficulties of navigating a narrow and irregular river channel combined with the advantages of high ground for defensive cannon placements. Indeed, topography determined where many of the major battles along the Hudson would take place.

Battling for Control of the River

In July 1776, General Howe sent several warships, including the *Rose* and *Phoenix*, up the Hudson. Favored by a flood tide and a strong breeze, the vessels passed little damaged through fire from American batteries at Forts Washington and Lee. From anchorages in the Tappan Zee, where the river's width provided safety from shore-based cannon, the warships harassed local residents. After several weeks, the British vessels were engaged by five American ships, including the *Lady Washington*. This only major naval battle of the Hudson proved indecisive; both sides withdrew, with the British eventually dropping downriver.

In fall of 1776, after defeats in Brooklyn and White Plains, the Americans retreated across the Hudson to New Jersey, leaving Fort Washington as their only remaining stronghold in Manhattan and southern Westchester. The British landed troops at Dobbs Ferry, advanced rapidly on Fort Washington, and on November 16 captured the fort and took over two thousand American prisoners. A few days later, a

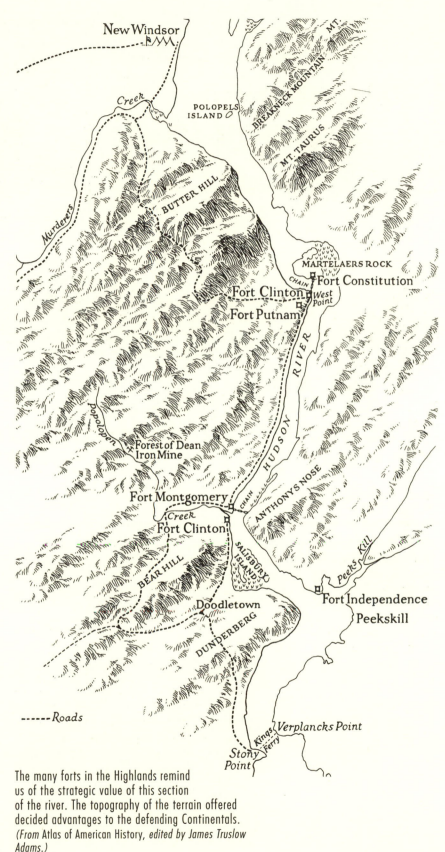

The many forts in the Highlands remind us of the strategic value of this section of the river. The topography of the terrain offered decided advantages to the defending Continentals. (From Atlas of American History, *edited by James Truslow Adams.*)

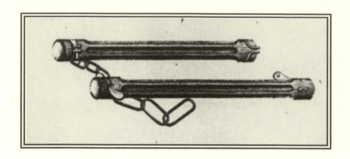

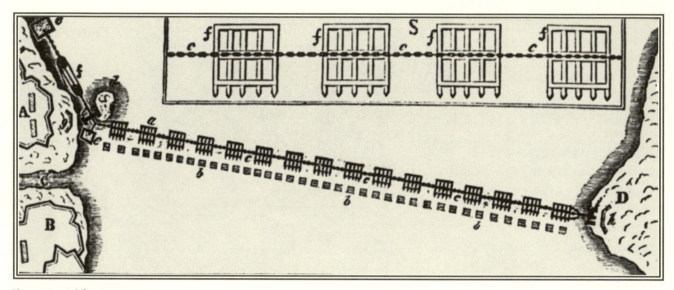

The patriots' defensive structures included chains on log booms and chevaux-de-frise placed across the river from Fort Montgomery to Anthony's Nose and from West Point to Fort Constitution. Links of the chain are on display in the West Point Museum.

British force ferried across the Hudson from Yonkers and seized Fort Lee.

Having secured Manhattan Island for the Crown, the British initiated their two-pronged attempt to seize control of the valley in 1777, moving north from the city and south from Canada. Americans hoped to check the British advance up the Hudson by relying on the defenses at Forts Clinton, Montgomery, and Constitution Island, and a chain and boom stretched across the Hudson from Anthony's Nose to Bear Mountain. In October, a British fleet sailed upriver and feinted an attack on Peekskill.

While the Continentals' attention and reinforcements were diverted, two thousand British soldiers landed at Stony Point in an early morning fog. Marching inland around Dunderberg Mountain, they attacked Forts Montgomery and Clinton from the rear, surprising the Americans and capturing these posts.

This victory enabled the British to dismantle the chain and sail northward, taking control of the Hudson and wreaking havoc along its shores. They burned all river vessels they encountered, cannonaded homes of Whigs, and set houses afire. The provincial capital of Kingston was a major casualty: put to the torch, only one of 116 houses was left standing.

Farther to the north, the second battle of Saratoga took place that October. The Americans under General Horatio Gates held Bemis Heights; Burgoyne hoped to drive them off and back toward the river. The Continentals prevailed and forced the British to surrender, thereby offsetting the advantages gained by the English victories in the Highlands. Burgoyne's defeat at Saratoga halted their advance from Canada and prevented them from completing their Hudson River strategy.

When the British withdrew to New York later that autumn, Washington decided to strengthen the fortifications at West Point and surrounding areas north of the city. A new Fort Clinton was constructed at West Point, and a second chain was planned for the narrow section of the river between West Point and Constitution Island, where a sharp bend would slow attacking ships, making them vulnerable.

The Gibraltar of the Hudson

In the summer of 1778 Washington again visited the Hudson, inspected the fortifications at West Point, and established headquarters in White Plains. Through the following winter the general shadowed British moves and feints up the Hudson. In 1779 he remained tied to the river with headquarters at New Windsor and West Point, watching the British take Stony Point and Fort Lafayette on Verplanck's Point in the spring. That victory gave them control of King's Ferry, a critical river crossing point, and was the prelude to Anthony Wayne's successful recapture of Stony Point.

The British, checked south of the

Highlands through the summer of 1780, decided on a bold stroke to capture West Point, gain control of the Hudson, and divide the Americans. The scheme involved General Benedict Arnold, at the time the disgruntled commanding officer at the Point. Arnold would surrender the "Gibraltor of the Hudson" for $50,000 in gold. Major John Andre, his British co-conspirator, came up the Hudson on the *H.M.S. Vulture*, disembarked, and met with Arnold between Stony Point and Haverstraw. At this meeting the details for the fall of West Point were worked out. Andre, armed with plans and notes on its defenses and a pass from Arnold, started back to the *Vulture*, only to find it had been chased downriver by patriot shelling from Tellers Point. Forced to cross the river and attempt return to British lines by land, he was captured at Tarrytown on September 23, 1780.

Arnold's plot was now exposed and he was forced to flee. He rushed to the Hudson, boarded his barge, and rowed downriver to meet the *Vulture* and eventually to escape to England. The Arnold conspiracy highlighted the importance of the Hudson to the conduct of the war and the key role of West Point in defense of the river. Washington called attention to West Point's significance by visiting it frequently from his winter quarters at New Windsor.

In the summer of 1781 Washington met French troops and officers at Dobbs Ferry and planned to attack New York City with the help of the French fleet. However, Admiral De Grasse put in at Yorktown, Virginia, instead of New York Harbor; consequently, the final battle of the Revolution was on the York River and not the Hudson.

Washington spent the Revolution's closing months (March 1782 to August 1783) headquartered at Hasbrouck House in Newburgh, struggling to hold his army

George Washington stayed at the Dutch Colonial–style Hasbrouck House in Newburgh from April 1782 to August 1783. Here he wrote the "crown letter" rejecting the offer of monarchy, and here he bid farewell to his army. Purchased in 1850 by New York, it was the state's first preservation effort.

together in a camp on the western banks of the Hudson. He made two journeys downriver: to Verplanck's Point to honor Rochambeau's French troops, and to Dobbs Ferry to arrange with Sir Guy Carleton for the evacuation of British troops. On the latter occasion British warships in the Hudson honored Washington with a seventeen-gun salute in the "first complimentary salute fired in honor of an officer of the American Army and indeed in honor of the New Nation."

America's River

The war came to a formal conclusion with the evacuation of British troops from the Bowery, Washington's entrance into the city, and the raising of the American flag at the Battery. The Hudson, which was the strategic key to the Revolution, the site of naval and land battles, and home for much of the duration of the war to Washington and the Continental Army, provided the new nation with a history and a series of memorials and associated places essential to the forging of a national identity. From the Battery to West Point, the Hudson River and valley marked the beginnings of a new history. One river traveler noted that "almost the name of every place" reminded him of "that glorious struggle for independence."

In the search for symbols of identity, the young Republic nationalized the Hudson, making it America's river with the hope that the new citizen would "feel the prouder of his native land" while sailing up the Hudson. For the first half of the nineteenth century, the Hudson, marked by Revolutionary shrines and memorials, embodied our national identity and reminded us of the struggle for independence. In their search for freedom, African Americans reaffirmed this historical association when they used the Hudson as a key section of the Underground Railroad providing runaway slaves with a direct north-south route to western New York and the safety of Canada.

The history of the Hudson now entered its second phase, in which the river served not only as an avenue for exploration and a waterway for commerce, but as a source of nationalist inspiration and instruction. The sanctification of the Hudson that began in the post-Revolutionary era is a process that has continued throughout the modern history of the river. A quick review of the roster of nineteenth-century steamers and twentieth-century bridges illustrates the persistence of the Hudson's Revolutionary associations and our desire not to forget them.

Chapter 8

The Romantic River

The Chapter in Brief
In search of a national identity, Americans turned to the landscape where they found God's blessing manifest in the land. The celebration of nature by painters and writers transformed the Hudson River and its valley into a sublime and picturesque landscape dotted with the great estates of the wealthy and into a source of pride for the young nation. The Hudson was America's river.

"A Spot of Earth with Soul"

Americans emerged from the Revolutionary War free and independent, yet uncertain about their national identity. The struggle for independence had provided Americans with the unifying catalyst of an external enemy around which diverse groups could rally.

After the conclusion of the War of 1812, Americans—having secured the original Revolutionary victory—turned to the consolidation of nationality, and the fostering of a consciousness of shared values and common history. They found examples of these values in their Revolutionary history and in the nineteenth-century landscape. Americans experienced the landscape in a deeply felt and meaningful way. It was rich in historical associations—as Nathaniel Parker Willis wrote, "a spot of earth with soul."

By the 1820s and 1830s Americans believed their destiny was made manifest in the gift of the land, a gift which made their history providential. Through discovery of God's presence in nature, Americans could verify their destiny—proof that they were a chosen people. This experience of discovery was not restricted to the few, but now, by virtue of the Romantic belief in knowledge available through feelings and intuition, open to all citizens. The search began for particular places in nature where the spiritual and the historical were united.

While the Revolution had already provided the Hudson River with abundant historical associations, it remained for the Romantic painters and writers of the nineteenth century to focus the public eye on the river and valley as sources of spiritual nourishment. Willis described nature as a "cathedral," the Hudson as the "grand aisle," and the Highlands as the "gallery."

Discovering the American Landscape

Thomas Cole, an English-born engraver, made his first trip up the Hudson in 1825 and visited the Catskills where he painted *Lake with Dead Trees* (1825). One of the first paintings of the Catskills, this canvas depicts a mountain lake rimmed with barren trees. After selling this and other landscape paintings in New York, Cole's reputation grew quickly and with it the popularity

Thomas Cole's *The Clove, Catskills*, c. 1827, contains some of the main elements in the painting vocabulary of the Hudson River School: a blasted tree and picturesque rock formations in the foreground, tension between dark and light portions of the middle ground, and a distant horizon filled with sky, clouds, and light. Looking out from the clove one can see the Hudson and the Berkshires.
(Courtesy of the New Britain Museum of American Art, Charles F. Smith Fund. Photo by E. Irving Blomstrann.)

of American landscape painting. He became the founding father of what would later be known as the Hudson River School.

Cole's paintings celebrated the *sublime*, elevating the awe and reverence inspired by nature into a religious, moral, and national force. In the picturesque valley of the Hudson the sublime could be found in the purity and transparency of water and sky, which for Cole was the "soul of all scenery." Such qualities were equated with the moral virtue so desirable in human undertakings. By Christianizing the sublime, Cole made it more accessible to the public—a kind of democratic aesthetic.

In large canvasses filled with detailed nature scenes that employed his engraving skills to the fullest, Cole began to document the American landscape and its representative example, the Hudson River and valley. His work, imbued with a strong sense of place, filled the young nation with pride and optimism and found in New York City a ready audience with the leisure to enjoy and the capital to purchase his works. The city, linked to the Hudson commercially, now found an aesthetic harvest was also to be had. The city's new wealthy, eager to show cultural maturity and to identify with the new nationalism, found these ideas fully expressed in Cole's work.

Cole, a painter-poet who wrote a great

deal about his attitude toward nature, felt the landscape offered by the Hudson was superior to any that one might admire in Europe. But Cole was apprehensive about the future. From his home in the Catskills, overlooking the Hudson, he noted the slow but inevitable movement of civilization into the wilderness. The march of civilization and speed of change were imperatives pushing Cole to document the threatened landscape. Cole expressed his fears in *The Course of Empire* (1836), five large canvasses which trace the transformation of an allegorical landscape from the savage stage through the pinnacle of civilization to desolation.

Later painters attempted to reconcile this early Romantic passion for wilderness with recognition of the work of civilization and the transforming power of technology. What they eventually came to celebrate in the valley and along the river was not its pristine natural quality but rather the domestication and adaptation of the landscape. Paintings began to document a riverscape where one could see the reworking of the land, ostensibly to enhance the experience of nature. The river and valley became the premier example of a new equilibrium between civilization and nature—a middle ground between the uncivilized wilderness and the overcivilized cities.

Disciples

After Cole's death, leadership of the landscape painters passed to Asher Durand, who had memorialized Cole in *Kindred Spirits* (1849), a work which depicts Cole and the poet William Cullen Bryant sharing a moment of contemplation in the Catskills. Durand studied and learned from nature. Like Cole, he believed art must capture the work of God expressed in nature. A second and third generation of painters, including John Kensett, Sanford Gifford, Frederic Church,

Asher Durand's *Kindred Spirits* (1848) was commissioned by a New York patron to commemorate William Cullen Bryant's friendship with Thomas Cole, who had died unexpectedly in February of 1848. The painting represents an idealized view of the Kaaterskill Clove. *(Collection of The New York Public Library, Astor, Lenox and Tilden Foundations.)*

and Jasper Cropsey, modified the work of the founder and in some instances pushed toward luminism, the celebration of American light.[1]

Discussions of the Hudson River School run the risk of neglecting some lesser-known landscape painters, one of them William Guy Wall, whose *Hudson River Portfolio* (1821) traced the path of the Hudson from Little Falls, Luzerne, to Governor's Island, New York, and is credited with being the first aesthetic tribute to river scenery. Plates from this work were used for a moving panorama at the Bowery

William Wade's 1845 *Panorama*, 12 feet long, is a detailed engraving showing farms, estates, villages, and commercial and industrial activities on the Hudson's east and west shorelines. The work is part of the panorama tradition of nineteenth-century landscape painting, which had a theatrical quality about it. This tradition was extended to photography in the late nineteenth and early twentieth centuries.

Theater in 1828. Some works by Cole and other Hudson River School painters were used to create what has been called "landscape theater"—panoramic paintings which extended appreciation of the topography and beauty of the Hudson to a larger audience.

The lure of the West and the growing popularity of the camera led to the decline of the Hudson River School in the 1870s and 1880s. But its artists had succeeded in sanctifying the Hudson as a place where God was manifest. Their work continued and deepened the nationalization of the Hudson, and by midcentury it was confirmed as America's river.

Kindred Spirits

Kindred Spirits, Durand's painting of Cole and Bryant, recognized the link between the Romantic artists and writers. They shared a common interest in the exploration of nature and the American wilderness as sources of national identity.

Between 1819 and 1820 Washington Irving published *The Sketchbook of Geoffrey Crayon Gent*, which described the Hudson as "that bright and holy influence of nature upon us." The scenery he described included the Hudson and the Kaatskill Mountains which had so influenced his imagination as a young man. In order to give the American landscape a poetic association, Irving created a folk history for the river, the valley, and New York City, setting characters derived from German folklore in the local landscape. His work created a new interest in the details of nature and inspired landscape painters to come to the Hudson and the Catskills and join with Rip who, looking down from the Catskill Mountain House, saw "the lordly Hudson, far, far below him moving on its silent but majestic course."

Irving's Knickerbocker friends James Kirke Paulding and William Cullen Bryant also contributed to the nationalizing of the regional landscape. In his 1828 work, *New Mirror for Travelers*, Paulding described the Hudson as "this magnificent river, which taking in all of its combinations of magnitude and beauty, is scarcely equalled in the new, and not even approached in the old [world]." Bryant echoed these sentiments in his travel accounts in the *Evening Post*, where he complained that so many Americans went to visit Wales or Scotland instead of the western shore of the Hudson, which was "as worthy of a pilgrimage across the Atlantic as the Alps themselves."

Some writers, sharing the concerns felt by Thomas Cole, expressed the tension be-

tween civilization and nature, few as clearly as James Fenimore Cooper in his *Leather-stocking Tales* (1823–1841). In these works Cooper maps the American wilderness, notes the incursions of humankind, and mourns the loss of innocence. Cooper describes in detail the regional landscape which he felt contained scenes distinctly American because they embraced both civilization and the forest. *Home As Found*

Sunnyside by the Hudson (artist unknown) depicts Washington Irving's "snuggery" set alongside two transportation innovations, the steamboat and the railroad. Some thought these new elements added to the picturesque quality of the landscape, as they seem to in this painting.
(Historic Hudson Valley, Tarrytown, New York.)

A. J. Downing recommended the bracketed cottage model because its projecting roof, supported by "brackets," produced "the kind of beauty called picturesque." The sketch appears in his 1850 work, *The Architecture of Country Houses*, the style book for hundreds of thousands of homes in the eastern United States.

(1838), *Satanstoe* (1845), *The Spy* (1821), and his short story "The Water Witch" provide examples of Cooper's eye for the topography of the valley and the river.

In listing the work of these nationally recognized American writers, one tends to overlook the contribution of Nathaniel Parker Willis, a valley journalist and editor. Late in his career Willis built his country house, Idlewild, near Cornwall, where he explored local history and the river landscape. There he wrote a series of popular essays for the *Home Journal* published later as *Out of Doors at Idlewild; or the Shaping of a Home on the Banks of the Hudson* (1855). Willis's Romantic sensibility extended to local place names, some of which he changed—Butter Hill to Storm King and Murderer's Creek to Moodna Creek, for instance.

The Romantic writers shared with the artists the sense of the Hudson and its valley as a source for an American literary identity. Although they embellished the landscape by peopling it with romantic characters and magnifying its grandeur and uniqueness, they genuinely felt this was the soul of the young nation.

The Velvet Edge

Many Hudson River painters and writers sought to awaken the romantic imagination through direct encounters with nature. Excursions up the Hudson and into the Highlands and Catskills in the 1840s and 1850s became romantic rituals. But for some artists and writers this occasional encounter was not sufficient to sustain their work, and they chose to live in close proximity to the river.

Beginning with Cole, who occupied a farmhouse at Cedar Grove in the Catskills, moving across the Hudson to Frederic Church's Olana (1870), and downriver to Jasper Cropsey's studio Ever Rest (1885) in Hastings, we have representative examples encompassing all the generations of the Hudson River School. But these examples of river living were not limited to artists. Newly wealthy urbanites in search of country seats joined the suburban migration of New Yorkers to the Hudson Valley, where their river estates can be found among the homes of the Romantic artists and writers.

The most extraordinary example is Washington Irving's Sunnyside, a Dutch farmhouse transformed into a Romantic stone mansion so remarkable that it inspired the landscape aesthetic of Andrew Jackson Downing and the architectural style of Alexander Jackson Davis.[2] Sunnyside, with its eclectic architectural style, located "with that glorious river before me . . . which has ever been to me a river of delight," was another attempt by Irving to give the Hudson a history. The landscaped grounds illustrate the Romantic manipulation and enhancement of nature and are one of the best examples of Romantic landscape practices.

Nathaniel Parker Willis's estate Idlewild, with a commanding view of Newburgh Bay, became one of the most famous Romantic retreats on the Hudson—an in-

This photograph of the Catskill Mountain House shows the viewing area at the edge of the escarpment.

Cozzens' Hotel (*below*) at Buttermilk Falls, located in the village of Highland Falls, was built on an escarpment 180 feet above the river. This representative nineteenth-century mountain house offered a panoramic view of the Hudson and abundant clean air for its three hundred patrons.

tellectual salon where one could enjoy nature, the river, and good conversation.

Almost overnight, living in the country became the fashion. A. J. Downing helped to set this pattern in 1842 with the publication of *Cottage Residences*, which served as a guide for country living. Businessmen in New York, flush with success and imitative of English gentry, sought to escape the city by building villas on the Hudson.

Country Living

The term "country living" defined the new domesticated landscape and distinguished it from the cult of wilderness that had dominated earlier Romantic thinking. The Hudson River fulfilled the ideals of the emerging middle ground landscape—human intervention which enhanced the glories of nature.

By the second half of the nineteenth century, the Hudson was in the grip of a frenzy of estate building. The riverscape was lined with a "velvet edge" of manicured landscapes and neo-Gothic cottages extending from Weehawken to Albany. A river journey could now be marked not by reaches but by great river estates: Wave Hill in Riverdale, Glenview in Yonkers,

Lyndhurst in Tarrytown, Castle Rock in the Highlands, the Vanderbilt Mansion in Hyde Park, the Mills Mansion in Staatsburg, Edgewater in Barrytown, and Montgomery Place in Annandale. New Yorkers who likened the Hudson to the Rhine appropriately built European-style castles, beginning with Fonthill in Riverdale and on to Ericstan in Tarrytown, Castle Rock in Garrison, and Bannerman's Castle on Pollepel Island.

The Mountain House

If one could not afford the luxury of a river estate there was always the mountain house, situated on high ground with a panoramic view of the river and offering fatigued New Yorkers refreshing doses of mountain air. The premier nineteenth-century mountain house was the Catskill Mountain House. Several variations quickly appeared along the Hudson, from the Fort Lee Hotel and the Palisades Mountain House in New Jersey to Cozzen's Hotel at Buttermilk Falls in the Highlands.

The emergence of a middle class with a measure of wealth and leisure contributed to the transformation of the Hudson into a therapeutic river, one which could heal both the body and the spirit. And as steamboats came to prominence, river excursions became recreational experiences attracting large numbers of the middle and lower classes. Amusement parks (some built by the steamboat companies) sprouted on the New Jersey Palisades and at Hastings, Indian Point, Iona Island, and Kingston Point.

The work of the painters, writers, and estate builders contributed to the development of a Hudson River aesthetic which envisioned the river, the land, and the home as key elements in the romantic sublime and picturesque. Unlike the raw American West, to which the painters of the Hudson River School would soon defect, the Hudson River valley provided the best example of humankind's ability to improve upon nature and live in harmony with it.

Chapter 9

Industrialization and the Transformation of the Landscape

The Chapter in Brief

Until the opening of the Erie Canal, the Hudson Valley was the breadbasket of the United States. The presence of New York as a commercial center, entry port, and growing city at the Hudson's mouth influenced the economic development of industries such as brickmaking, iron making, lumbering, and quarrying. Completion of the Erie Canal enlarged the market area served by the Hudson and lifted the valley's economy out of its provincial status. Industrialization of the valley required a transportation revolution including development of the steamship and railroad. The process reshaped the landscape and led artists and writers to develop new and broader definitions of the sublime.

A Republic of Small Farmers

The nineteenth century was not only an age which celebrated nature and discovered the American landscape, but also one which witnessed the industrialization of the United States and the transformation of the very landscape the artists and writers were honoring.

Industrialization of the Hudson was preceded by a long and prosperous commercial and agricultural history. Agriculture flourished in the valley and along the river until the second quarter of the nineteenth century. The production of wheat, barley, and rye on choice soils in the valley was so successful that the region was known as the "Bread Basket of the Nation." In addition to commercial farming, which made use of the Hudson for transportation and encouraged the development of sloop landings along the river, subsistence farming was commonplace throughout the valley. Axe-wielding settlers transformed the landscape: most of the valley's original forest cover had been cleared for agriculture by the time of the Revolution.

Industrial Development: The First Stage

Early signs of industrial development appeared along the Hudson during the eighteenth century, limited by modest capitalization, few local markets, and restricted means of transportation. The valley's industrial growth was driven by the needs of New York City at the river's mouth; the expanding city served as a commercial center for trade and a consumer of natural resources from the valley.

Among the earliest of these industries was lumbering, which provided materials for home construction and shipbuilding, fuel for steam engines, and pulp for paper production. Lumbering stimulated the expansion of milling, dependent on water power and thus frequently located on tributaries of the Hudson. Milling included not only sawmills but also gristmills and paper mills.

Bricks and Quarries

Quarrying in the Palisades and the Highlands began as early as 1736 and accelerated in the nineteenth century with the increase in New York City's building needs, especially road construction. In the Catskills, quarry operations produced slabs of bluestone used as paving on city streets and sidewalks.

Brickmaking appeared in Haverstraw in 1815 and expanded rapidly, employing at its peak twenty-four hundred workers, making Haverstraw the brickmaking capital of the valley. Local forests supplied the wood needed to fire the kilns; clay deposits and anthracite coal dust provided the basic ingredients. The industry's energy needs gobbled up the cedar which formerly stood in great abundance along the western shore of the river. Broken and misformed castoffs from brick production still litter the Hudson's banks in Haverstraw, Kingston, Fishkill, and other river communities.[1]

The success of quarrying and brickmaking provided impetus for the growth of shipbuilding. Between 1815 and 1828, Nyack shipyards turned out a sloop a year,

making the town the shipbuilding center of the Hudson. Nyack was succeeded by Newburgh and Rondout in steamboat production later that century. The latter continued shipbuilding activity through World War II.

Upriver industrial activity included ironmaking in the Highlands, cement production near the foot of the Catskills, and tanning along Catskill Creek. Ironmakers cleared large tracts of forest to manufacture charcoal, constructed forges and furnaces, and played an important role in arming the Union forces during the Civil War. Nineteenth-century iron production in the valley was concentrated in the Cold Spring area.

Beds of limestone found near the river proved suitable for cement making, but the river itself was the key factor in establishing the industry. Powdered cement, made by burning chunks of limestone in kilns, was a bulk cargo most easily and cheaply shipped by water. Even today, up-

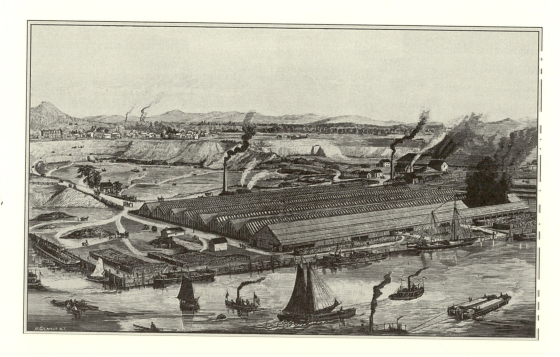

The brickworks of John Derbyshire, one of the largest brick producers of the late 1800s, were set in a treeless landscape at Haverstraw. Clay unloaded from barges along the southern dock was stockpiled adjacent to the works; schooners tied up at the long wharf to the east transported finished bricks to New York.

A standard ice house was made of wood and measured 200 feet by 150 feet with a storage capacity of 20,000 to 30,000 tons. Most were located on the Hudson's western shore and set broadside to the river. For insulation, the space between their double outer walls was packed with sawdust.

river cement factories ship their product downriver in barges.

Leather and Ice

Tanning required tannic acid from hemlock trees, which were found in the Catskills in conjunction with large supplies of fresh water also necessary to the operation. Untanned hides, some from South America, could easily be transported up the Hudson by steamer, and finished hides reshipped to New York City.

One of the best examples of the influence of New York City on industrial development along the Hudson is ice harvesting. In 1826, ice blocks were cut from Rockland Lake and shipped downriver to be stored in city ice houses. The newly incorporated Knickerbocker Ice Company built an inclined railway from the landing to the lake, ran a fleet of thirteen steamboats, and eventually employed twenty-four hundred to three thousand men.

Similar growth occurred upriver, where ice was cut from the Hudson itself. Ice houses were found along the river from Marlboro to Troy. One firm, the Mutual Benefit Ice Company, had ice houses in West Park, Port Ewen, Staatsburg, and Barrytown, where the house could hold sixty thousand tons of ice. This kind of growth depended on demand from a readily accessible major urban market.

Industrial Development: The Second Stage

Industrial growth in the early 1800s provided the precedent for a second stage of industrial development in the late 1800s and early 1900s, including automobile assembly plants, cable wire production, Portland cement manufacturing, electrical power production, oil refining and shipment, sugar refineries, and paper making.[2]

Many of these industries attracted immigrant workers to river towns, where they provided cheap industrial labor and the basis of a heterogeneous population. The immigrant workers tended to concentrate in the towns' older sections, close to the river, to industrial facilities, and to the railroad, while old-stock residents and new suburbanites moved up the hill, thereby creating the town/hill split which marks so many river villages.

The rearrangement of river towns was only a small part of the industrial transformation of the landscape along the Hudson and throughout the valley. Visible industrial scars from quarrying, for example, raised concerns about the vulnerability and beauty of the landscape. But the response was not rejection. Artists and travelers, including Nathaniel Parker Willis and Benson Lossing, believed that mills and factories added to the picturesque.

But before this second stage of industrial development could blossom, key obstacles needed to be overcome. The Erie Canal and the steam engine were major forces in this process.

The Erie Canal

While the river had always provided inexpensive transportation, until the nineteenth century this service remained limited by the provincial economies of the river-based towns and nature's uncertain winds and changing tides. Completion of the Erie Canal in 1825 provided a major avenue for economic expansion, linking the Hudson and New York City with the Great Lakes and the Middle West. The canal opened the hinterland to the New York/Hudson commercial network and became the principal commercial route on the continent; one year after completion it was carrying nineteen thousand boats.

New York City, at the nexus of interstate trade via the Erie Canal and international trade from Europe and the Far East, became a center for banking, insurance, and shipping, while Albany, at the key juncture of the Hudson and the canal, became an inland port and a thriving seaport.

Drawn by the fertile soils of the Midwest, wheat farmers moved west, accompanied by flour milling operations. The low costs of raising wheat in those rich soils and shipping it back to the Hudson Valley via the canal allowed Midwestern wheat to be

Entering the Lock (E. L. Henry). Canal boats had colorful and evocative names including *The Chief Engineer, The Seneca Chief, The Young Lion of the West,* and *Noah's Ark.* Boats were named for love, pride, patriotism, and even the exotic—the *Breath of Cashmere,* for example.
(Collection of the Albany Institute of History and Art.)

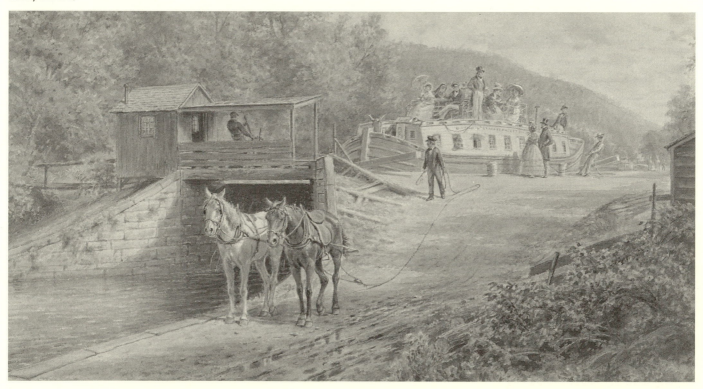

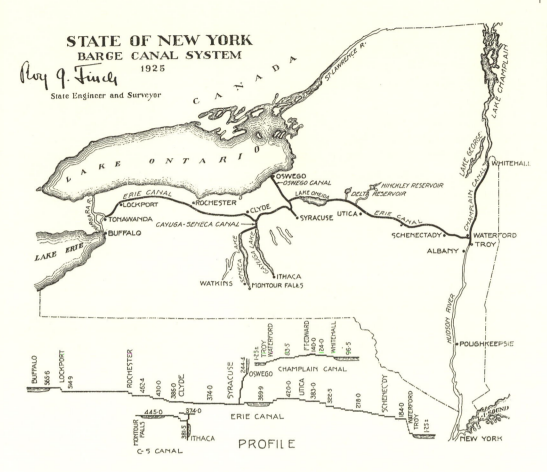

STATE OF NEW YORK
BARGE CANAL SYSTEM
1925

Roy G. Finch
State Engineer and Surveyor

"The Erie Canal rubbed Aladdin's Lamp. America awoke, catching for the first time the wondrous vision of its own dimensions and power."—Francis Kimball, canal historian.

sold more cheaply than that grown along the river. New York lost its function as the breadbasket of the nation and was forced to shift to more specialized dairy and fruit farming.

The Erie Canal extended the network of river transportation to Lake Erie, creating a larger market, broadening the resource base, and elevating the region's economy out of its provincial status. The canal offered savings in shipping costs and time that attracted more traffic and stimulated expansion and investment. And in overcoming the obstacles of nature, it illustrated the central role of engineering and technology in economic development.[3]

"A Monster Moving on the River Defying Wind and Tide, and Breathing Flames and Smoke"

The Dutch sloop, because it depended on nature, often found its passengers and cargo were held captive by the Hudson's winds and tides, introducing uncertainty and irregularity to commercial activity. Industrialization and modernization of the valley's economy required a transportation system that could reach more distant markets and carry goods in a regular and timely manner. As demonstrated by the Erie Canal, engineering and technology helped expand markets; they were also needed to overcome the remaining obstacles of winds and tides.

In May of 1804 James Renwick and his Columbia College classmates observed a crowd moving quickly toward the Battery to see "Jack Stevens going over to Hoboken in a queer sort of boat." When they arrived at the Battery the boat—"with no visible means of propulsion"—was speedily under way. What Renwick and his friends had observed was the first known successful application of steam to twin screw propellers.

Robert Fulton is thus neither the inventor of the steamboat nor the first to build one on the Hudson; this honor belongs to New Jerseyan John Stevens of Hoboken. What distinguished Robert Fulton from Stevens and others was the commercial backing of Robert Livingston of Clermont, who had the capital to underwrite Fulton and the legal expertise to monopolize steam travel on the Hudson.

On August 17, 1807, off the west side of Manhattan near the old state prison and in front of a large crowd, Robert Fulton left the dock on his *North River* (later dubbed the *Clermont*), 130 feet long with a beam of 16 feet and open paddle wheels. Making his way up the Hudson, he arrived at the Livingston estate, a distance of 100 miles, in twenty-four hours. The next day Fulton continued to Albany, completing a journey of 150 miles in thirty-six hours. The steamboat age had begun.

The full impact of this new technology was delayed by the legislative monopoly Fulton and Livingston had secured to protect their invention, fix prices, and eliminate competition. This chokehold on river steamboat travel slowed the transportation revolution until the monopoly was broken by the U.S. Supreme Court in the case of *Gibbons v. Ogden*, decided in 1824.[4] Very

The Clermont *making a landing at Cornwall on the Hudson, 1810* (E. L. Henry). The interlocking nature of the transportation system was documented every day at river landings large and small. Here turnpike, coach, inn, dock, and the *Clermont* all meet with the exchange of goods, passengers, and gossip.
(I. N. Phelps Stokes Collection, Miriam and Ira D. Wallach Division of Art, Prints and Photographs, The New York Public Library, Astor, Lenox and Tilden Foundations.)

quickly competition increased, rates fell, and river traffic expanded.

Keeping to a Schedule

By 1850 over a hundred steamboats were carrying more than a million passengers and arriving on schedule. Speed was all. Steamboat captains, crews, and owners competed with reckless abandon to be the fastest on the river. The passion for speed was so consuming that the safety of passengers was sometimes secondary. One infamous steamboat race, pitting the *Armenia* against the *Henry Clay* in July of 1852, ended with the *Clay* in flames and many dead, including Andrew Jackson Downing, the noted landscape architect.

The steamboat was conquering time, promising to arrive and depart on schedule.

Hudson River Day Line,

NEW YORK & ALBANY DAY BOATS.

General Offices, Desbrosses St. Pier, New York.

DIMENSIONS OF STEAMERS.

	"New York."	"Albany."
Length over all	341 feet.	325 feet.
Breadth " "	74 "	75 "
Breadth of Hull	40 "	40 "
Tonnage	1,850 tons.	1,415 tons.
Horse Power	3,850	3,200
Stroke of Piston	12 feet.	12 feet.
Diameter of Cylinder	75 in.	73 in.

DAY LINE TIME TABLE, 1899.
DAILY EXCEPT SUNDAY.

GOING NORTH.	A. M.	GOING SOUTH.	A. M.
Brooklyn by Annex, 8.00		Albany, - - -	8.30
New York:		Hudson, - -	10.40
Desbrosses St.,	8.40	Catskill, - -	11.00
22d St., N. R.,	9.00		P. M.
Yonkers, -	9.45	Kingston Point,	12.25
West Point, -	11.50	Poughkeepsie,	1.20
	P. M.	Newburgh, - -	2.15
Newburgh, -	12.25	West Point, -	2.50
Poughkeepsie,	1.15	Yonkers, - -	4.30
Kingston Point,	2.10	New York:	
Catskill, - - -	3.25	22d St., N. R.,	5.30
Hudson, - -	3.40	Desbrosses St.,	6.00
Albany, - - -	6.10	Brooklyn by Annex, 6.20	

The celebration of technology was always tinged with apprehension about human ability to control the machine. The *Henry Clay* disaster served as a reminder that the machine could quickly become the monster in irresponsible hands.

Interior of the steamer Drew. *"River palace" aptly describes the* Drew *with its luxurious interior. The cost of early steamboat travel may have compelled designers to embellish the interiors to offer passengers a "travel experience"—something more than a speedy connection between two points. While falling rates (which helped democratize travel) made such luxury unnecessary, a similar pattern of interior design appeared in railroad cars as well.*
(Collection of The New-York Historical Society.)

One of the most significant documents in the history of transportation may be the schedule—the commitment to regularity and predictability so necessary to the development of an industrial economy. Schedules for steamboat travel made their appearance on the Hudson as early as September 1807, long before they appeared on any other American river. With the introduction and widespread use of the steamboat on the Hudson, the machine had entered the garden.

Hudson River painters and lithographers have provided us with a rich visual record of the steamboat's progress. The best of these are the works of the Bard brothers, who captured the efficient beauty of the machine. They saw the "technological sublime" in the Hudson River steamboats.[5] These artists seem to express an optimism that nature and technology could coexist and share in a common sublime.

The deep and abiding faith of nineteenth-century Americans in the inevitability of progress impelled technology to search beyond the steamboat, which, though it had conquered time, remained river-bound and ice-locked. Engineers transferred steamboat technology to land transportation, leading to the development of the railroad.

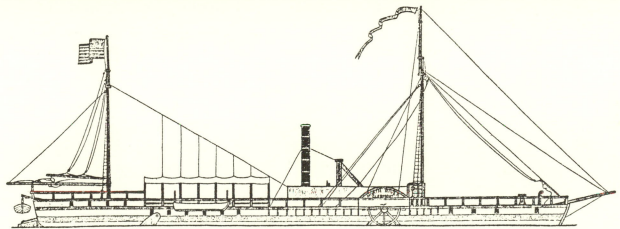

NORTH RIVER · 1807-1808

Robert Fulton and Robert R. Livingston

1807: 142 × 14 × 4 feet ⊄ 79 T ⊄ 43,280 × 4,267 × 1,219 m

1808: 149 × 17.92 × 7 feet ⊄ 182 T ⊄ 45,414 × 5,462 × 2,134 m

The elaboration of steamboat design is clear in comparing a diagram of Fulton's *North River* (*bottom*) with the *Drew* and the *St. John* (*top*), depicted passing in the Highlands by Currier and Ives. The extension of the deck out over the narrow hull increased passenger capacity. Triple decking also underscored the designers' intention to provide a visual travel experience. The decorated paddle box was one of the distinguishing characteristics of each vessel.

(Collection of The New-York Historical Society.)

Syracuse (James Bard). The art of the Bard brothers, James and John, stylized the steamboat as a fast, sleek, and modern-looking vessel—a nineteenth-century prefiguring of the streamlined style we identify with twentieth-century design. Their representations have become icons, defining our image of the Hudson River steamboats. (Collection of the Albany Institute of History and Art, Gift of William Gorham Rice.)

Railroads: The Great Machine

Land travel along the Hudson had remained a primitive affair over the Albany Post Road. Competing stage lines merged in 1835 and provided regular passenger service between New York and Albany. Winter ice and snow required the use of sled runners, clearly a preindustrial means of transportation.

Beginning in 1831, when the Mohawk and Hudson Railroad reached Albany, and in 1841 when the Erie connected to the Hudson at Piermont, stage travel declined and the steamboat had its first real competition. In 1851 the Hudson River Railroad was completed along the Hudson's eastern bank from New York City to the town of Greenbush, across the river from Albany. The first railroad trip from New York to Greenbush in October 1851 took four hours. Fulton's steamboat had taken thirty-six hours to make the same journey, an improvement over the several days it might have taken a sloop to cover that distance. For both sloop and steamboat, their days of prominence on the Hudson were now numbered.[6]

Travel, now freed from the natural limits of the river, stimulated commercial development, population growth, and the suburbanization of many river towns. The railroad not only linked the river valley more closely to the city, but established a corridor of industrial activity all along the right-of-way. It completed the revolution begun by the steamboat and the Erie Canal, namely the expansion and integration of markets.

And the railroad announced its

First Railroad Train on the Mohawk and Hudson Road
(E. L. Henry). *Scientific American* reported in April
1851 that "one of the grandest sights is a locomotive
with its huge train dashing along in full flight . . .
when a large train is rushing along at the rate of
30 miles per hour, [it] affords a sight both sublime
and terrific."
*(Collection of the Albany Institute of History and Art, Gift of
Friends of the Institute.)*

By the mid-1800s the new railroad lines had been
linked to established steamboat landings, creating a
travel network in which passengers were likely to move
from one means of transportation to another in the
course of a single journey. Steamers from New York
took vacationers to the landing at Catskill; from there
they were conveyed by stagecoach and railroad to the
Mountain House.

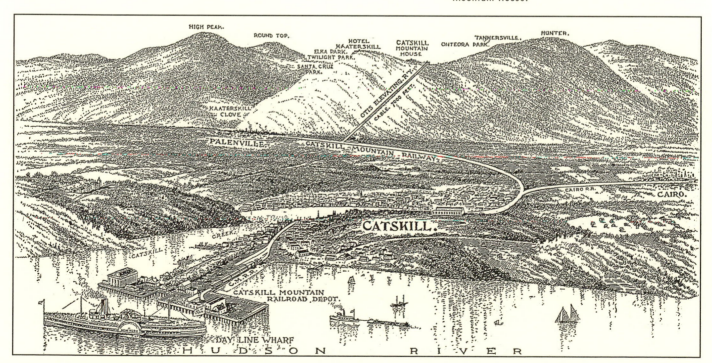

The first bridge to span the Hudson below Albany was the railroad bridge at Poughkeepsie, completed in 1888. Bridges are only one reminder of how engineers were central, though too often neglected, figures in the river's history. In the 1800s they played key roles in exploiting the valley for transportation and water supply. John B. Jervis, for example, had major reponsibilities in building the Delaware and Hudson Canal, the Croton Aqueduct, and the Hudson River railroad.
(Courtesy Adriance Memorial Library, Poughkeepsie, New York.)

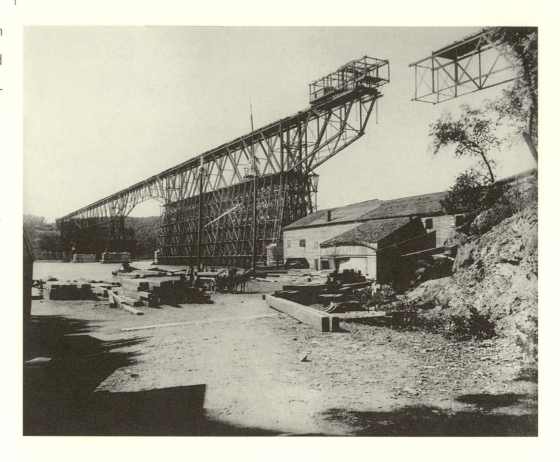

presence in the riverscape with bold and powerful marks. No one could miss the size, sound, and smoke of this new engine of progress, which promised to complete the conquest of the wilderness and the domination of nature. Residents of river towns and estates daily felt its transforming power close at hand. The Hudson's shoreline was now bounded by a steel highway that regularized the water's edge and, with electrification, kept people from the river.

The Machine Enters the Garden

Nineteenth-century responses to the railroad were ambivalent. Lovers of the Hudson like Thomas Cole, while they welcomed the advance of civilization which the railroad represented, were angered by the destruction of nature that accompanied it.

Cole witnessed scenes of beauty made desolate in the name of improvement. The Hudson River, which the Romantic painters and artists viewed as a special creation of God, was—in the hands of railroad builders and land developers—quickly becoming the work of civilization.

Because of its power to break through the boundaries of space and transform the landscape, the railroad more than the steamboat underscored the tension between civilization and nature. How were these forces to be balanced to ensure the beauty of the Hudson River and the valley?

While some critics saw these forces as irreconcilable, others believed the railroad and the river were complementary agents of the sublime. As the portrayal of the valley became less wild and more pastoral, the railroad offered a vehicle for public enjoyment of the domesticated landscape. It seemed to a majority of nineteenth-century Americans that a reconciliation was possible.[7]

The railroad, in choosing the Hudson's shoreline for its right of way, followed the topography of the river and the route of least resistance and lowest cost. This decision, based on economics and not aesthetics, established the precedent for later riverside highway travel by automobile.

Driving to the Country

Apologists for the twentieth-century highway, like the railroad's nineteenth-century defenders, argued that it brought humankind's engineering skills to nature, enhanced the landscape, and made the river and valley accessible to more people. Advertisements for both the railroad and the automobile shared a common emphasis on the virtues of the countryside and the great outdoors—the river and the valley—now within reach of many city dwellers because of the transportation revolution.

The shift to the automobile and truck as principal means of transportation in the valley was a signal of a deeper shift in the economic growth pattern of river communities. Industries no longer dependent on the Hudson or the railroad eventually began to leave the river for other sections of the country. River-based industrial facilities became vacant, ghostly monuments to an older order.[8]

In the mid-twentieth century, newer manufacturing and service industries settled in the Hudson Valley, but not necessarily near the river. The service businesses in particular were attracted by the new phenomenon of suburbanization, which created new population centers and customers. Such changes were the result of the increasing importance of the automo-

bile. River communities once linked by the Hudson are now connected by highways.

Over and Under

Engineers were stymied by the difficulty of burrowing underneath the Hudson River until 1904, when a tunnel (now used by Port Authority transit trains) was completed

African-Americans played a role in the construction of major Hudson River public works projects including the West Shore Railroad. In this kind of unskilled labor they shared a common experience with Irish and Italian immigrants who found similar work in the building of the two Croton aqueducts.

linking Hoboken in New Jersey and Morton Street in New York City. In 1924 the Bear Mountain Bridge, the first vehicular spanning of the Hudson below Albany, was completed. More bridges and tunnels followed, and the Hudson no longer stood as a natural boundary between states and counties, urban and rural.

The transformation of river communities formerly separated by the Hudson and now linked by a bridge or tunnel was rapid. Inevitably the newly accessible communities in the lower valley grew in population and became twentieth-century suburbs. A modern example of this is the surge of growth in Rockland County following the completion of the Tappan Zee Bridge in 1955. The 1950 pre-bridge census showed a population of 89,000; by 1970 the figure

CROSSING THE RIVER
Bridges and Tunnels Located Between *Albany and New York City*

1. Parker F. Dunn Memorial Bridge *(1969)*
2. Castleton Thruway Bridge *(1959)*
3. Castleton Railroad Bridge *(1923)*
4. Rip Van Winkle Bridge *(1935)*
5. Kingston-Rhinecliff Bridge *(1957)*
6. Poughkeepsie Railroad Bridge *(1888 - no longer in use)*
7. Mid-Hudson Bridge *(1930)*
8. Newburgh-Beacon Bridge *(1963 - 2nd span completed 1980)*
9. Bear Mountain Bridge *(1924)*
10. Tappan Zee Bridge *(1955)*
11. George Washington Bridge *(1931 - lower deck opened 1962)*
12. Lincoln Tunnel *(1937 - first of 3 tubes)*
13. Pennsylvania Railroad Tunnel *(1906 - now Amtrak)*
14. Holland Tunnel *(1927)*
15. Hudson & Manhattan Railroad Tunnel *(1904 - now PATH uptown tube)*
16. Hudson & Manhattan Railroad Tunnel *(1909 - now PATH downtown tube)*
17. Verrazano Narrows Bridge *(1964)*

The Bear Mountain Bridge seems to be the perfect example of the technological sublime in which the work of the engineer is fully absorbed into and compatible with the work of nature. Such a view is typical of America's basic faith, rooted in the nineteenth century, in harmony between civilization and nature. *(Photo by Charles Porter.)*

had jumped to 230,000. The river had historically affected population distribution and growth; now engineers had successfully limited its role.

Bridges and tunnels, unlike the old ferries and steamers, insulate the public from direct physical experience of the river: its smells, sounds, and even its spray. Today's commuters are moved across the Hudson in an engineered space that is repetitious and unnatural. Modern society's mastery over nature and the river has detached us from experience of the present-day Hudson and may contribute to public indifference about its future. Recent restorations of ferry service and an increasing number of excursion boats may bring the public back into closer contact with the river and expand the political base of those who feel that the health of the river is important.

The nineteenth century established the Romantic image of the Hudson as an example of the sublime in nature. At the same time, the Hudson River valley was the setting for a revolution in transportation and the ensuing advance of industrialization. By the end of the nineteenth century a basic historical and cultural pattern of river history was in place: the forces of nature and civilization pushing and pulling against each other in a battle over the future of the Hudson.

Chapter 10

Conservation and Environmentalism

The Chapter in Brief

By the end of the nineteenth century, America faced a crisis in the struggle between the forces of progress and preservation. Critics argued that the benefits of industrialization needed to be balanced with needs for long-term economic growth and land preservation. Fears over depletion of the resource base and the natural environment led state governments to intervene to preserve the Adirondack Forest and the Palisades. This was the beginning of the conservation movement, an effort to protect the beauty of the landscape and effectively manage natural resources. The battle over Storm King, a struggle that engaged a power company, the federal government, and citizen action groups, not only involved issues of scenic beauty and use of natural resources but also issues of health and habitat, the concerns of the new environmental movement of the 1960s and 1970s.

Woodsman, Spare the Axe

The end of a century has always been a time for soul-searching and grandiose prophecy about either impending disaster or a new age of progress. As the nineteenth century approached its end, Americans swung between extremes of fear and exhilaration. The cultural crisis deepened with the knowledge that the frontier was closing; its character-forming power would soon disappear, and with it America's youthful vigor and natural resources.

The signs of crisis were visible to Americans in the destruction of wilderness and desecration of the landscape. The abundance of natural resources seemed threatened by aggressive businessmen driven only by immediate profits. The pattern of depletion and destruction was visible along the Hudson River, where intensive lumbering in the Adirondacks and quarrying of the Palisades posed a threat to the Hudson's watershed and its geological beauty.

In 1870 Verplanck Colvin called attention to the watershed problems caused by the "chopping and burning off of vast tracts of forests" in the Adirondacks. A water shortage in Albany also underscored the Adirondacks' value as a water resource. The state legislature examined various uses of the Adirondacks and in 1885, after several reports and investigations, established the Forest Preserve in the Adirondacks and the Catskills, preserving the "nurse" of the Hudson.[1]

The preserve was created not only to protect the Hudson's watershed and manage a forest but also to guarantee a wilderness experience for wealthy New Yorkers. Two wings of the conservation movement clashed over these different goals—one side committed to planned long-term use of resources rather than short-term plunder, the other committed to defending nature from any land or resource development that did not preserve its beauty.

The preserve was the result of intervention by the state to protect nature against the depredations of civilization. As confidence in the idea of limitless resources and the durability of nature faded, local, state, and national governments moved forward to become key players in the twentieth-century history of the Hudson and its val-

The nineteenth-century response to the Adirondacks has been described as essentially masculine. Such a conclusion may reflect bias in the readily available texts. Women did share in the enthusiasm for the outdoors and—as we have recently begun to discover—wrote a great deal about their experiences. *(Courtesy of the Palisades Interstate Park Commission, Trailside Museum.)*

ley. One could no longer trust some invisible ecological hand to balance the demands of development and preservation.

New York State would now be an active, if at times reluctant participant in the conservation movement. Yet in spite of the state's role and the organizing work of groups like the Sierra Club, the movement continued to have an elitist underpinning. Public consciousness and participation remained low until the 1960s.

Dynamite, Dynamite, Dynamite

The most visible signs of destruction were to be found in the Palisades and Hook Mountain, just north of Nyack on the Hudson's western shore. Quarrying had intensified greatly in the 1870s and 1880s with the aid of dynamite and earth-moving equipment. A river traveler could not help but notice the scars and deep cuts in the Palisades, Hook Mountain, and Breakneck

Ridge in the Highlands. Some Palisades landmarks, including Washington Head and Indian Head, were destroyed.

Dynamiting, a daily reminder of the relentless destruction, galvanized the union of residents of landscaped Palisades estates, influential landowners from Riverdale, and the Women's Clubs of New Jersey into a pressure group advocating an end to the quarrying. In March 1890, state commissions from New York and New Jersey finally recommended that a permanent interstate park be established to protect the Palisades.

Preservation and Recreation

The New York and New Jersey legislatures established the Palisades Interstate Park Commission (PIPC) to buy and administer land on the Palisades. The PIPC's jurisdiction extended from the top of the Palisades to the river's edge and by 1906 included

Establishment of the Palisades Interstate Park in 1900 stopped the quarrying along the Hudson only south of the Tappan Zee. The 1931 purchase of one thousand acres on Mount Taurus (in Cold Spring) by the Hudson River Stone Company led to formation of the Hudson River Conservation Society, which lobbied unsuccessfully to stop the quarrying there.
(Courtesy of Scenic Hudson)

Hook Mountain in Rockland County. In addition to saving the Palisades and Hook Mountain from the quarrymen, the motive here was to encourage managed use in which Manhattanites, in search of a respite from city life, would be able to enjoy the river and the Palisades.

The recreational objectives, which included bathing, hiking, and camping, expanded and democratized use of the river while serving the interests of the elite conservationists who sought to preserve the landscape and bring the common person into contact with nature. It took the active leadership of well-connected citizens along with the direct intervention of two state governments to produce this pioneering cooperative effort in conservation.

In 1909 the Palisades Interstate Park was formally dedicated as part of the Hudson-Fulton Tricentennial Celebration. The celebration's parades, memorials, and speeches became civics lessons for old and new stock Americans, who may have forgotten or not known that this once was America's river, with the history and power to instill national pride. At the same time that conservation efforts in the Adirondacks and on the Palisades attempted to protect the river's Romantic landscape, the Hudson-Fulton Celebration hoped to reinvigorate the historical associations identified with the river and valley.

The Roads Roll On

The PIPC also prepared surveys for new river roadways, the Henry Hudson Parkway in 1905 and the Palisades Parkway in 1909, which would provide automobile access to the recreational experience of the Hudson. The traveling public would come to know the riverscape in a horizontal way, as something one moved through.

The energy of the first wave of conservation extended into the 1920s as the geographical territory administered by the PIPC was expanded to include the Harriman and Bear Mountain Parks. These years also saw construction of connections to those sights—the Bear Mountain Bridge (1924) and the Storm King Highway (1919–1922) running two hundred feet above the Hudson and across the face of Storm King Mountain. The pattern of improving automobile access continued into the 1930s with the construction of the George Washington Bridge (1931) and the New Deal's Storm King Highway (1940), built around the back of Storm King by the Civilian Conservation Corps (this road is now part of State Route 9W).

The automobile was quickly becoming a major force in a new transformation of the riverscape. The pace of change was so rapid that two additional lanes had to be added to the George Washington Bridge in 1946 and a six-lane lower level in 1960. As

New Deal public works projects transformed the American landscape. Bear Mountain caught the attention of WPA planners who sponsored the construction of Perkins Memorial Drive and the rustic Bear Mountain Inn in which they attempted to integrate design with the natural elements of the surrounding region. Most of the highway work was done by hand labor. *(Courtesy of the Palisades Interstate Park Commission.)*

described in chapter 9, completion of the Tappan Zee Bridge in 1955 transformed Rockland County, formerly an artist/vacation colony set apart by the natural barrier of the Hudson, into a bedroom community for New York City.

While the forces of civilization dominated these decades with road and bridge building and ongoing quarrying at Little Stony Point and Mount Taurus in Cold Spring, the critics were not without voice. The Hudson River Conservation Society was founded in 1936 to challenge the quarrymen by appealing to preservation and the Romantic sublime. In 1939 Carl Carmer's *The Hudson* was published in

Rinehart and Company's "The Rivers of America" series. Carmer hoped his work would help reconstitute the Romantic and historical Hudson, and indeed, *The Hudson* became one of the cornerstones for the Hudson River renaissance of the 1960s and 1970s.

The Hudson: "That River's Alive"

The new conservationists of the 1960s and 1970s would build on the tradition of the Romantic sublime, historical association, and the work of the first river conservationists. They would draw heavily, too, on the relatively new science of ecology with its concern for human impact on the balance of nature. The public health questions first raised by Rachel Carson's book *Silent Spring* in 1962 helped distinguish the environmental movement from the classical conservation movement of the turn of the century.

Over the next twenty years the history of the Hudson River would center around questions that engaged both the preservation ideals of the classical conservation movement and the health and ecology concerns of the new environmentalism.

Storm King

In 1962 Consolidated Edison (Con Ed), searching for new sources of power to satisfy New York City's enormous appetite for electricity, announced a proposal to build a pumped storage generating plant at Storm King.[2] The proposal launched one of the major environmental battles of this century, which in turn contributed to a rebirth of interest in the Hudson.

Carl Carmer and others formed the Scenic Hudson Preservation Conference (today known as Scenic Hudson) to oppose Con Ed, appealing to the aesthetic tradition established by the nineteenth-century Ro-

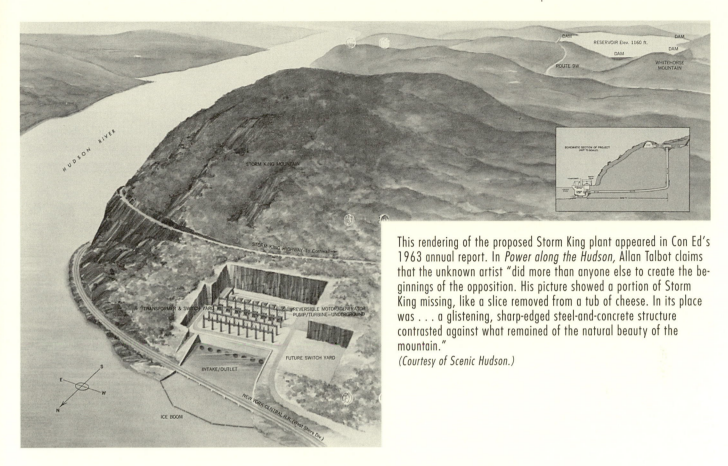

This rendering of the proposed Storm King plant appeared in Con Ed's 1963 annual report. In *Power along the Hudson,* Allan Talbot claims that the unknown artist "did more than anyone else to create the beginnings of the opposition. His picture showed a portion of Storm King missing, like a slice removed from a tub of cheese. In its place was . . . a glistening, sharp-edged steel-and-concrete structure contrasted against what remained of the natural beauty of the mountain."
(Courtesy of Scenic Hudson.)

mantic painters. They argued that Storm King should be held inviolate given its special place in the cultural life of the river. For Carmer and friends, Con Ed's pumped storage plant was another example of modern society's desecration of the Hudson's landscape in order to serve the needs of the city at the river's mouth.

At the outset the issues seemed to center on the traditional conservation objective of preservation. But as time went on, scientific and technical questions came to play a more central role. Concerns for impacts on fish life and the health of the river intensified with revelations in 1963 of fish kills at the Indian Point nuclear power plant. This plant, and all other generating stations on the Hudson, have "once-through" cooling systems that constantly suck in cool water from the river and discharge heated water.[3]

The kills occurred at the intakes, where river water was sucked in at a rate of thousands of gallons per second. The proposed Storm King plant would likewise draw in enormous volumes of water. Would the Hudson's fish populations, particularly young fish for which the estuary is a vital nursery, be endangered by Storm King and other power plants that were expected to follow quickly?

As the debate grew, Con Ed obtained a license to build the plant, only to be met with legal challenges contesting the licensing process. These challenges led to a precedent-setting ruling recognizing that aesthetic and environmental impacts must be considered during licensing procedures, in which only matters of economics, property rights, and technology had previously had standing. In addition, government

While Con Ed's power plant was scrapped and Storm King spared its scars, the mountain was not inviolate. The Storm King Highway was opened in 1922 to provide access for motorists wishing to enjoy the scenic view. But in spite of this road cut, Storm King retains its majesty.
(Photo by Charles Porter.)

agencies charged with environmental protection became increasingly concerned about the fish kills and moved to require the utilities to build cooling towers at their nuclear and fossil-fueled plants. By recycling cooling water, these towers would reduce the intake of Hudson River water. The utilities opposed this requirement because of the towers' significant costs.

These controversies dragged on through frustrating years of hearings and lawsuits. Faced with the prospect of many more, the parties to the dispute reached a mediated out-of-court settlement in 1980. In the settlement's major trade-off, the utilities gave up the planned Storm King plant and instituted measures to reduce fish kills at other power plants in return for not being required to build cooling towers for ten years.[4]

Unnatural History

In 1969, amidst the power plant controversies, one of the most vocal environmentalists involved in the struggles, Robert Boyle, published *The Hudson River: A Natural and Unnatural History*. This book did for the Hudson's environmental movement what Rachel Carson's *Silent Spring* had done for the movement nationwide in 1962. It became the environmental handbook for the Hudson, documenting the long-term and

systematic pollution which he felt threatened the life of the river.

In stating his case against the "Unnatural Hudson," Boyle described in great detail the natural history of the river, deepening our understanding of its ecology and our sense of responsibility for its survival. This work accelerated the shift in focus from the aesthetic to the scientific and compelled recognition of the Hudson as an eco-

As the river is cleansed of sewage, warning signs like this one are coming down.
(Photo by Paul Cohen.)

system filled with life, some of it seriously endangered. One could no longer fully comprehend the Hudson without some basic knowledge of its ecology.

Public interest in and understanding of the Hudson was heightened by the battle over Storm King and Boyle's indictment of a polluted river. Accordingly, the ideas of conservation and environmental protection gained much broader support. From its origins among a relatively small and elite group, the Hudson River environmental movement grew to encompass a wider segment of the region's populace. Many individuals joined advocacy groups like Scenic Hudson, the Hudson River Fishermen's Association, and the Hudson River Sloop Clearwater.

Setting Sail to Restore the River

In the same year that *The Hudson: A Natural and Unnatural History* was published, the sloop *Clearwater* was launched to, in Pete Seeger's words, "clean up this polluted stream" and make it "the way it was on the river a hundred years ago." The *Clearwater* combined the traditions of classical conservation and the new environmentalism.

The choice of a sloop provided a Romantic reminder of a simpler preindustrial time when the Hudson was not yet transformed by modern technology. The *Clearwater* connects us to the history of the river by re-creating the experience of sailing the Hudson and linking river travel with nature.

But it also fights for a cleaner river. In

Clearwater, launched in May 1969, is a reminder of the central role of the sloop in the rich maritime history of the Hudson, and also a symbol of contemporary efforts to restore the river to its past health. *(Courtesy of Clearwater.)*

keeping with the ecological character of the environmental movement, the *Clearwater* educates and informs the citizenry about key issues such as PCB contamination, heightening public consciousness and broadening participation in decisions about the river's future. In the end it seeks to make us all stewards of the river.

It is right indeed that this history of the Hudson should conclude with a historical replica. The river's story is a dynamic one filled with changes and surprises. But while it unfolds anew this history also reminds us of its continuities: threads leading back to an earlier time. One cannot experience the modern river or reflect on its future without feeling the pull of its rich past.

Chapter 11

Resolving River Conflicts

The Chapter in Brief

In current environmental disputes, Romantic era arguments over whether nature and civilization can coexist are joined by debate over ecology, economics, property rights, and the quality of scientific data. Such disputes, originating in conflicting value systems, are resolved through the political process and within a framework of legislation interpreted and enforced by regulatory agencies and the courts. Federal and state laws require disclosure of possible environmental impacts before major projects get underway. Wetlands laws regulate activities potentially harmful to these habitats. Public trust doctrine establishes public ownership of and right of access to tidal wetlands. The Hudson could increasingly be tapped as a municipal water supply, but New York City, the largest potential user, has chosen to lower demand through conservation rather than augmenting supply. Coastal zone, estuarine management, and Hudson Valley Greenway programs encourage input from many interested parties in formulating policies guiding development in a context of environmental protection.

A Question of Values

Near the end of the twentieth century, many contemporary Hudson River issues replay the conflict between civilization and nature which preoccupied the Romantic artists in the nineteenth century. However, nineteenth-century optimism that nature and civilization could exist in harmony has waned, allowing frictions at the root of this conflict to come to the fore. Will strict pollution controls cost jobs as industries move to regions with less stringent laws? Does owning a piece of marshland give one the right to fill it in, or can society prevent destruction of wetlands and the ecological values they provide? If river shallows are destroyed by landfilling, can scientists accurately predict whether fish there will perish or survive by moving elsewhere?

For society to make decisions about environmental matters, individuals and groups must examine their own deeply held ideals and beliefs—their values. Typically a spectrum of opinion develops as environmental values are weighed against other important concerns.

At one end of the spectrum are those who desire an environment as unspoiled as possible. Their position is grounded in the belief that protecting ecosystems and organisms also protects the biological support systems necessary for human survival, or even in the belief that these systems and species are as intrinsically valuable as humans and their civilization. To these individuals, the most admirable aspects of the quality of life in the Hudson Valley are symbolized by a healthy and attractive river. They feel that nature (as represented by the Hudson) has been severely stressed and needs stronger protection.

At the other extreme are those who believe that human endeavor should be minimally restrained by ecological concerns. They feel that negative ecological impacts are of minor importance relative to benefits accruing to society and to individual, institutional, and regional economic well-being. They have faith that the environment is resilient enough to adjust to alterations, or that in cases where ecological upset has major repercussions for people, human ingenuity and technology can solve such problems.

But the majority of people and the greatest weight of opinion are balanced somewhere in the middle. Their shifts toward one end of the spectrum or the other, perhaps in response to arguments made by those at the extremes, will likely determine society's values on environmental matters.

Politics and Law

The first Earth Day in 1970 marked a major shift of society's values in favor of greater ecological protection. This shift translated into popular support for legislative action. In the late 1960s and early 1970s Congress enacted significant environmental laws including the National Environmental Policy Act, the Clean Water Act, and the Clean Air Act.

Existing executive branch agencies were reorganized and new ones created to administer these laws. The U.S. Environmental Protection Agency (EPA), New Jersey's Department of Environmental Protection (DEP), New York State's Department of Environmental Conservation (DEC), and county and municipal entities

EPA	**PCB**	MGD	*EIS*
FHWA	*NYSDOH*	USFWS	USCG
LWRP	DEC	**DDT**	CZMA	FDA
NEPA	*HRFA*	**CPUE**	SEQRA
SPDES	**FWPCA**	PPM	NYSDOT
USGS	**CERCLA**	*NMFS*	**DEPE**

Debate about environmental controversies can present a confusing array of acronyms. Those used in this chapter and the next are defined where they first appear as well as in the glossary.
(Nora Porter Graphic.)

(health departments, planning boards, etc.) established regulations in accord with the new legislation. In specifying standards, decision-making procedures, and enforcement measures, the agencies created a regulatory framework for resolving disputes.

However, conflicts over environmental values did not end then. In the decades since, these conflicts have been politically expressed in legislative attempts to tighten

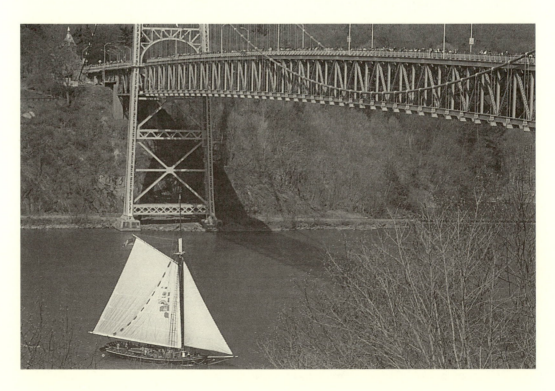

The sloop *Clearwater* sails under the Bear Mountain Bridge during a Hands Across the Hudson demonstration marking Earth Day 1990, the event's twentieth anniversary.
(Photo by Nora Porter.)

or loosen environmental restrictions. Public officials, environmental groups, business interests, and individual citizens continue to express their views and pressure legislators. The resulting laws reflect the political give and take necessary for enactment. They typically call not for absolute environmental protection but for protection that takes into account a variety of interests, a balance evident when the National Environmental Policy Act was written: "It is the continuing policy of the Federal government . . . to create and maintain conditions under which man and nature can exist in productive harmony, and fulfill the social, economic, and other requirements of present and future generations of Americans."

Such wording creates opportunities to influence environmental decisionmaking beyond the legislative realm. After enactment, even legislation clearly intended to protect the environment may give executive agencies room to balance competing interests in carrying out the law's aims, and often requires that agencies provide an opportunity for public comment as part of the regulatory process.

The need to balance conflicting public attitudes may require judgment calls by agency managers. These decisions may additionally reflect the philosophies of elected officials who appoint key agency staff, particularly in high profile cases where major ecological or economic resources are at stake. While few in number compared to the day-to-day routine decisions, these cases can generate enormous pressures on agency decision-makers, attract intense media attention, and greatly mold public opinion on how well government is managing environmental concerns.

When a party to a dispute feels that agencies have decided improperly or failed to enforce the law, they may take the matter to the third branch of government—the judiciary. The courts are the ultimate arbiters of whether a law's provisions have been properly interpreted and enforced.

In addition to political lobbying, regulatory process, law enforcement, and legal action, another avenue of conflict resolution is being explored as groups with divergent aims and roles sit down together to design management plans that will guide use of the Hudson's natural resources within a context of environmental protection. If accepted by the parties involved, such plans may in the future reduce the number of costly and time-consuming regulatory and legal wrangles.

Even within the bounds of the Hudson Valley, discussion of environmental law, values conflicts, and dispute resolution must cover a wide range of topics. For clarity's sake, this chapter covers issues of managing the river's natural resources and planning for development while protecting the environment. Chapter 12 covers pollution control.

Assessing Environmental Impacts: Storm King's Legacy

In the dispute over the proposed Storm King power plant (see chapter 10), a major achievement of conservationists worried about the plant's impacts on the mountain's scenery and the Hudson's striped bass was to earn a hearing for these concerns. They established that these environmental interests were valid and worthy of review alongside economic and engineering considerations as the proposal's fate was decided.

The National Environmental Policy Act

This achievement led to congressional enactment of the National Environmental

Policy Act (NEPA) in 1969. While the act does not require that projects with the potential to harm the environment be stopped, it does mandate that the potential impacts be recognized and weighed in deciding whether or not to go ahead. The law mandates that a detailed environmental impact statement (EIS) be prepared regarding proposals for "major Federal actions significantly affecting the quality of the human environment." This public statement must cover the following:

(i) the environmental impact of the proposed action,
(ii) any adverse environmental impacts which cannot be avoided should the proposal be implemented,
(iii) alternatives to the proposed action,
(iv) the relationship between local short-term uses of man's environment and the maintenance and enhancement of long-term productivity, and
(v) any irreversible and irretrievable commitments of resources which would be involved in the proposed action should it be implemented.

NEPA's mandate is chiefly procedural: requiring full disclosure of potential impacts based on accurate investigation of the affected environment and its resources. Those who try to halt a project by claiming that NEPA has been violated must prove that the required EIS does not meet these standards—a situation illustrated in the fight over Westway.

A Case History: Westway— Right Way or Wrong Way?

In 1973, two vehicles traveling on Manhattan's elevated West Side Highway unexpectedly exited to the street below when a portion of the road collapsed beneath them. The collapse accelerated efforts to build a replacement roadway; the proposed design, dubbed Westway, called for a 4.2-mile-long expressway built on two hundred acres of landfill in the Hudson River. Creation of this new land, which would also support parks and residential, commercial, and industrial development, accounted for more than half of the project's $2.3 billion price tag (as of 1983).

The proposal quickly generated controversy. Opponents sought to protect air quality and the Hudson's wetlands, and argued that such a huge sum of money was better spent on a less costly replacement highway built on shore, with the remainder traded in to earn funds for mass transit improvements. Supporters valued the economic benefits of development on the landfill and felt that Westway would result in a better highway and rehabilitation of a decaying waterfront.

Federal law required Westway's sponsors to obtain a landfill permit from the Army Corps of Engineers (see Landfill Permits section). The Corps' decision in this matter would be a "major Federal action" under NEPA, so an environmental impact statement was necessary. The initial EIS dealt extensively with issues of air

Westway was intended to replace the decaying West Side Highway. Along with the rest of the old elevated highway, the remnant shown here has been demolished.

The Westway landfill would have extended from the current shoreline to the end of the West Side's piers for much of the proposed highway's 4-mile length. Proponents saw this area as a decaying waterfront in need of revitalization; opponents saw it as valuable wetland habitat in need of protection.

and noise pollution, traffic congestion, and mass transit alternatives. This multi-volume document also discussed—in just four paragraphs—the project's potential impacts on estuarine habitat, and concluded that they were not significant since the area to be filled was "biologically impoverished."

Westway Goes on Trial. To halt the project, Westway opponents sued, charging that the statement's analysis of these concerns was less than adequate. They claimed that meeting NEPA's procedural standards would require a new EIS based on more thorough and accurate research. The court dismissed most of these claims, finding that the highway agencies had satisfactorily assessed potential impacts from air pollution, noise pollution, and traffic congestion, and had adequately analyzed transit alternatives.

That left only the question of whether the EIS was correct in concluding that impacts on estuarine habitat would be insig-

nificant. Here the court agreed with Westway opponents that research supporting this conclusion was inadequate, making its accuracy questionable.[1] Westway went on trial over this concern.

Further research established that, like other Hudson River wetland habitats, this area was home to a diverse and abundant array of creatures, most notably winter flounder, white perch, and striped bass. But in releasing these data, the highway agencies stood by their original conclusion that Westway's impacts on estuarine life were of little importance. Opponents believed that the new information required preparation of a supplemental EIS more fully assessing these impacts. After hearing the case the court agreed, finding that the highway agencies had presented data in a "misleading" manner, and had "acted in willful derogation of the requirements of [NEPA] in failing to issue a corrective supplemental environmental impact statement." The judge's 1982 decision directed

Much of the controversy over Westway centered on its impacts on significant numbers of young striped bass which winter in the area that was to be filled.
(Photo by Chris Lake.)

them to complete such an EIS before Westway went forward.

After a third round of research and assessment, a draft supplemental EIS concluded that the landfill would indeed have "significant adverse impacts" on striped bass. The document underwent public review and was then rewritten into final form. In the process, the conclusions about impacts were changed to "minor" without explanation or substantiation—a change examined closely when the new impact statement was brought before the court in 1985. Its authors argued that their basic conclusion hadn't changed: that the finding of minor impact was intended all along. Writing "the court finds this position incredible," the judge again halted the project. In his view, making such a change without substantiation constituted a failure to meet NEPA obligations for accurate assessment.

By itself, this decision might not have been enough to kill the project. The highway agencies could have done more research, prepared yet another EIS, and tried again to meet NEPA's standards. However,

the deadline for applying to trade Westway funding for mass transit money was only weeks away. Another attempt to produce an acceptable EIS would have needed more time, with no guarantee of success; pursuing this course risked losing large sums of money. Not willing to gamble, New York opted for a less expensive roadway on shore and for the trade-in of leftover money for mass transit funds.[2]

Policy and Politics. While the controversy was resolved largely through the courts, one should not exit Westway with the impression that the battle was a cut-and-dried legal matter. To supporters the idea that concern for fish could stop a billion-dollar construction project was ridiculous. They tried end runs around the law: New York's governor persuaded like-minded members of Congress to introduce legislation exempting Westway from the environmental review required by NEPA. In response, the state's attorney general telegrammed New York's congressional delegation to say, "Whatever your position on the merits of Westway, exempting any particular project from the impartial application of environmental laws could do great and lasting harm to the national effort to clean our rivers and streams." Congress did not act on these bills.

Critics from environmental groups have observed that EIS documents often contain superficial or unsubstantiated findings, and seem to be written not with a true sense of NEPA's intent of complete and accurate disclosure but instead simply to meet the requirement for an assessment. The judge in the Westway case concluded that problems with the Corps of Engineers' assessments could "only be explained as resulting from an almost fixed predetermination to grant the Westway landfill permit," a purpose to which full disclosure was a hindrance. Challenging inadequate environmental assessments in court is often the only way to force full disclosure and review of impact statements.

Environmental Assessment: The Local Perspective

Westway was a major federally funded project with large-scale costs and impacts. Other environmental controversies involving development, different only in their smaller scale, simmer all along the Hudson, perhaps made fiercer since the parties involved are not just law firms, government agencies, or corporations but familiar faces—people known in a community. The impacts of local development may be small-scale, but they have an immediacy that engages community residents in a personal way.

These controversies may do more than involve politics—they may dominate local politics. Typically, the officials making the decisions are more exposed to the wrath of dissatisfied constituents than administrators of major state and federal agencies. When the outcome of the required regulatory process leaves many citizens unhappy, the next election may offer the most immediate recourse.

Environmental assessments of local development projects may be required by state laws modeled after NEPA, such as New York's State Environmental Quality Review Act, or—as in New Jersey—by similar requirements established under executive order. These reviews can be required by state agencies or by local governments—for example, as town planning boards consider approval of site plans for large subdivisions. Projects may also require variances under existing zoning laws, in which case

Through recent economic upturns and downturns, river-front property has remained highly desirable to developers. Though local development projects may be relatively small, their cumulative impacts along the Hudson may be quite large, significantly changing the distinct character of the region, altering river vistas, and eliminating areas of open space.
(Photo by David Bernz.)

zoning boards of appeal provide a forum for environmental review.

The local role in environmental review is important, since along the Hudson most planning and land use decisions are made by individual communities, following a strong tradition of home rule—local primacy in such decisions. The public hearings required during review often address community values beyond the ecological. The process may provide the only formal opportunity for residents to comment on how a project might affect their deeply held sense of what the community should be—a quiet residential village or a bustling commercial center, for example.

Like NEPA, state environmental review regulations mandate only the comprehensive and accurate disclosure of potential impacts; they do not require that a project be halted if potentially serious negative impacts are disclosed. This situation begs the question of which laws can actually restrict environmentally damaging projects. Of such statutes, those most important in protecting the Hudson have been state wetlands laws and the federal Clean Water Act.

Protecting Wetland Habitats

Wetland habitats serve as feeding areas for waterfowl and other creatures, nurseries for young fish, and breeding sites for birds and mammals. They filter out sediment and pollution as they slow tidal currents. These habitats also offer economic benefits such as buffering damage from storms and floods and maintaining fish stocks that support valuable commercial fisheries. In addition, many wetlands possess great scenic beauty.

However, recognition of these values has been a long time coming. Wetlands were once seen as mosquito-infested waste-

lands, a view that countenanced destruction of over 50 percent of the coastal and estuarine wetlands acreage in the continental United States. By the mid-twentieth century, urbanization had claimed most of the best building land along the northeast coast. Wetlands were among the last large open spaces available to absorb the building boom of the 1950s and 1960s; many were filled in then. In the Hudson Valley, it is estimated that 4,850 acres of such habitat have been filled in to create land for highways, railroads, industrial facilities, housing, and parks. Another 6,800 acres have been buried by sediment and dikes as a result of dredging operations. Wetlands have also suffered from activities on adjacent uplands, which changed runoff or drainage patterns and increased pollution.

In response to growing awareness of their importance and the pressures on these habitats, governments have enacted regulations protecting wetlands. Such laws are lightning rods for disputes, perhaps because it is here that disparate underlying values are most clearly exposed. Largely stripped of concern about human health, these battles come right down to the belief that ecological health should be maintained versus the belief that property interests should prevail.

Economic arguments can be used by both sides in wetlands disputes. Westway is again a useful example. Proponents decried the loss of promised economic benefits—a new highway, construction jobs, and urban renewal—due to concern over fish habitat. Opponents, having framed Westway's economics differently, praised the preservation of the multimillion-dollar recreational and commercial fisheries for striped bass. They pointed out that, for the cost of building Westway on landfill, New York City would

Historic attitudes about wetlands are illustrated by this sign, which suggests that filling in a tidal swamp to create a sanitary landfill—a dump—is a worthy use of such habitats.
(Photo by Steve Singer.)

Several Hudson River wetlands, including the North Bay marsh bordering the city of Hudson, have been impacted by such use.
(Photo by Charles Porter.)

now get both a new highway on shore and money for needed mass transit improvements, all promising construction jobs.

Landfill Permits

The major federal wetlands protection law is the Clean Water Act. As implied in the name, it is primarily an antipollution law. However, Section 404 of the act mandates that projects requiring landfilling or discharge of dredged material obtain a permit from the Army Corps of Engineers. In considering whether to grant the permit, the Corps must weigh costs and benefits, both ecological and economic, and the desirability and availability of alternatives. In addition, legal guidelines established under Section 404 state that "no discharge of dredged or fill material shall be permitted which will cause or contribute to significant degradation of the waters of the United States . . . [including] loss of fish and wildlife habitat."

Prior to passage of the Clean Water Act,

the Corps of Engineers had issued dredge and fill permits based on its historic mission of keeping navigational channels open. To insure that these permit decisions also reflected an ecological perspective, Congress directed EPA to develop guidelines for issuing Section 404 permits and gave the agency the power to veto Corps permit decisions. By vesting power in two agencies with different missions, Congress was trying to strike a balance that insured consideration of both the needs of commerce and the ecological values of wetlands.

This arrangement does not eliminate conflict, however, and disputes between the Corps and EPA reflect the different values and uses society finds in wetlands. A case in point is dredging in Newark Bay, part of the port of New York and New Jersey. Without dredging, silt would accumulate at the bay's docks and prevent their use by large ships. In testing done for a 1990 dredging permit application, dioxin was found in the silt. Concerned about this toxic chemical's effects in the environment where the dredged silt would be dumped, EPA withheld approval of the permits. The Corps felt that the risks posed by dioxin levels in the sediments did not justify the economic damage likely if the docks were closed. The ensuing discussions between the Corps, EPA, and other agencies took years, during which time silt continued to accumulate, eventually requiring new rounds of testing and evaluation. In 1993 EPA finally allowed the project to go forward with the provision that the disposal site be covered with clean sand to prevent release of dioxin into the environment.[3]

State Wetlands Regulations

The states also play important roles in wetlands protection. Under Section 401 of the Clean Water Act, states must certify that fill, dredge spoils, and other discharges into waterways will not violate their water quality standards. In addition, New York and New Jersey have their own comprehensive wetlands laws, and these require permits for activities that may have impacts on these habitats.

Two New York State statutes apply to the Hudson: a freshwater wetlands law that covers the river south to the Tappan Zee Bridge, and a tidal wetlands law that applies below the bridge. Both use scientific parameters of flooding and vegetation types to define wetlands and mandate preparation of inventories and maps of the state's wetlands. The laws allow DEC to develop land use rules for wetlands, and to regulate activities occurring on adjacent uplands.

These laws do not provide complete protection. In New York, for example, the freshwater wetlands statute requires that wetlands larger than 12.4 acres (one hectare

High Schoolers Act to Save a Marsh

In the early 1970s a Lakeland High School ecology class discovered that the New York State National Guard was filling in a Hudson River marsh at Camp Smith, north of Peekskill. The fill was not the "clean" variety (sand, gravel, etc.); according to Robert Boyle in *The Hudson River: A Natural and Unnatural History*, it included "lumber, a dead dog, and a bundle of conservation department leaflets on what citizens could do to save the environment." The high school group notified Boyle and the Hudson River Fishermen's Association, who took the matter to court. The court ordered the filling halted and required the Guard to remove the debris and restore the marsh. *(Photo by John Sedgwick.)*

in the metric system) must be mapped and protected, but some scientists consider current maps and inventories to be far from complete. Smaller wetlands of special significance can be included in the inventory, but are for the most part ignored. As a result, less than 50 percent of New York's freshwater wetlands are protected under this statute.[4]

To be successful, these regulations must be aggressively enforced. Be they saltwater or fresh, large or small, wetlands are frequently subject to piecemeal degradation that goes unnoticed or is low on the priority lists of enforcement agencies with limited staff and funds. Pressure from citizens is often key to enforcement of wetlands laws.

Protection by Purchase

One form of protection for wetlands and other coastal habitats is ownership or management by environmental agencies or conservation groups. Four of the river's largest wetlands—Piermont Marsh, Iona Island Marsh, Tivoli Bays, and Stockport Flats—are included in the Hudson River National Estuarine Research Reserve, managed by New York State's DEC in cooperation with other regional and federal agencies. The Scenic Hudson Land Trust, National Audubon Society, and Nature Conservancy are among the organizations that own or manage Hudson River wetlands and bordering uplands as preserves or sanctuaries.

Protecting habitat by government purchase with tax dollars has become increasingly controversial in recent years. Here again, values come into conflict as people debate the wisdom of buying land to preserve it when land prices have soared, tax burdens seem high, budget shortfalls are a problem, and development might add to the tax base.

The Public Trust Doctrine

Even in the best of times only a limited amount of wetland habitat can be protected by purchase. However, under a longstanding principle of common law, the public already owns lands subject to tidal influence (strictly, lands below average high tide). This public trust doctrine, by which the state holds these underwater lands in trust for the public, guarantees access for swimming, boating, fishing, and other water-related pursuits, although the public cannot cross adjacent private land without the owner's permission.[5]

States can sell or rent public trust lands, a practice common in the seventeenth and eighteenth centuries when large parcels were sold to adjacent upland owners to promote commerce and economic growth. New York State's Office of General Services, which administers this property, estimates that 25 to 30 percent of tidal lands around Manhattan and along the Hudson have been conveyed into private hands.

Day-to-day management of public trust lands is difficult when agencies must rely on tenets of common law rather than specific statutes. In 1992 New York took a step toward codifying the public trust doctrine through enactment of an Underwater Lands Act. The law requires that anyone proposing to place a large structure or fill on these lands obtain a lease, easement or other interest from the Office of General Services; it also provides for DEC review and regulation of such proposals to prevent harm to wetland habitats.

Putting the Hudson on Tap

The very substance of the Hudson—its water—is also held in trust for the public by the states. As is the case with wetlands, debates over use of this resource have generated much controversy.

The Hudson Riverkeeper

In Britain, riverkeepers have traditionally protected fish and habitat in trout and salmon streams. Inspired by this model, in 1973 four Hudson River environmental groups joined together to hire a riverkeeper, Tom Whyatt, to protect the river in the public interest. Financial pressures ended that first experiment after about two and a half years, but the Hudson River Fishermen's Association tried again, hiring John Cronin as the new Riverkeeper in 1983 and providing him with a patrol boat. Since then, the Riverkeeper's successes in bringing pollution to light have inspired imitators around the country: a Long Island Soundkeeper, a New York Baykeeper, and a San Francisco Baykeeper, to cite a few.
(Photo by Charles Porter.)

In 1983, local residents alerted the Hudson River Fishermen's Association and their Riverkeeper to unusually frequent appearances of large tankers off Hyde Park and Port Ewen. Upon investigation, the Riverkeeper discovered that the tankers, owned by Exxon, were filling up with Hudson River water and carrying it to the Caribbean island of Aruba, which has limited freshwater supplies. There the firm used the water in refinery operations and offered it for sale, reportedly receiving $2 million that year. Exxon did not have the necessary state permit to transport and sell the water, but avoided a court trial over that issue by ending the practice and agreeing to pay settlements of $500,000 to the Fishermen's Association and $1.5 million to New York State.[6]

In breaking the story, the Riverkeeper characterized Exxon's operations as "a deliberate theft of water, a valuable commodity." Hudson River water *is* a valuable commodity, considered a viable drinking water supply (after treatment) over much of the freshwater river. For the water system serving over thirty thousand residents of Pough-

keepsie, the Hudson is the only source. Other communities use the river for backup or partial supply, and more may do so in the future. Over the years, the largest proposed withdrawals, and those of most concern to environmentalists, have been for New York City.

A Thirsty City

New York is a thirsty city: water consumption there averages 1.5 billion gallons per day and reached a peak of 1.8 billion gallons daily in summer 1988. Ninety percent of this water comes from reservoirs in the Catskills, the rest mainly from the Croton Reservoir complex in Westchester County. However, the estimated safe yield of this system—the amount it could deliver each day during the worst drought on record—is only 1.3 billion gallons. Additionally, the city's water consumption was on the rise for twenty-five years up to about 1990, increasing even while population decreased through the 1980s. New York's response was twofold: identifying new sources of supply, notably the Hudson River, and lowering consumption through conservation efforts.

The city has one tap on the Hudson, a pumping station in Chelsea, a hamlet just above the Beacon-Newburgh Bridge. One proposal for increasing New York's supply was to operate the Chelsea station continuously and to construct additional pumping plants in Newburgh or Kingston, adding up to 300 million gallons daily (mgd) to the system. A more ambitious plan called for construction of an intake, pump station, filtration plant, and aqueducts in or near Hyde Park. This complex, estimated to cost $2.5 billion, might have taken in as much as one billion gallons daily during spring, when freshwater flow into the river usually peaks (an operation known as "high-flow skimming"). It would not have operated in

Intended for emergency use during droughts, the pumps at New York City's Chelsea station can contribute 100 million gallons of Hudson River water per day to the city's supply. By comparison, Poughkeepsie's plant, next largest on the Hudson, is rated at 12 million gallons per day.
(Photo by Cara Lee.)

late summer and early fall, when freshwater flow typically is minimal. Thus the project's annual yield would have averaged about 400 mgd.

Intake Impacts

The potential environmental impacts of these plans generated much controversy. One point of concern recalled a major issue of the Storm King struggle (see chapter 10). Along with enormous volumes of water, the intake pipes would have sucked up fish, especially juveniles, larvae, and eggs that swim weakly or not at all. Given the river's role as a nursery for young fish, damage to fish populations could have been considerable.

Other potential impacts on estuarine

organisms would have been more indirect. Detouring large quantities of water from Chelsea (or points farther north) to faucets in New York could shift the salt front's position.[7] One might assume that plants and animals would simply move with the salt front. However, salinity is but one of many factors controlling their distribution, and staying in water of the proper salinity may put an organism in areas where other factors—substrate, current, or depth—are unsuitable.

The withdrawals proposed by New York City also caused concern among communities upriver. Poughkeepsie depends entirely on Hudson River water and cannot dilute salty water with fresh water from another source, as New York can by mixing river water with reservoir water. In past droughts the salt front has reached Poughkeepsie's intakes; the city worried that increased pumping by New York might have made that a more regular occurrence. Other communities looking to the river as a potential supply worried that New York's demands would preempt theirs.

Increase the Supply or Lower the Demand?

Another approach to closing the 200 mgd gap between the reservoirs' safe yield and the city's demand was not to increase supply but to lower demand by conserving water and improving system management. By the city's own estimates, up to 240 mgd were being lost to leaks, water running in vacant buildings, open fire hydrants, and illegal connections—more than enough water to fill the gap.

Developing new supplies would also have been a costly proposition, and not simply for new intakes, pump stations, and aqueducts. Should the Hudson have become a permanent source of supply, the state Department of Health would have required the city to build expensive filtration plants. New supplies would have increased flow into New York City's sewage treatment plants and required expansion there. Six of these plants were already receiving greater flows than they were designed to handle.

Faced with such realities, New York increased emphasis on conservation efforts. In 1986 the city began a leak detection survey in the supply pipes running under its streets, followed up by repairs to leaky pipes. In parts of Manhattan and the Bronx, the city has also begun a door-to-door leak detection program to reduce overflows at two sewage plants.

Knowing exactly how much water is used, wasted, or lost due to leaks requires metering. Metering also makes people pay for water according to how much they use, and encourages individuals to conserve to save money. In 1988 the city began a ten-year program to install 630,000 water meters at a cost of $290 million.[8] Estimates of expected savings range from 105 to 355 mgd when the program is completed. These savings should be augmented by recent laws requiring installation of water-saving plumbing fixtures in new construction and in renovation of existing structures.

Through these measures, conservation education programs, and individual water-saving efforts, New York City's water consumption has fallen below projections since December 1991, and decreased by 110 mgd between April 1991 and April 1992. As a result, the city put plans to use the Hudson as a regular source of supply on hold, though it continues to investigate the feasibility of river withdrawal options.

As one means of addressing water supply issues, representatives of New York City, other local governments, state agencies, and environmental groups formed the Southeastern New York Intergovernmental Water Supply Advisory Council. This group attempted, with some success, to balance conflicting mandates, needs, and values through joint planning and priority setting as an alternative to more adversarial approaches.

Managing the Estuary

Applied to the Hudson River, such a process might head off at least some conflicts by establishing policies for protecting the ecosystem's vitality in ways that would allow sustainable development and use of its resources. The end products of the process would be management plans intended to guide decision-making along the river. Optimism about the utility of such an approach has led to the creation of a variety of programs: the coastal zone management program, state and federal estuarine management programs, and the Hudson Valley Greenway.

Coastal Zone Management

Of all the resources the Hudson offers to those who live along its shores, perhaps the one in most limited supply is its very shoreline. With public recognition that the river is becoming cleaner, coupled to increased awareness of its beauty and recreational po-

In 1986, New York's leak detection program surveyed 5.25 million feet of supply pipe, finding and repairing leaks losing over 24 mgd of water. By 1990, the length of piping surveyed yearly had doubled to 10 million feet, but the amount of leakage discovered had dropped by nearly half, to 12.6 mgd. This trend indicates that the program is reducing overall leakage.
(Courtesy New York City Department of Environmental Protection/Carl Ambrose.)

The Hudson and its shoreline offer an abundance of resources and support a great variety of human uses, among them:

environmental education programs like this one at the Tivoli North Bay Marsh;

shipping, which requires docking facilities for tugboats and other vessels;

swimming and picnicking at riverfront parks like this Kingston beach;

housing, here in a renovated industrial building at Yonkers;

boating, with services provided by marinas such as this one in Haverstraw;

and industrial production, represented by this cement plant and loading dock just south of Catskill.
(Photo by Charles Porter.)

tential, riverfront property is now a valuable commodity. Jostling for space along the river are developers with proposals for housing, restaurants, and new marinas, industries which require waterfront locations, and groups seeking to increase public access and protect scenic values and habitats.

Conflicts over shorefront land use have been a concern not only here in the Hudson Valley but throughout the nation. In response, Congress passed the Federal Coastal Zone Management Act in 1972. This law provides financial assistance to the states to develop management programs that will

New Jersey's Hudson River Waterfront Walkway: Preserving Access in the Face of Development

New Jersey's Hudson River shoreline offers spectacular views of the river, the harbor, and Manhattan's skyline. Recognizing its scenic and recreational value and foreseeing that residential and commercial development would replace declining port and industrial facilities, New Jersey's DEP moved to require that public access be provided in exchange for permits to develop on the waterfront. Its goal is establishment of a continuous waterfront walkway running 18 miles from the Bayonne Bridge to the George Washington Bridge and the Palisades. Since 1988 the project has been facilitated by the Hudson River Waterfront Conservancy, representing developers, property owners, nonprofit groups, state and local governments, and interested citizens. While progress on the ground has been fitful, coming primarily when proposals for private development are put on the table, some sections are in place and the Conservancy has aided efforts toward solving management issues. *(Courtesy of the Hudson River Waterfront Conservancy.)*

preserve and, where possible, restore or enhance coastal resources. Participation is voluntary; incentives to get on board include the funding assistance and a provision that, once a state program receives federal approval, any federal actions affecting the state's coast must be consistent with that program. Both New Jersey and New York have approved management programs. Since the Hudson is tidal, New York's extends up the river to the Troy Dam.

In parallel fashion, river communities in New York may prepare Local Waterfront Revitalization Plans which spell out land use guidelines and activities allowed along their shorelines. Since most land use decisions are made at the local level, such planning can be very helpful in dealing with intense development pressures along the Hudson. Preparation of these plans can allow a community to clarify its values and appropriately balance ecological protection, public access, and economic development in shaping the future of its riverfront. Community adoption of such a plan, once it is

approved by the state, asserts a fair degree of local control since all state and federal agency actions within that community's coastal zone must then be consistent with the local plan.

The state provides technical assistance to communities trying to establish local waterfront plans. Such aid might include guidance in interpreting wetlands laws or in developing criteria for local ordinances to protect shoreline habitats. This aid is particularly helpful in small communities where planning boards and waterfront advisory boards are not usually trained specialists but rather citizens from all walks of life, elected or appointed mostly on a volunteer basis.

In the decade or so since New York State established its Coastal Management Program, half of the towns and cities lining the Hudson have participated in the program, and thirteen communities had state-approved local waterfront plans by the end of 1994.

In New Jersey, coastal management is

governed by the Coastal Area Facility Review Act, administered by the DEP. Projects with impacts on the coastal zone must receive permits from the agency, which evaluates proposals based on coastal resource and development policies promulgated under the Facilities Review Act. Unlike New York, New Jersey has no provision for delegating such review to communities through approval of local waterfront plans.

Estuarine Management Plans

Given the importance of the Hudson, the need to maintain its ecological health while supporting sustainable human uses, and the history of controversy over such concerns, development of management plans for the estuary has received particular attention. In progress are several efforts to identify estuarine resources and values in need of protection, determine what factors degrade those resources and values, and recommend possible solutions to problems.

New York State's DEC is developing a Hudson River Estuary Management Plan to "protect, restore and enhance the productivity and diversity of natural resources of the Hudson River Estuarine District to sustain a wide array of present and future human benefits."[9] With similar goals in mind, the EPA has designated New York Harbor, including the Hudson south of the Piermont Marsh, an estuary of national significance and initiated a five-year research and planning process leading to development of a management plan for this area. The process involves a host of agencies, authorities, interstate commissions, and private groups, and is moving forward in cooperation with similar efforts in the New York Bight and Long Island Sound.

These are ambitious undertakings given the ecosystem's scale and dynamics, overlapping and often conflicting agency mandates, budget constraints, and underlying disagreements between participants from environmental groups and those representing development or industrial interests. But the Hudson estuary is an entity greater than the sum of its many parts. Preserving its ecological health, a task now parceled out among many regulations and bureaucracies, may analogously require a system greater than the sum of these parts. Comprehensive management plans may establish the overarching goals and policies necessary to the task.

The Hudson Valley Greenway

The web of jurisdictions overseeing the Hudson River stems in part from the fact that ecological boundaries and regional identities often don't correspond to political boundaries. The Hudson Valley is recognized as a distinct region from historical, cultural, commercial, and ecological perspectives. Yet from the Mohawk River's mouth to the Battery, some eighty-two political jurisdictions (villages, towns, boroughs, and cities) govern the Hudson's shorelines—not counting counties or New Jersey jurisdictions. In this situation, local decisions made without reference to a regional identity could, in piecemeal fashion, erode the assets that make the region as a whole so attractive and distinctive.

Recognizing this problem, the New York State legislature established the Hudson River Valley Greenway program in 1991. While intended to preserve open space in and around densely inhabited regions, greenways are more than a patchwork of open lands. Greenways try to link these lands both physically, via creation of trails and preservation of small parcels linking larger open areas, and perceptually, fostering the sense that all these parcels are valuable parts of a larger entity defined by its natural heritage.

Responsibility for designing and implementing a regional planning strategy rests with the Greenway Community Council. Past efforts to regionalize Hudson Valley planning and land-use decisions have been stymied by firm belief in home rule and distrust of bureaucratic control by outsiders. Aware of this history, the council will begin at the local level, encouraging (with financial incentives) communities to develop their own plans addressing Greenway objectives. These plans will guide preparation of subregional plans and ultimately a planning document for the entire region. This regional plan then goes back to the localities for review. Those that elect to be guided by the plan's provisions will be entitled to special funding consideration for projects which advance Greenway goals.[10]

In a 1991 Greenway report to New York State's governor and legislature, one hears echoes of Romantic-era belief in an equilibrium between preservation and development:

> The Valley is a place where the future must be built in harmony with the region's natural and historic heritage. We are convinced that economic development will not occur in areas that tolerate a deteriorated environment.

> We emphasize that there must be places for the residents of the Valley to live and to work just as there must be places for them to have access to the Hudson River and the Valley's beauty and history.

But any equilibrium attained through the Greenway or other programs, doctrines, regulations, and management plans will be a dynamic one. The struggle between development and preservation has characterized the Hudson's history for the past 150 years. It will no doubt continue to challenge both the activists at opposite poles and the many conscientious citizens in the middle as they make democratic choices to shape a Hudson River environment in keeping with their values.

Chapter 12

Is the Hudson Getting Cleaner?

The Chapter in Brief

The Hudson, once an "open sewer," is cleaner now. The Clean Water Act deserves much of the credit, requiring sewage treatment and funding treatment plant construction. Some sewage problems remain: disposal of sludge left after treatment, overflows from combined sanitary and storm sewers, and pretreatment of industrial wastes discharged into sewer systems. The act also established the National Pollution Discharge Elimination System to control point sources of pollution, and required planning to control non-point source pollution. Oil pollution, a major concern given the volume of oil transported on the Hudson and in New York Harbor, is also covered by the Clean Water Act. Superfund, intended to clean up hazardous waste left by past disposal practices, is being applied to cadmium contamination in Cold Spring and PCB hotspots in the upper Hudson. Preventing discharges rather than just regulating them is increasingly seen as the best solution to pollution problems, especially those involving toxic chemicals.

An Open Sewer

"Life Abandoning Polluted Hudson" ran a 1966 headline in the *New York Times*. Government reports of that time referred to the river as an "open sewer." Old-time river rats pull the legs of newcomers by telling how, before going for a swim back then, one tossed in a few boulders to clear holes in the scum.

Much of this ill repute came from the enormous volume of untreated human sewage discharged into the Hudson. Sewage may carry pathogens that make swimming in or eating shellfish from polluted waters dangerous to human health. It also contains nitrates, phosphates, and other nutrients that may cause unpleasant blooms of algae (see chapter 2). Additionally, sewage becomes food for microorganisms in the river, and more sewage means more microbes. As their numbers increase, they use up more and more of the dissolved oxygen in the water.[1] Ultimately oxygen levels can be reduced nearly to zero, killing off most higher forms of life in the affected area.

Sewage pollution, aggravated by other untreated organic wastes from pulp mills and tanneries, once made the "Albany Pool" (stretching roughly from Cohoes southward past Albany) infamous as the most severely polluted section of the Hudson. In *The Hudson River: A Natural and Unnatural History*, Robert Boyle quotes from a press report that described a hearing about the pool's problems: men "grit their teeth and women left the room."

The Albany Pool mess was but one of the Hudson's horror stories. The river's sewage problems along Manhattan were as bad as those in Albany; off Tarrytown the water would be colored with whatever paint the General Motors plant there happened to be using on its cars that day; grease and oil poured into the Hudson from railroad repair facilities in Croton. But the rising tide of environmental concern in recent decades has produced a flood of antipollution laws. Today, when those who teach about the Hudson are asked, "Is the river getting cleaner?" the answer is a qualified "yes."

The Clean Water Act

Much of the credit for improvements over the past two decades should go to the Clean Water Act (formally the Federal Water

At plants such as New York City's Newtown Creek facility, incoming sewage first undergoes primary treatment, entering tanks where some solids settle to the bottom. Water and remaining suspended solids go on to secondary treatment, in which microbes digest organic material. This may occur in a trickling filter—a bed of rocks coated with a slime of microorganisms—or in an activated sludge tank, where a suspension of solids is aerated to promote the desired microbial action. After another round of settling, clarified water is chlorinated to kill bacteria and then discharged to the river. The solids left behind become sewage sludge. *(Courtesy New York City Department of Environmental Protection/Marion Bernstein. Diagram courtesy of Clearwater.)*

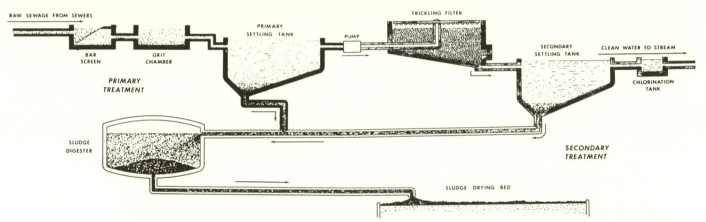

Pollution Control Act) enacted in 1972 to "restore and maintain the chemical, physical, and biological integrity of the Nation's waters." The act aims directly to curb pollution by improving municipal sewage treatment, regulating *point discharges* of pollutants (from a specific pipe, discharge canal, or similar facility) through a permit system, planning for control of *non-point source pollution* (polluted runoff from streets, parking lots, farm fields, lawns, and the like), and preventing oil pollution.

Municipal Sewage Treatment

The Clean Water Act requires that municipalities provide secondary treatment for their sewage, a process that can remove 85 percent of its organic materials. Originally, the act also committed federal funds toward the great expense of building sewage treatment plants.[2] Most river communities quickly moved to construct such plants, the notable laggard being New York City owing to the scale of its discharges and a fiscal crisis. Some 150 million gallons of sewage per day flowed untreated from Manhattan's West Side until 1986, when the North River plant, located on the Hudson in Harlem, began operation.[3] Completion of this plant and Brooklyn's Red Hook facility, finished in 1987, rounded out the city's planned set of fourteen treatment plants.

Certain measures of water quality have improved greatly as a result of sewage treatment. Dissolved oxygen levels have increased even in the Albany Pool and New York Harbor. Fecal coliform bacteria counts are lower. These nonpathogenic bacteria live in the human digestive tract; when numerous in water samples, they usually indicate the presence of sewage and, potentially, of more dangerous microbes that sewage might contain. As numbers of coliforms go up or down, there is a correspondingly greater or lower probability of pathogens being present.[4] Off Manhattan, startup of the North River plant resulted in a 78 percent decrease in fecal coliform counts between 1985 and 1986.

Dealing with Sewage Sludge. Left behind after these plants have discharged treated water is sewage sludge, a semisolid substance rich in organic matter and nutrients. Ideally, sludge should be a resource valuable either as a fertilizer or, after composting, as a soil conditioner. In some Hudson Valley communities this is the sludge's fate, and in New Jersey about 23 percent of the sludge is spread on land. But in many cases the sludge goes to landfills or is incinerated, wasting this potentially valuable resource.

For years, New York City and parts of Long Island, Westchester County, and New Jersey shipped their sludge to dumpsites in the Atlantic Ocean, a practice banned by Congress as of 1991. All eventually complied with the ban, the last sludge barge

sailing from New York in summer 1992. The city has begun a composting program for its sludge. In Westchester, plans for sludge incineration next to the Hudson in Peekskill were opposed by a coalition of advocacy groups and local residents. While studying other options, the county presently spreads its sludge as a landfill cap.

Sludge sometimes contains heavy metals and other hazardous substances which the sewage treatment process cannot break down or neutralize. These pollutants limit its use in agriculture and pose problems even when sludge is disposed of as solid waste. They may leach out of poorly designed or operated landfills or spread widely through the air if incompletely incinerated. Sources of such pollutants include water and sewer pipes (copper and lead leach from these) and industries that discharge wastes into sewer systems.

To avoid contamination of sludge and disruption of the sewage treatment process, industries discharging into municipal sewage systems must establish pretreatment programs to clean their wastewater before it empties into the sewers. These programs are administered by local governments on the basis of federal and state standards.

Effective pretreatment is vital if sewage sludge is to be used beneficially and widely. For example, to achieve its goal of composting and land application of sludge, New York City has had to identify and require pretreatment of sewer discharges from metal-finishing and electroplating industries. Between 1975 and 1989, this effort led to a 90 percent decrease in inputs of five heavy metals—cadmium, chromium, copper, nickel, and zinc—from such industries to sewage treatment plants.[5] However, in 1992, the date by which New York expected its composted sludge to meet state standards for land application, the city comptroller reported that contamination remained a problem due in part to budget shortfalls and associated cutbacks in staffing and inspections of dischargers.

Combined Sewer Overflows. Continued progress in sewage cleanup will require solving the problems posed by combined sanitary sewers and storm drains in New York City and other older urban areas. After storms, runoff from storm drains may increase total flow beyond the capacity of the sewage plant at the receiving end. When this happens, the treatment process may not work thoroughly; it may even be bypassed, sending this combined sewer overflow, waste and all, into the river. Scientists estimate that 90 percent of the coliform bacteria found in New York Harbor at present come from these overflows. Solving this problem will require separating storm water pipes from sanitary sewers, or building storage tanks which collect overflows for later treatment in drier weather. The cost of these

solutions, reckoned in billions of dollars, is one reason the problem remains.

Capacity is also exceeded as more residences are built and hooked into sewage systems, more water is used in new commercial and industrial facilities, and people form habits that consume more water. All of this water ultimately flows to sewage plants. Expanding capacity through new plant construction is very expensive, so there is increasing emphasis on lowering flows to existing plants through water conservation.

Ready for a Swim? On hot summer afternoons at Kingston's bathing beach on the Hudson, lifeguards keep watch over hundreds of people crowding the sand and water, trying to ensure their safety. Also vital to their safety is regular water testing by the county health department, making sure that this swimming spot is free of contamination by sewage. Such contamination, which may carry harmful bacteria and other patho-

Effective sewage treatment, including solving problems posed by combined sewer overflows, is necessary to maintain and increase safe use of Hudson River swimming areas like this Kingston beach.

gens, is a major factor limiting swimming in the Hudson.

Nonetheless, New York State classifies the length of the river from Castleton to the New Jersey line as swimmable. This classification doesn't necessarily mean that it always is swimmable; a check with the county health department about conditions at one's favorite beach is advisable.[6]

Controlling Point Discharges: The National Pollution Discharge Elimination System

While sewage pollution is of major concern to swimmers, it is only one of many waste discharges that have degraded the Hudson. At the heart of the Clean Water Act is a program intended to control all point discharges: the National Pollution Discharge Elimination System (or State Pollution Discharge Elimination System—SPDES—when administered by states, as it is in New York and New Jersey). The system covers not only sewage discharges but other forms of pollution as well—hazardous chemicals, heavy metals, food-processing wastes, and heated wastewater, for example.

The National Pollution Discharge Elimination System has three parts. Part 1 is a classification scheme intended to designate the best use of every waterway. These use classifications are as follows:

A. Suitable for drinking, cooking, or food processing;
B. Suitable for primary contact recreation (swimming);
C. Suitable for fishing and fish propagation; and
D. Suitable for secondary contact recreation (i.e., boating) and fish survival.

Classifications reflect the current best use of the waterway; much of the mid-Hudson, which supplies drinking water to Pough-

keepsie and other communities, is classified A. They are also intended to be goals for the eventual quality of a particular stretch of water; sections of the Hudson classified B may not actually be swimmable yet, but can reasonably be expected to attain that quality. Classifications are made with input from the public and reviewed every five years.

Part 2 of the Discharge Elimination System is determination of water quality standards. These numerical limits define the maximum amount of a pollutant allowed to be present in water bodies and may vary according to use classification.

With classifications established and standards set to protect water quality to the degree required by each classification, state

A People's Pipewatch Program

After the Clean Water Act became law, some polluters ignored it or were slow to comply. Clearwater initiated a People's Pipewatch Program in which volunteers searched out noxious discharges, identified their sources, and investigated whether or not the dischargers had the required permits. In one instance, pipewatchers discovered that Tuck Industries in Beacon had twenty-nine discharge pipes but held permits for only two. The information, including analyses of pollutants from the pipes, was presented to the U.S. Attorney, who filed a twenty-four-count indictment. The company eventually pleaded guilty to twelve counts and paid a fine of $43,500. (Photo by Karin Limburg.)

environmental agencies carry out part 3 of the program: issuing SPDES permits to control the quantities of wastes going into a waterway. Every pipe through which any facility discharges wastes into the river must have such a permit; it specifies what pollutants can be discharged, limits for each pollutant, and the frequency and type of testing that must be performed to monitor the discharge. Violations can result in fines and prison terms. Permits must be renewed every five years, at which time discharge limits can be made more stringent. By this means the SPDES "E"—for elimination— could be realized, as was intended in the Clean Water Act's national goal that "discharge of pollutants into the navigable waters be eliminated by 1985."

Has SPDES worked? 1985 has come and gone; discharges into the Hudson River continue. Whether a glass of river water remains half filled or half emptied of pollution depends on one's point of view.

Enforcement agencies argue that, while they are working to eliminate discharges, what is vital is establishing a balance of chemical constituents that does not threaten human health or the river's ecology. They feel that substantial progress has been made in achieving such a balance. According to statewide DEC data from 1990– 1991, 95 percent of New York's rivers and streams and 67 percent of its tidal waters support the uses called for by their classification. Problems with point discharges accounted for less than 10 percent of the cases in which these uses had not been achieved.

Environmental advocacy groups are more likely to see SPDES permits as licenses to pollute, arguing that even when compliance with permit limits is good, large amounts of toxic chemicals are discharged

into the Hudson and other waterways. According to Clearwater, some 190,000 pounds of known or suspected cancer-causing agents were discharged into the Hudson River basin in 1987.[7]

Enforcement of permit requirements is a particular concern for agencies and advocates alike, especially as budgets are cut in difficult fiscal climates. Under SPDES, responsibility for testing and reporting on permit compliance rests with the polluter. While this self-monitoring seems akin to the fox guarding the henhouse, even advocacy groups feel that the arrangement could work, provided that regulatory agencies examine polluters' reports thoroughly and back up this review with on-site inspections, random sampling of discharges, and firm action when violations are found.

Monitoring Self-Monitoring. DEC conducts an annual sampling program to check the self-monitoring reports prepared by dischargers. Data for fiscal year 1989–1990 show that 83 percent of significant dischargers sampled statewide were in compliance with their permits, apparently a fairly good record. However, the data cover only 37 percent of the major dischargers, and some facilities may not be checked for three to four years. In response to growing financial constraints, DEC intends to place more emphasis on review of monitoring reports and less on site inspections and discharge sampling, claiming that false reporting will be easy to detect.[8]

Environmentalists aren't so sure; there are known cases of polluters getting away with data falsification for up to a year. And by their reckoning, even when violations are reported, the enforcement reaction is weak. Clearwater studies of SPDES permits in the Hudson basin from 1979 to 1984, another period when budget woes restricted on-site inspections and sampling, revealed that 40 to 44 percent of major dischargers reported permit violations more than half the time, and that 43 to 54 percent reported exceeding their discharge limits by a factor of two or more. In response to these admitted violations, enforcement actions by DEC numbered only nineteen in the Hudson basin between 1975 and 1984, and in these cases "fines were not assessed in a consistent fashion or in a manner to deter future violations of the law."

Controlling Non-Point Source Pollution

Non-point source pollution can be seen on a rainy day in the parking lot of any Hudson Valley shopping mall. Rather than simply dodging puddles in a rush to get out of the rain, take a look at what they often contain: oil, antifreeze, and other fluids leaked from cars, as well as plastic wrappers, cigarette butts, and other solid waste, all bound for the nearest storm drain and ultimately the Hudson. Now multiply that scene by the valley's many square miles of parking lots and highways to begin to understand the magnitude of non-point pollution.

Other major components of the problem are fertilizers and pesticides applied to farm fields and lawns, animal wastes (especially where many animals are kept together in a small area, the case in cattle feedlots), and soil eroded off land left bare by farming or construction activities. These pollutants typically are not discharged through a specific pipe; instead, they are carried by runoff as it drains downhill and enters waterways at many scattered locations. These many small contributions of pollution add up; according to DEC, non-point source pollution is now the major factor impairing water quality across New York.

While state and federal agencies en-

Non-point sources of pollution include:

sediment eroding off construction sites and into streams,

motor oil, antifreeze, and other liquids leaking from automobiles,

and fertilizers and pesticides washed off lawns and agricultural lands.

Taking Individual Action Against Non-Point Pollution

Household closets and garages may contain potential pollutants: paints, paint thinners, motor oil, antifreeze, and lawn and garden pesticides, to name a few. All too often these find their way into storm drains (or down the sink where they may contaminate sludge or septic systems). Such substances should be used only in prescribed amounts. Leftover chemicals can often be turned in at household hazardous waste pickup days sponsored by county environmental councils or other local agencies; used motor oil can be returned to auto repair shops for recycling.

courage local governments to prevent non-point pollution through land use controls, the Clean Water Act does not require specific remedies. Appropriate remedies will vary greatly depending on the degree of urbanization in a region and particular land uses there. The act directs the states to inventory waters affected by such discharges and to prepare plans for dealing with the problems. Once plans are approved by the EPA, projects proposed in the plans can receive funding grants from the federal government.[9]

Preventing Oil Pollution

Eighteen billion gallons of petroleum are transported through New York Harbor each year, so it shouldn't be surprising that spills are a problem here. In two months' time early in 1990, spills of 565,000, 25,000, and 120,000 gallons blackened the Arthur Kill between Staten Island and New Jersey. While only the largest spills gain public attention, this type of pollution occurs virtually every day in the harbor.[10]

Only about 5 percent of the petroleum entering the harbor goes up the Hudson, but the river has not been spared. Larger spills include 26,000 gallons spilled from a grounded tanker in 1989, 102,000 gallons from a barge that hit Diamond Reef in 1987, and an infamous encounter between a barge and a reef in the Highlands in 1977 that released 480,000 gallons.

Oil's impacts go beyond the oil-soaked

On February 4, 1977, the Hess Oil barge *Ethel H.* grounded on Con Hook Rock just north of the Bear Mountain Bridge. Before the barge was freed and towed away four days later, 480,000 gallons of heavy fuel oil had spilled, forming a slick which covered some 30 miles of the Hudson.
(Photo by Charles Porter.)

birds and beaches shown during nightly newcasts. During the Arthur Kill spills, the herons that nest there avoided oiling; they were wintering in warmer climes. But food webs on which the birds depend were damaged: large swaths of *Spartina* grasses in the area's marshes were killed; populations of killifish, on which some heron species depend, were decimated, as were fiddler crabs and some types of clams. In the two years following the spills, nesting success of snowy egrets suffered: more than 80 percent of chicks died, and some scientists speculate that the young egrets died of starvation associated with the destruction of food supplies. The slicks are gone now, and killifish numbers are rebounding, yet oil remains in the marsh sediments and will probably contaminate this habitat for years, affecting benthic creatures and the animals that feed upon them.

Clean Water Act regulations prohibit the discharge of oil into navigable waterways, require inspections of vessels and waterfront oil terminals, and provide for fines when violations occur. The law mandates preparation of contingency plans to deal with spills, including creation of cleanup "strike forces" and prompt notification of authorities when accidents occur. The act also authorizes government takeover of cleanup efforts when responsible parties' efforts are inadequate, with later recovery of cleanup costs from those parties.

Oil and water may not mix, but they are inextricably linked since the Hudson and the complex of waterways around New York Harbor are vital to oil transport in this region. Measured both by volume and number of trips, petroleum is by far the major commodity shipped on the Hudson. While a number of federal and state agencies have authority over oil production, transportation, refining, and storage, the U.S. Coast Guard has the most prominent role in dealing with oil pollution on these waterways.[11]

An Ounce of Prevention Is Worth a Pound of Cure

Given human imperfection, a few spills are inevitable. Yet noting the regularity of such accidents and the sorry record of cleanup efforts (only 10 to 15 percent of spilled oil is usually recovered), it is worth recalling the adage about an ounce of prevention being worth a pound of cure. Environmentalists advocate adoption of more preventive measures to reduce the number of spills, their scale, and the severity of their impacts.

More rigorous inspections of vessels and facilities handling oil is one such measure. The largest of 1990's Arthur Kill spills poured from a ruptured Exxon pipeline that was uninspected due to gaps in agencies' statutory responsiblities, and in which a faulty leak detection system went uncorrected for more than twelve years. Improvements in navigational aids would also reduce the chance of collision or grounding. The potential for human error could be reduced through better training and tighter licensing requirements for mariners, along with increased use of pilots skilled in the intricacies of navigating the harbor and the Hudson.

Changes in the design of tankers and tanker barges would reduce the impacts of inevitable accidents. For decades, environmentalists called for these vessels to be constructed with double hulls and bottoms, which offer a second layer of protection against tank rupture due to collision or grounding. After finding that the infamous *Exxon Valdez* spill in Alaska, largest in U.S. history, would have been reduced by 25 to 60 percent had the ship been constructed with a double bottom, the Coast Guard and Congress moved to require that all

Who you gonna call? Reporting oil spills and other pollution

Should you witness an oil spill or other environmentally damaging incident, whom would you call? Given the many agencies involved, it can be difficult to determine which one has authority over the problem in question. For example, sewage discharges from pipes could be the concern of either a municipal agency, or of the state if violation of an SPDES permit is involved, while such discharges from boats on the Hudson are regulated by the Coast Guard. One can also report incidents to environmental watchdogs. Below are some toll-free phone numbers intended to put citizens in touch with organizations able to do something about immediate environmental problems such as spills.

New York State DEC hotlines:
to report polluters, 1-800-TIPPDEC; to report spills, 1-800-457-7362.

New York State Attorney General's Environmental Crimes hotline:
to report intentional or reckless release of hazardous substances that endanger people or the environment, 1-800-ENCRIME.

U.S. Coast Guard's National Response Center hotline:
to report oil spills, chemical spills, or illegal ocean dumping, 1-800-424-8802.

New York/New Jersey Harbor Baykeeper hotline:
1-800-8BAYKPR.

In response to a call from a concerned citizen, DEC directs a cleanup of home heating oil leaking into a marsh along a tributary of the Hudson.

new tankers delivered after 1994 for operation on U.S. waters be constructed with double hulls.

More effective response to spills could reduce their impacts. Contingency plans are required, but their implementation in real-life situations can be problematic, as was evident with the Exxon pipeline break. Since the leak alarm system was known to be faulty, its warnings were ignored and the pipeline was not shut off for six hours. When the spill was discovered, estimates of its size were far too low, resulting in delayed and inadequate deployment of booms intended to contain the mess. As the oil spread, Exxon and the Coast Guard discovered that the containment and cleanup equipment on hand in the harbor—on pa-

per enough to handle the spill—was in actuality not sufficient or available; additional equipment had to be flown in from as far away as Alabama. Wetland areas identified as sensitive habitats in an existing Coast Guard contingency plan were not boomed off promptly, and were soaked with oil.

Debate over instituting these changes swirls around questions of higher tanker construction costs and pilotage fees, resulting oil price hikes, and increasing staffing and training for spill response personnel in a time of budgetary restraint. With spill impacts widely known and decried, disputes about the validity of research findings and health risks are minimal; the basic issue is how much to spend to prevent oil disasters.

Through regulation of oil pollution,

point and non-point discharges, and sewage treatment, the Clean Water Act is intended to control ongoing pollution. But what about the legacy of years of toxic discharges into the Hudson?

A Superfund for Super Messes

To remedy problems caused by abandoned or uncontrolled hazardous waste sites, Congress passed the Comprehensive Environmental Response, Compensation, and Liability Act—more popularly known as Superfund—in 1980. Superfund, administered by the EPA, is supported by a tax on the chemical and petroleum industries. When those responsible for the waste can be identified, the EPA may seek reimbursement from the polluters for cleanup costs. New York has enacted a fairly similar state Superfund law.

Mention of Superfund brings to mind industrial wastelands piled with rusty barrels leaking their noxious contents onto the ground, perhaps with workers in spacesuit-like protective garb examining the mess. At the two Hudson River sites on Superfund's National Priorities List, the serious dangers posed by hazardous chemicals are masked by the river's beauty.

One site covers Cold Spring's picturesque Foundry Cove and nearby areas of the river, set in the spectacular scenery of the Hudson Highlands. The cove has the dubious honor of containing the world's highest known levels of environmental contamination by cadmium. The second site is a stretch of the Hudson from the Troy Dam north to Hudson Falls, where the river's surface reflects the lush pastoral landscapes of Saratoga and Washington Counties. In the bottom here are "hotspots," areas of sediment with especially high concentrations of toxic PCBs, which are the crux of the

Hudson's most serious contamination problem.

Cadmium is a heavy metal known to cause kidney damage and suspected of causing cancer. PCBs are suspected of causing liver damage and cancer and have been shown to have serious negative effects on brain chemistry, reproduction, and infant development. Human exposure to the Hudson's PCBs and cadmium comes mostly via consumption of fish and other river life—hence the issuance of the health advisories described in chapter 5.

This former battery factory in Cold Spring discharged cadmium into Foundry Cove and adjacent portions of the Hudson. Decontamination of the plant's interior and nearby residential yards was completed in 1992. Cleanup of the plant grounds and dredging to remove cadmium-laden sediments from the cove—here shown staked out to guide the process—finished in 1995.

Highly Chlorinated

Lightly Chlorinated

Polychlorinated biphenyl molecules consist of two linked phenyl groups—rings of six carbon atoms (C) and some hydrogen atoms (not shown)—with chlorine atoms (Cl) attached in various numbers and positions. Over 200 varieties can be formed. Those with many chlorine atoms are implicated in causing cancer; less-chlorinated varieties alter levels of chemicals vital for proper brain functioning and negatively impact reproduction and infant development.

Correcting hazardous waste problems through Superfund involves a complicated sequence of studies, hearings, and administrative decisions, all with the requisite descriptive jargon. Briefly, once a site is placed on the National Priorities List, the EPA conducts a two-part study—part 1 a remedial investigation into the nature and extent of the problem, part 2 a feasibility study examining options for dealing with the contamination.[12] After completing these assessments and seeking public comment, the EPA issues a record of decision, committing the government to specific remedies for the problem. At this point, the EPA may enter into a consent decree with the polluters responsible for the contamination; such a decree details financial and other responsibilities for the cleanup. In final preparation for the actual cleanup—the remedial action—a remedial design study details the engineering and construction of the chosen solutions. The entire process can take years, as can be seen in examining progress toward cleanup of cadmium in Cold Spring and PCBs in the upper Hudson.

Cadmium Cleanup in Cold Spring: A Case Study of Slow but Steady Progress

In 1981, Foundry Cove and nearby areas contaminated by cadmium were placed on the National Priorities List as the Marathon Battery Site, since the contamination came from a battery factory operated in Cold Spring between 1953 and 1979. The initial remedial investigation (1985) found that "high levels of cadmium, nickel, and cobalt existing in the site sediments pose a health hazard from direct contact, inhalation of heavy metal contaminated dust from the sediment, and bioaccumulation in the biota with subsequent ingestion of contaminated crabs and other biota." In one 50-by-

100-foot section the cove's sediments contained up to 17,000 ppm of cadmium.

After several feasibility studies examined cleanup alternatives within different portions of the site, EPA issued three records of decision. The first called for highly contaminated sediments to be dredged out, chemically fixed, and deposited in a landfill outside the Hudson Valley. The second specified limited dredging in other, less heavily contaminated portions of river bottom and marsh within the site, since removal work might cause more ecological harm than the cadmium present there. This portion of the project also included restoration of marsh habitats affected by dredging. The third required decontamination of the factory, its contents, and grounds, plus excavation of nearby residential yards, where there were high levels of heavy metals in the soil.

In 1991, a consent decree between the EPA, the Marathon Battery Company, and the U.S. Army (which built and initially operated the plant) provided nearly $11 million toward cleanup of the factory and its grounds. The sum represented about 70 percent of the costs of cleaning up this portion of the site, with federal and state Superfunds covering the remainder.

Remedial designs for dredging and the other cleanup and restoration efforts at the site were completed in 1992. Early in 1993 the EPA announced an agreement with the army, Marathon, and Gould Inc. (another firm that once operated the factory) on a consent order covering this work. The $109 million settlement is expected to pay for these efforts without requiring additional money from federal or state Superfunds.

PCBs: A Case Study in Ongoing Struggle

The story of attempts to cleanse the Hudson of PCBs is more complex and far from

The bulk of the river's PCBs came from this General Electric factory in Hudson Falls and another one in neighboring Fort Edward. These plants manufactured heavy-duty capacitors, in which PCBs were used as an insulating fluid.

over. Cleanup proposals have been forward, shot down, and reincarnated in a manner recalling popular horror movies with their endless sequels.

According to the EPA, from 1946 to 1977 as many as 1.3 million pounds of PCBs were discharged from two General Electric Company (GE) plants in Hudson Falls and Fort Edward. Washed downriver, the chemicals entered food chains throughout the Hudson and traveled with migrating fish, notably striped bass, into coastal waters.

Levels of PCBs in fish (see chapter 5) began to worry environmentalists, anglers, and researchers in the early 1970s. Their concerns captured public attention in 1975 with a *New York Times* front-page story headlined "State Says Some Striped Bass and Salmon Pose a Toxic Peril." The article described an alert from the DEC advising the public not to eat Hudson River stripers. In 1976 the agency prohibited commercial fishing for all Hudson species other than American shad and adult Atlantic sturgeon.[13]

General Electric had an SPDES permit from the DEC to discharge PCBs. However, increasing evidence that PCBs damaged fisheries prompted the DEC to conclude that the discharges violated state environmental laws, and the agency took legal action against GE. The ensuing hearings concluded that the contamination resulted from corporate abuse *and* regulatory failure. In a 1976 settlement, GE agreed to end its PCB discharges and put up $4 million for monitoring and investigation of the problem and possible remedies. The settlement also required DEC to contribute $3 million to the research effort.

A PCB Cleanup Proposal. It was soon clear that cleanup costs would far exceed $7 million. Forty million dollars was the 1978 estimate for the DEC's proposal to dredge the hotspots and place the contaminated sediments in a landfill in Fort Edward. Though uneasy about the landfill, most Hudson River environmental groups supported the plan. They felt that, uncontrolled, the hotspots would continue to feed PCBs into the estuary, and that a major flood might scour out PCB-laden sediments and send a heavy slug of contamination downriver. Thus timely removal of PCBs, even if to a landfill, was vital. In 1980, Congress authorized $20 million for the project via an amendment to the Clean Water Act. The amendment specified that this money was not to be released if other funds were available from a hazardous substance cleanup fund.

Many Fort Edward residents were unhappy with the idea of siting a hazardous waste landfill in their community. The location chosen—labeled Site 10—was an abandoned farm in a thinly settled part of town; however, these residents felt that the landfill would lower property values and threaten working farms nearby. They were able to legally overturn a state decision approving use of Site 10. This initiated a new review and site selection process, adding another layer of scientific study and administrative procedures to those ongoing in preparation of a cleanup plan.

The DEC was required to prepare an environmental impact statement and submit it to the EPA for approval before the project could proceed. The EIS, completed in October 1982, evaluated eight alternatives for dealing with the PCBs, including simply leaving them undisturbed in the river. The report recommended dredging the worst of the hotspots.

In December 1982, the EPA denied approval of the EIS and barred release of funds authorized by the Clean Water Act amendment, on the basis that cleanup money was available under Superfund. Environmentalists cried foul: at the time, the contaminated sites were not on the National Priorities List, nor was there any guarantee that the project would qualify for Superfund status or funding. Claiming that the decision was a political shell game aimed at killing the project, Clearwater, Scenic Hudson, the Hudson River Fishermen's Association, and others sued the EPA for release of the cleanup money, and were joined in that suit by the DEC.

Superfund Enters the Fray. In 1983, the EPA did assess the problem under Superfund, and the Hudson River PCBs Site was placed on Superfund's National Priorities List. Following the requisite studies, the agency's 1984 record of decision identified GE as the responsible polluter. However, based on analyses that "used matrices and weighting factors that were never clearly explained or motivated," the EPA found that the proposed remedies were not cost-effective given the lack of a defined threat to public health and at that time chose to take no action on a Superfund cleanup of the river bottom.[14]

This blow against the proposed cleanup was blunted by settlement of the lawsuit over the Clean Water Act funds. The settlement allowed release of that money once the DEC resurveyed the hotspots and secured a landfill site, so the agency proceeded to seek approvals for dredging and a landfill

A citizen advisory committee, appointed to provide input to research and cleanup efforts funded by the 1976 settlement between DEC and GE, views Site 10, a potential location for a landfill to hold PCB-laden sediments from the river.

at a new location. Hearings began in 1987. In fall 1988, the hearing judge found that the project was necessary for environmental safety and recommended issuing the required permits. His recommendations went to New York State's Hazardous Waste Facilities Siting Board for a final decision. Here progress was halted again, as the board agreed that the project was necessary but found the new landfill site unacceptable.

At this point the DEC decided to "rescope" the project, reevaluating use of the first site selected (remember Site 10?), and assessing technologies for destroying PCBs rather than just landfilling them. This led to the release of another version of the dredging and landfill plan late in 1989. Meanwhile, the EPA was mulling over a DEC petition to review the 1984 Superfund no-action decision. In December 1989, the two agencies jointly announced that the EPA would reconsider a Superfund cleanup of the PCBs.[15]

That reassessment, to be accomplished in three phases, was ongoing at 1994's end. The agency's consultants completed Phase One, a review of existing data on PCB contamination, in 1991. Phase Two, additional sampling along with ecological and human health risk assessments, was to be completed in 1995, with a feasibility study due in 1996.

PCBs and Politics. The political side of the PCB controversy has involved virtually every level of government from local town halls to Congress and the White House. GE, individual citizens, and organized activist groups on both sides of the issue are trying to speed or stall the proposed cleanup by pressuring elected officials and government administrators.

Decisions about hazardous waste cleanup are usually thought to be above politics, since toxics affect people regardless of their political affiliation. However, evidence gathered for the lawsuit over EPA's 1982 impoundment of the Clean Water Act funds showed that it was based on political pressure to stop the project rather than on scientific or resource management concerns.[16]

One example of such pressure were the efforts of Congressman Gerald Solomon, a Republican representing Fort Edward. In 1982 the *Troy Times Record* quoted him as vowing to stop the project by "using every ounce of influence I have with the [Reagan] Administration." And in 1990, Hudson Valley newspapers published a letter from Congressman Solomon to John Sununu, then chief of staff to President George Bush, requesting that this "environmentally useless" dredging program being considered under the Superfund reassessment be stalled because a cleanup would "help Governor [Mario] Cuomo politically."

Both proponents and opponents of the dredging plan have been placed on various citizen advisory committees reviewing the reassessment. Some of these individuals have been chosen to chair their committees, leading to debate about the potential for exercise of undue influence. In one case, after state officials and environmental groups protested to the EPA, a GE scientist serving as chair of the key Scientific and Technical Committee was replaced by a researcher viewed as more impartial. Under Superfund, GE—as the party responsible for the contamination—might have to pay cleanup costs, now estimated to approach $300 million for the option of dredging and destroying the PCBs. The company actively opposes dredging, claiming that bacteria are degrading PCBs in the river and that the chemical poses a lower risk to public health than has been thought.

HEALTH RISKS LINKED TO PCB EXPOSURE

HEALTH EFFECT OBSERVED IN STUDIES OF:	HUMANS	WILDLIFE	LAB ANIMALS
Cancer (*skin, liver, brain, respiratory & gastrointestinal*)	✔		✔
Circulatory disease	✔		
Respiratory impairment	✔		
Birth defects in offspring of exposed females	✔	✔	✔
Development disorders in offspring of exposed females	✔	✔	✔
Severe skin rashes	✔		
Increased blood pressure	✔		
Abnormal liver function	✔		✔
Impaired immune system	✔	✔	✔
Reproductive disorders/failure		✔	✔
Neurological disorders			✔

(Data from EPA.)

The PCB Controversy Today. As the Superfund reassessment proceeds, the following points are argued in public and scientific debate over the PCB problem and the state's proposed dredging project.

The toxicity of PCBs. Opponents claim that the cancer-causing potential of PCBs, based on feeding laboratory animals large doses, is overstated, and that serious health effects are caused mainly by highly chlorinated varieties uncommon in the river; public health and environmental advocates point out that carcinogenicity is also supported by studies of occupational exposure, and that recent research has shown that the less-chlorinated varieties of PCBs also have major negative effects on human health.

Trends in PCB levels. Levels in striped bass have gone down, but most of the decline occurred over the four years following cessation of PCB discharges in 1977; levels have remained fairly constant since the early 1980s (with some yearly fluctuation thought to be due to rainfall and river flow conditions) at a level that exceeds federal guidelines for dietary safety.

Sources of PCBs in the river. GE points to reports estimating that there are significant contributions of PCBs from sources downriver; even if these estimates are correct, GE's discharges still account for the majority of the PCBs in the Hudson.

The impacts of dredging. The image of a clam-shell scoop dripping muddy water leads to fears about stirring up the PCBs, but sediments would actually be removed by hydraulic suction dredges (akin to vacuum cleaners) in a manner that has been shown not to create an extensive plume of contaminated water.

Biodegradation of PCBs. GE scientists have demonstrated that microbes will degrade PCBs under controlled conditions in the laboratory; the company's claims that such degradation is happening at a significant rate in the river are unconfirmed and disputed by outside scientists.

Landfill safety. While the proposed landfill would be a state-of-the-art facility, it cannot be guaranteed against leaks; landfilling is at the bottom of New York State's ranking of solutions to hazardous waste problems; the intent that it be a temporary containment facility must be underlined by rapid identification of treatment measures to break down the PCBs.

After decades of argument and inaction, the PCB story may seem like stale news to the larger public. It shouldn't be. From 1977 to 1989, roughly the time between release of the DEC's first cleanup

proposal and announcement of the Superfund reassessment, over 33,000 pounds of
PCBs flowed over the Troy Dam and into
the lower Hudson. They continue to enter
the lower Hudson as the reassessment goes
on. Twenty years after PCBs became headline news, they remain the most serious
toxic hazard in the river.

Pollution Prevention versus Pollution Control

The history of the Hudson's PCB problem makes clear the difficulties in trying to
clean up *after* a pollutant has been released.
As a result, environmentalists and regulatory agencies are now looking beyond controlling the ongoing release of hazardous
pollutants and focusing on preventing their
release.

In his 1990 book *Making Peace with the
Planet,* well-known environmental scientist
Barry Commoner evaluated the success of
the Clean Water Act, Clean Air Act, and
other similar laws. Choosing common pollutants known to be dangerous to human
and ecological health, he reviewed studies
that allowed comparisons of their levels in
the environment before and about a decade
after passage of these laws. While some specific waterways had shown improvement,
the picture nationwide was disappointing.
In the few cases where levels of a pollutant
had substantially declined, he attributed the
decrease to elimination of the pollutant in
production processes. Lead levels, for example, had dropped dramatically due to
elimination of leaded gasoline. Commoner
summed up by making the case for pollution
prevention rather than pollution control:
"When a pollutant is attacked at the point
of origin—in the production process that
generates it—the pollutant can be eliminated; once it is produced, it is too late. This

A New Source of PCBs in the Upper Hudson?

In 1992, routine tests found unexpectedly high PCB levels in the water of the upper Hudson.
When concentrations in fish also jumped that year, a search began for a "new" source of PCBs
other than the identified hotspots. The hunt led back to GE's Hudson Falls plant, where researchers found PCB-contaminated water, oil, and sediments seeping from the plant and its
grounds and moving through abandoned pipes and other water courses into the river. In 1993
GE signed consent orders to collect and treat the seepage and to remove and dispose of 3,000
cubic yards of PCB-contaminated soil adjacent to the factory. In 1994, portions of river bottom
next to the plant were revealed when water was diverted for work on a dam; nearly pure PCBs
were oozing from the exposed bedrock.

(Photo by Charles Porter.)

is the simple but powerful lesson of the two decades of intense but largely futile effort to improve the quality of the environment."

The lesson is now being heeded. New Jersey, for instance, enacted a Pollution Prevention Act in 1991. The law requires certain industries to reduce the generation of pollution at the source by 50 percent over five years, and provides incentives for developing new industrial processes that reduce use and discharges of harmful pollutants. New York passed a Hazardous Waste Reduction law in 1989, establishing reduction and elimination as the most preferred methods of hazardous waste management. In both states, industries must develop and implement hazardous waste reduction plans that are subject to scrutiny and approval by environmental agencies.

Reducing pollution at the source can be accomplished by using different raw materials, changing manufacturing processes, redesigning products, and improving maintenance and housekeeping at factories. If production of wastes cannot be avoided, its management may be improved through reuse and recycling. Such changes may result in savings for manufacturing firms through more efficient use of raw materials and lower waste disposal costs, making environmental protection good for business as well as for the Hudson.

In cases where reduction or reuse of wastes is not possible, they must by treated and disposed of in an environmentally sound manner. Here pretreatment, SPDES permits, and other Clean Water Act programs discussed above come into play. To avoid the possibility that these controls may encourage industries to discharge their wastes elswhere—in the ground or up a smokestack instead of into the river—New York's DEC is coordinating its many regulatory divisions and programs in a new Multi-Media Pollution Prevention effort. This should allow comprehensive review and regulation of a polluter's impacts on air, water, and land.

Pollution prevention philosophy is also apparent in the DEC's proposed Water Quality Enhancement and Protection Policy. This policy would protect particularly sensitive waters (those used as drinking water supplies, for instance) by prohibiting some or all discharges into them, prevent degradation down to the legal limit where waters are cleaner than required by applicable classifications and standards, and ban the manufacture, importation, and use of some environmentally persistent toxic substances.

Adoption of this policy and other pollution prevention measures, complementing the pollution control programs of the Clean Water Act, promise a real reduction in the threat of toxic contamination. With such progress, those who ask, "Is the Hudson cleaner?" in the not-too-distant future will be answered with a more resounding "yes!"

Afterword

When a large quantity of information is packed between the covers of a book like this one, readers may view it as a final authority on the topic covered. While we hope and trust that *The Hudson* will be an invaluable reference, it is not intended to and cannot possibly be the last word.

One obvious reason is length: a work of this magnitude lacks comprehensive detail. But in addition, and contrary to what one might expect, the experience of researching and writing this book did not make the authors feel more expert and comfortable in their increasing knowledge of the Hudson. Rather, it made clear the degree to which many specific statements of fact must be qualified because important questions about the ecology and history of the river are at present unanswered.

Thus the book should serve as a basic skeleton of information, suggesting the direction of deeper investigation and supporting fuller understanding of fields in which the reader has a personal interest. At the same time, it points out the connections to be made between relevant yet diverse fields of knowledge.

We encourage readers to undertake such investigations, leavening the academic research with trips to the river, letting it spark curiosity and inspiration. In earlier times, this happened as a matter of course, since much of everyday life centered on the Hudson. The river is not so "in the face" of valley residents today, yet it still defines this region and remains at the mercy of natural and social forces that have determined its past and present condition. Through a fuller understanding of these forces, we hope our readers will be better able to insure that the Hudson River continues to inspire in the future.

Sources and Notes

Materials used in preparing this book are described below, accompanied by notes. For each chapter, the first paragraph lists the most important and readily available works, using an abbreviated citation. See Suggested Readings for complete, annotated citations of these sources. The second paragraph lists materials that provide more limited amounts of information, or which may be more difficult to obtain. Complete citations are provided for those readers who wish to find these items.

1. A Physical Overview of the Hudson

The first chapter of Karin Limburg et al., *The Hudson River Ecosystem*, provided information on length, width, depth, flow, salinity, and flushing rates. The New York State Geological Survey's *Geology of New York: A Simplified Account* by Y. W. Isachsen et al. describes the impacts of ice age glaciers on southeastern New York and the Hudson Valley. Tide data were drawn from the National Ocean Survey's annual publications, *Tide Tables: East Coast of North and South America* and *Tidal Current Tables: Atlantic Coast of North America*.

More specifics concerning the geological history of the Hudson came from scientific papers, most notably "Late Quaternary Geology of the Hudson River Estuary: a Preliminary Report" by W. S. Newman, D. H. Thurber, H. S. Zeiss, A. Rokach, and L. Musich, in *Transactions of the N.Y. Academy of Sciences*, series 2, vol. 31 (1969), and "Oceanographic and Geologic Framework of the Hudson System" by Nicholas K. Coch and Henry J. Bokuniewicz, in *Northeastern Geology*, vol. 8, no. 3 (1986). Added detail came from John H. Johnsen, professor of geology at Vassar College (retired), via his *The Hudson River Guide*, a 1987 edition of a field book for geological trips on the Hudson.

1. All depths given in this book are referenced to average low tide.

2. Glacial Lake Albany is thought to have extended nearly 200 miles from Glens Falls to New York City, but there is some disagreement about whether it was one lake or several separate lakes occupying the valley, and the point or points where the melting water was dammed up is an enigma.

3. Other deltas formed in Glacial Lake Albany at the present-day sites of Newburgh, Kingston, Red Hook, Hudson, Kinderhook, Albany, and Schenectady.

4. Because the moon is in motion, revolving around the earth, a complete tidal cycle actually takes twenty-four hours and fifty minutes. Imagine yourself on the spinning earth's surface, checking your watch as you pass directly under the moon. As you wait for the earth to whirl you around full circle, the moon is not standing still. It is moving ahead, toward the east as you view things, so that you will need more than twenty-four hours and 360 degrees to catch up. You must wait an extra fifty minutes for the spinning earth to put you directly under the moon again. For this reason, the timing of a given tidal event will fall back by fifty minutes each day, on average. For example, if low tide on Monday morning is at 9:00, low tide Tuesday morning would be at 9:50.

5. The flood tidal current should not be confused with flooding due to heavy rains. Destructive floods of the latter sort do occur in the Hudson above the Troy dam; their effects are dampened by tidal action farther to the south. Even in high floods, river levels south of Catskill fall within ranges determined by ocean tides.

6. Parts per million are units commonly used to describe a chemical's concentration in a given substance such as water. Imagine one part per million as one letter of a million printed in a book. There are about 500,000 printed in this volume; thus the letter "v" in volume would be one per million in a book twice the length of this one. Concentrations are also commonly expressed as milligrams per liter (mg/l); with very dilute solutions, the units are practically equivalent.

7. As of 1995, Waterford, Port Ewen, Rhinebeck, Highland, and Poughkeepsie depend on the Hudson for all or part of their water supply. New York City has drawn water from the river during drought emergencies. Hyde Park is constructing an intake on the river. Two institutions, the Hudson River Psychiatric Center and the Castle Point Veterans Administration Medical Center, also obtain water from the Hudson.

2. Energy Flow and Nutrient Cycles in the Hudson

The first chapter of Karin Limburg et al.'s *The Hudson River Ecosystem* provides an overview of the estuary's food webs and was the main source of data on productivity and inputs of organic carbon, nitrogen, and phosphorus to the estuary. Our more general descriptions of food webs, energy flow, and nutrient cycling depended on standard ecology texts, notably Eugene P. Odum's *Fundamentals of Ecology.*

Energy flow and nutrient cycling in the Hudson have been important foci of recent scientific study. J. J. Cole, N. M. Caraco, and B. L. Peierls, "Phytoplankton Primary Production in the Mid-Hudson" (1989), Final Report to the Hudson River Foundation, reviewed primary production estimates for a number of rivers and estuaries and discussed limiting factors controlling algal growth, a subject expanded upon in their paper, "Can Phytoplankton Maintain a Positive Carbon Balance in a Turbid, Freshwater, Tidal Estuary?" *Limnology & Oceanography,* vol. 37, no. 8 (1992). The importance of bacterial production was addressed by Stuart Findlay in personal communication and Findlay et al., "Weak Coupling of Bacterial and Algal Production in a Heterotrophic System: The Hudson River Estuary," *Limnology and Oceanography,* vol. 36, no. 2 (1991). Finally, Robert Howarth et al. provided estimates of organic carbon inputs to the freshwater tidal Hudson in "Ecosystem Respi-

ration and Organic Carbon Processing in a Large, Tidally Influenced River: The Hudson River," *Biogeochemistry,* vol. 16, no. 2 (1992).

1. The amphipod example also points out a major difference between taxonomic classification, by which organisms are given a scientific name, and categorization based on ecological considerations. In taxonomy, organisms are grouped based on anatomy, physiology, and evolutionary development; ecological categorizations depend on roles and placement within ecosystems and can group taxonomically unlike organisms together. Amphipods and bald eagles are far apart taxonomically but could be grouped together ecologically as scavengers; both will eat dead fish.

2. Heat energy is expressed in random motion and vibration of molecules. This is transferred to other nearby molecules and results ultimately in the dispersion, not the destruction, of energy.

3. Energy loss along the food chain has practical effects on the numbers and size of consumers. For instance, the Hudson River can support many more Canada geese than great blue herons. Though similar in size, geese eat plants; their position lower in the food chain means that there is more energy available for them than for herons.

4. These estimates, along with those in the section "The Bottom Line" and the figure titled "The Hudson's Income Budget" are from Limburg et al. While somewhat dated, we used them because they cover the entire tidal Hudson. More recent data (Howarth 1992) for the freshwater tidal portion of the Hudson puts the watershed's contribution of organic carbon at 87 percent of the total, primary production by phytoplankton at 9 percent, and sewage at 4 percent. However, its geographic limitation means that this study leaves out sewage inputs from the New York metropolitan area and primary production in the Tappan Zee, Haverstraw Bay, and New York Bay.

5. Nitrogen is an important component of many compounds vital to the functioning of living organisms, among them amino acids (the building blocks of protein) and nucleic acids (constituents of genetic material). Phosphorus is found in phospholipids (part of cell membranes) and vertebrate bone, and is important in energy transformations within cells.

6. This description is very simplistic. The nitrogen cycle can be traced through many steps involving bacteria and fungi that alter the form of the fixed nitrogen before it is reused by green plants.

7. This process of enrichment in aquatic ecosystems is called *eutrophication.* It occurs naturally as lakes and ponds

age. In regions of heavy human habitation, the process may accelerate due to pollution and is then called *cultural eutrophication.*

3. The Hudson's Habitats and Plant Communities

A wide-ranging source of information for this chapter was *Hudson River Significant Tidal Habitats: A Guide to the Functions, Values, and Protection of the River's Natural Resources,* produced jointly by the Division of Coastal Resources and Waterfront Revitalization, New York Department of State, and the Nature Conservancy. Also useful was *The Ecology of Tidal Freshwater Marshes of the United States East Coast: A Community Profile* by W. E. Odum et al. The Boyce Thompson Institute's *An Atlas of the Biological Resources of the Hudson Estuary* was helpful in developing our general discussion of plant communities and their productivity and in describing representative plant species. Information in those descriptions also came from *A Field Guide to Coastal Wetland Plants of the Northeastern United States* by Ralph W. Tiner, Jr.

Valuable for its descriptions of wetland habitats and species was Erik Kiviat's *Hudson River East Bank Natural Areas, Clermont to Norrie* (The Nature Conservancy, Arlington, Va., 1978). Robert E. Schmidt and Erik Kiviat's 1988 report to the Hudson River Foundation, "Communities of Larval and Juvenile Fish Associated with Water-Chestnut, Water-milfoil, and Water-Celery in the Tivoli Bays of the Hudson River," offers specific information on the plants and communities associated with them.

1. Technically, the euphotic zone extends to the point where light available to plants allows photosynthesis to produce just enough energy to meet their respiratory needs. This is roughly the point at which one percent of surface light remains.

2. While these are generally used, terms may vary from reference to reference (the intertidal zone may be called the *littoral zone,* for instance), and some authors include more divisions.

3. Also encountered in discussions of this community are the terms *periphyton* and *aufwuchs,* referring to plants and animals living underwater attached to surfaces, including plant leaves and stems, that project above the bottom. Epiphytes would be included in the category defined by these two terms.

4. Low and high marsh are the most basic divisions of the marsh community. Scientists who study these communities have subdivided further, using a number of classification systems.

5. Extensive single-species stands of marsh plants—stands that appear to be many individual plants packed closely together—may actually be one plant with above-ground stems and leaves growing from an underground network of rhizomes.

6. Notable examples of tidal swamp communities are found at Tivoli Bays near Red Hook, and at Rogers Island and Ramshorn Creek near Catskill.

4. The Hudson's Invertebrate Animals

Ralph Buchsbaum's *Animals without Backbones* provided background information about invertebrates as a group. Material about many significant invertebrate species of the estuary came from the Boyce Thompson Institute's *Atlas of the Biological Resources of the Hudson Estuary.* Additional information on freshwater invertebrates came from Robert Pennak's *Fresh-water Invertebrates of the United States;* on saltwater creatures from Kenneth Gosner's *A Field Guide to the Atlantic Seashore.*

Some details on specific organisms or groups of organisms came from a variety of scientific papers, fact sheets, and articles. Particularly useful was David Strayer's "Ecology and Zoogeography of the Freshwater Mollusks of the Hudson River Basin," a report prepared for the Hudson River Foundation in 1986, and "Oysters in the Hudson" by Chuck Keene in the winter 1993 member bulletin of the Museum of the Hudson Highlands, Cornwall on Hudson, New York.

1. For these reasons and more, we will not cover the smallest of invertebrates, the protozoans. However, they play a key role in food chains and other aspects of Hudson River ecology, and readers interested in them should check the invertebrate references listed in Suggested Readings.

2. *Polychaete* and *oligochaete* are imposing words, but easy to interpret once one knows that *chaeta* means "bristle" and the prefix *poly* means "many," the suffix *oligo* "few." The bristles of polychaete worms grow in a bundle from a sac in the skin; only a single bristle grows from each sac in the skin of oligochaetes.

3. The moon snail drills into the shells of bivalves with its radula; the whelk hammers at bivalve shells, chipping a hole into its prey.

4. Compound eyes are made up of many individual lenses and provide the crab with sight. The simple eyes respond to the absence or presence of visible light and to ultraviolet light.

5. The New York State Department of Health recommends limiting consumption of Hudson estuary crabs to six

per week and advises against eating the soft green substance—commonly called tomalley or mustard—found in the body. It contains high levels of chemical contaminants, including PCBs and heavy metals.

5. The Hudson's Fishes

General information about fish came from the text *Ichthyology* by Karl F. Lagler et al. The Boyce Thompson Institute's *Atlas of the Biological Resources of the Hudson Estuary* provided information on the critical zone and on important Hudson River fishes. Descriptions of individual species also drew from C. Lavett Smith's *The Inland Fishes of New York State*.

A listing of fish species recorded from the Hudson (north of the Battery) and its tributaries can be found in C. Lavett Smith and Thomas R. Lake's paper, "Documentation of the Hudson River Fish Fauna," *American Museum Novitates*, no. 2981, from the American Museum of Natural History in New York City. It does not include species recorded only from New York Harbor. Our discussion of the critical zone came from testimony entitled "Analysis of Fisheries Sampling Programs Conducted in the Hudson River with an Overview of the Biological Productivity of That System," prepared for the U.S. Environmental Protection Agency by fisheries scientist William Dovel. Information about consumption of Hudson River fish came from the New York State Department of Health's *1994–95 Health Advisory: Chemicals in Sportfish or Game*; this document is updated regularly.

1. Though significant from an evolutionary point of view, lampreys are of minor importance in the Hudson. The species found here—the American brook lamprey (*Lamptera appendix*), silver lamprey (*Ichthyomyson unicuspis*), and sea lamprey (*Petromyzon marinus*)—are elusive and seldom seen. The latter two have round mouths with rows of rasplike teeth and are parasitic, burrowing through a host's skin to feed on blood and tissue.

2. Sharks and their kin take water in through the mouth and pass it out through five to seven pairs of gills, each in its own pouch. Muscle contractions pump water over the gills, but this pumping ability is limited in many sharks. They are only able to take in sufficient water for respiration while in motion, and suffocate easily when immobilized. Sharks, rare in the Hudson above the Battery, are occasionally caught in New York Harbor.

3. Fish breathe molecular oxygen (O_2) dissolved in water, not the oxygen atom of the water molecule (H_2O).

4. Assuming that growth rings are close together only

in winter is not always correct. A more accurate method of assessing age in fish is by examining growth rings on otoliths, calcareous structures that are part of the organs for hearing and balance.

5. In many species the young must at first fill their swim bladder with air taken in at the surface. They can then maintain inflation with blood gases.

6. A parent stream is the stream or area within the stream where an individual fish was born. Many anadromous fishes return to their parent stream to spawn. If the stream is altered in any way, it may be unrecognizable to the returning adults, the result being reproductive failure.

7. The jelly-covered hairs may be exposed on the surface of a fish's body, embedded in sheltering pits, or enclosed in canals running under the skin.

8. These health advisories are updated yearly. To obtain the latest version, call the Department of Health at 1-800-458-1158, ext. 409.

6. The Hudson's Birds and Beasts

Most information in this chapter came from scientific reports rather than books intended for the general public, though the *National Audubon Society's Encyclopedia of North American Birds* by John K. Terres, and Roger Tory Peterson's *Field Guide to the Birds* provided data on individual species.

Discussion of the Hudson's amphibians, reptiles, and mammals depended largely on publications by Erik Kiviat, including *Hudson River East Bank Natural Areas, Clermont to Norrie*, published by the Nature Conservancy in 1978, and "Reptiles and Amphibians of the Hudson Estuary," from *Clearwater's North River Navigator*, October 1977. The section on birds owes much to checklists produced by bird clubs and nature centers. "Birds of the Hudson River National Estuarine Research Reserve" is especially useful and available free from the Reserve (c/o Bard College Field Station, Annandale, NY 12504). Reports by Bryan L. Swift of the New York State Department of Environmental Conservation, "Avian Breeding Habitats in Hudson River Tidal Marshes" (1989), and by Charles Keene of the Museum of the Hudson Highlands, "1984–1985 Survey of Bald Eagles, Peregrine Falcons, and Osprey along the Hudson River," both prepared for the Hudson River Foundation, were important references. Also valuable was a 1990 report to the U.S. Environmental Protection Agency's New York–New Jersey Harbor Estuary Program by Dr. Joanna Burger of Rutgers University and coworkers, "Toxicant Accumulation and Effects on Birds: The Reproductive Biology and Effects of Pollutants on Estuarine and Marine Birds of the New York/New Jersey Harbor Estuary," and Dr. Burger's later presentation, "Biomonitoring Using Selected Marine Birds from Massachusetts to Southern New Jersey," at a February 1992 conference sponsored by the Estuary Program.

1. Some aquatic turtles "breathe" through the lining of the pharynx in the throat and also through the lining of the cloaca, an internal cavity into which the genital and excretory systems discharge.

2. The poisonous copperhead (*Agkistrodon contortrix*) is found locally in rocky areas bordering the Hudson, but is a mild mannered, retiring snake. The chances of being bitten are minimal unless one tries to handle the snake, which is not advisable.

3. The diving ducks need a running start because they have smaller wings for their size than surface-feeding ducks.

4. Celebration of these achievements may be premature. From 1988 to 1991, pairs of nesting peregrines in New Jersey declined from fourteen to ten. Increasing levels of DDE, a metabolic residue of DDT, were observed in their eggs, the shells of which were becoming thinner and more fragile. These phenomena were implicated in reproductive failure during the falcon's earlier population decline. The source of the DDT is not known, but speculation includes limited use of DDT in current pesticide formulations, and release from decades-old deposits in sediments dredged or otherwise disturbed today.

5. Another warning involving toxic chemicals and birds comes from the New York State Health Department, which advises hunters not to eat mergansers. These ducks feed chiefly on fish, and tend to concentrate the PCBs found in the Hudson's fish.

7. *Exploration, Colonization, and Revolution*

The historical framework and factual details for a description of the colonial period were drawn from Carl Carmer's *The Hudson*. Discussions of Native Americans depended on Herbert C. Kraft's *The Lenape: Archaeology, History and Ethnography*, and Julian Harris Salomon's *Indians of the Lower Hudson River: The Munsee*. Descriptions of land use and settlement patterns in the 1600s and 1700s relied on Raymond O'Brien's *The American Sublime: Landscape and Scenery of the Lower Hudson Valley*, and D. W. Meinig's innovative geography of early American history, *The Shaping of America: A Geographical Perspective on 500 Years of History: Atlantic America, 1492-1800*, vol. 1.

Other sources included John Seelye's *Prophetic Waters: The River in Early American Life and Literature* (New York: Oxford University Press, 1977), which influenced the chapter's emphasis on the centrality of the Hudson in colonial and Revolutionary New York, and Paul Wilstach's *Hudson River Landings* (Indianapolis: The Bobbs-Merrill Co., 1933), which provided a clear overview of the Revolutionary battles.

1. Muhheakantuck is spelled in various ways, including Muhheakunnuk, Mahicannittuck, and Mahicantuck.

2. A lively addition to the literature of local native history is a five-part series of articles by Robert S. Grumet in the magazine *Hudson Valley* (January–May 1991). Grumet is an archaeologist who draws on the findings of this discipline to create a political and cultural history of the valley's natives.

3. Even after Columbus's discovery Europeans continued to hope for a natural passageway through the barrier of the American continent to the South Sea. An alternative Northeast Passage, sailing to the north of Europe and Asia, was not as popular as the northwest route.

4. The Dutch applied the term "Walloons" to Huguenot refugees from the southern Netherlands. The Huguenots were French Protestants persecuted by Catholic monarchs.

5. The Hudson's reaches included (from south to north) the Great Chip Rock, the Tappan Reach, the Haverstroo, Seylmakers, Crescent, Hoges, Vorsen, Fishers, Claverack, Backerack, Playsier, Vaste, and Hunters.

6. The term "North River" distinguished the Hudson from the Delaware, which was the South River and the southern boundary of Dutch hegemony in seventeenth-century America. It may also have been a term used by traders to distinguish the Delaware from the Hudson. Even today the river's professional mariners use North River to refer to a portion of the Hudson along Manhattan; the term is reflected in the naming of the North River Sewage Treatment Plant at West 135th Street.

7. Rooted in medieval practices, the manorial system was based on the grant of land and feudal rights to a lord by royal charter. The land in turn was rented or leased by the lord of the manor to tenants or peasants for a fixed dues or service.

8. The first federal census found seven free, non-white households in Albany in 1790. Legislation abolished slavery there in 1799, and the 1810 census counted more than three hundred free residents of African ancestry. This information comes from the Colonial Albany History Project, which has been studying the ethnic makeup and daily lives of Albany's

minorities before 1800. Using innovative research methods, the project has offered insights into the lives of slaves and free people of color, whose history had long been neglected.

9. This quote is from Meinig's *The Shaping of America*.

8. The Romantic River

Discussion of the sublime and basic analysis of the work of the Hudson's painters comes from Barbara Novak's *Nature and Culture: American Landscape and Painting 1825–1875*. Raymond O'Brien provides a definition of the sublime more directly tied to its use in the Hudson Valley in his *American Sublime: Landscape and Scenery of the Lower Hudson Valley*. The section on literature relied on Arthur Adams's *The Hudson River in Literature*, and treatment of estate architecture on John Zukowsky and Robbie Pierce Stimson's *Hudson River Villas*.

Additionally, Leo Marx's *The Machine in the Garden* (New York: Oxford University Press, 1967) shaped discussion of the struggle between nature and civilization.

1. Luminism, sometimes referred to as "air painting," flourished in the middle decades of the century. It concentrated on capturing weather, light, and air effects. The leading painters in the movement included Sanford Robinson Gifford, John Frederick Kensett, Fitz Hugh Lane, and Martin Johnson Heade.

2. Alexander Jackson Davis (1803– 1892) was a most prolific New York architect, notably successful in his Greek Revival style and in his anticipation of the use of cast iron. He designed many river estates, the best examples of which include Locust Grove in Poughkeepsie and the neo-Gothic Lyndhurst in Tarrytown. Andrew Jackson Downing (1815– 1852) was the nation's most popular theorist of architecture and landscape gardening. He also urged the development of public open spaces. His magazine, *Horticulturist*, and his many publications on rural residences and landscape gardening exercised enormous influence over the Romantic movement and nineteenth-century estate building in the valley. Downing and Davis were close friends and collaborators. *Charmed Places: Hudson River Artists and Their Houses, Studios, and Vistas*, edited by Sandra Phillips and Linda Weintraub, discusses their influence on river estates (see Suggested Readings.)

9. Industrialization and the Transformation of the Landscape

Information about development of cities, towns, and villages as well as industrial growth in the nineteenth century was found in D. W. Meinig's *The Shaping of America: A Geographical Perspective on 500 Years of History: Atlantic America, 1492– 1800*, vol. 1, and Carl Carmer's *The Hudson*. Discussion of the railroad's impact on the valley landscape was based on John Stilgoe's *Metropolitan Corridor: Railroads and the American Scene*.

Additional sources included F. Daniel Larkin's *John B. Jervis: An American Engineering Pioneer* (Ames: Iowa State University Press, 1990), offering background on Jervis's work; John Seelye's *Beautiful Machines: River and the Republican Plan 1755–1825* (New York: Oxford University Press, 1991), which examines the cultural and political significance of rivers, canals, and steamboats in the early republic; and Paul Wilstach's *Hudson River Landings* (Indianapolis: The Bobbs-Merrill Co., 1933), covering the development of communities and industrial growth along the river.

1. Brickmaking in the valley began to decline in the 1920s with the importation of European brick and innovations in use of building materials including glass, aluminum, and poured concrete. The Depression also hit the industry hard; production in Haverstraw had just about ended in the 1940s.

2. Some economic historians describe three stages of economic development: a primary, or agricultural, stage; a secondary, or industrial, stage; and finally a tertiary, or service, stage. Thus we tend to refer to the present as a postindustrial, or tertiary, stage.

3. Overemphasis on the Erie Canal may lead one not only to ignore other canals but also to miss the canal fever that gripped the region at this time. Another example was the Delaware and Hudson Canal, completed in 1828 to transport anthracite coal from Pennsylvania coal fields to tidewater at Rondout for transshipment to New York City.

4. Fulton and Livingston's monopoly rights had passed to Aaron Ogden, who sued Thomas Gibbons to restrain him from engaging in steam navigation between New York and New Jersey. In *Gibbons v. Ogden* the court invalidated the New York monopoly and curbed state authority to restrict interstate transportation. This ruling contributed to the expansion of steam navigation on eastern rivers, harbors, and bays.

5. The technological sublime celebrated the machine as a mark of progress and American creativity. This definition countered the generally held view of the sublime to be found in nature.

6. Faced with dual competition from railroads and steamboats, the sloops were relegated to freight service, and by century's end were largely gone. Steamboats were to

meet the same fate, as automobiles and trucks joined the railroads in providing a greater share of transportation services. The steam engine itself was replaced by the more cost-efficient diesel engine. The last Hudson River passenger steamboat, the *Alexander Hamilton*, ended service in 1971. In 1989 its successor, the diesel-powered excursion vessel *Dayliner*, ceased regular passage on the river. Commercial traffic is now dominated by diesel tugs with their barges.

7. John B. Jervis, the chief engineer of the Hudson Line, saw no tension here. In fact, he argued that the railroad would enhance the experience and beauty of the shoreline and river.

8. The most prominent of the remaining industrial facilities along the Hudson are power plants that use the river as a source of cooling water (see chapter 10). Tank farms are also common; the river is still an important shipping route for petroleum products—bulk cargoes most cheaply shipped by tanker barges.

10. Conservation and Environmentalism

The historical background for themes of conservation and environmentalism was drawn from Roderick Nash's *Wilderness and the American Mind*. Raymond O'Brien's *American Sublime: Landscape and Scenery of the Lower Hudson Valley* helped connect these two national movements to the Hudson. Sections on the Storm King controversy and pollution of the Hudson relied on Robert Boyle's *The Hudson: A Natural and Unnatural History*, and Allan Talbot's *Power along the Hudson*. More recent treatment of environmental issues in the Highlands can be found in Frances Dunwell's *The Hudson River Highlands*.

Discussion of the history of the conservation and preservation movements also drew from Hans Huth's *Nature and the American: Three Centuries of Changing Attitudes* (Berkeley: University of California Press, 1957), and Kate H. Winter's pioneering discussion of women and the wilderness experience, *The Women in the Mountain: Reconstruction of Self and Land by Adirondack Writers* (Albany: State University of New York Press, 1989).

1. The Forest Preserve, consisting of 681,374 acres, received additional protection when it was designated "forever wild"—never to be leased to any person or corporation—by constitutional amendment in 1894. In 1892 New York created the Adirondack State Park, 2.8 million acres that included the Forest Preserve and other lands held by private individuals. The state did not treat public and private lands within the park in the same fashion, allowing development to continue on the privately owned sections.

2. The proposal involved pumping river water up to a storage reservoir to be located behind Storm King Mountain. This would occur during times of low electrical demand (late at night, for example). During times of peak demand, water released from the reservoir would drive turbines to produce electricity. The turbine house was to have been carved out of Storm King's northeast flank, which looks out over Cornwall and Newburgh Bays.

3. In power plants using fossil or nuclear fuels, the heat produced boils water to create the steam that drives turbines to generate electricity. The steam, and the water used to make it, run through a closed system of pipes which includes a condenser. Here the steam condenses to liquid water by losing its heat to cooler water flowing through the condenser in a separate set of pipes.

4. The settlement also required the utilities to contribute $12 million to endow an independent research foundation (the Hudson River Foundation), spend $2 million per year on biological monitoring, and to fund the establishment of a hatchery to stock the river with 600,000 young stripers annually. However, ten years have elapsed since the settlement was signed, and the utilities, government agencies, and environmentalists are renegotiating many of the terms of the agreement.

11. Resolving River Conflicts

Much of the information in the Westway case study came from *The Hudson River Ecosystem* by Karin Limburg et al. Descriptions of wetland values, coastal management, and responsibilities of agencies overseeing Hudson River environmental quality can be found in the New York Department of State's *Hudson River Significant Tidal Habitats: A Guide to the Functions, Values, and Protection of the River's Natural Resources*. Robert Boyle's *The Hudson River: A Natural and Unnatural History* includes some information on landfill controversies.

Since many of the disputes described in this chapter are ongoing, books about these controversies can quickly become dated. Thus periodicals, current agency policy statements and bulletins, environmental impact statements, and studies by environmental groups were most useful in writing this chapter. *Wetlands of the United States: Current Status and Recent Trends* by Ralph W. Tiner, Jr. (U.S. Fish and Wildlife Service, Washington, D.C., 1984) provided historical data on loss of wetlands. Data on lost wetland acreage along the Hudson is from Jennifer Anne Young's M.A. thesis, "Human Manipulation of the Historical Hudson Shoreline" (University of Connecticut, 1990). Information about the Hudson River National Estuarine Research Reserve's wetlands is available from the Reserve (c/o Bard College Field Station, Annandale, NY 12504). Discussion of water supply issues depended on bulletins produced by Scenic Hudson (9 Vassar St., Poughkeepsie, NY 12601), and on the New York City Department of Environmental Protection's "Third Annual Report on Water Conservation" (July 1992). Information on coastal zone and estuarine management programs came from the following: "Coastal Resources and Development Policies," published by New Jersey DEP's Division of Coastal Resources (Trenton, NJ 08625); the "Draft Hudson River Estuary Management Plan" (1990) and "Hudson River Quarterly Issues Update and State of the Hudson Report" from the Estuary Management Program at DEC-Region 3 (21 South Putt Corners Road, New Paltz, NY 12561); and New York/New Jersey Harbor Estuary Program newsletters available from the Hudson River Foundation (40 West 20th Street, New York, NY 10011). Finally, Hudson River Greenway information came from documents put out by the Greenway Council (P.O. Box 2080, Albany, NY 12220).

1. Study had been limited to two summer months when low oxygen conditions made the area inhospitable to fish and other aquatic life. Also, researchers had used only a limited array of equipment for collecting estuarine creatures.

2. This eleven-year battle closed debate over the location of a new roadway, but development issues raised during the dispute are still hotly contested. Opponents of a major redevelopment plan for the waterfront claimed that the plan was going forward without the environmental assessment required by state law, and in January 1995 a court agreed, halting implementation until an EIS was prepared.

3. The situation did prompt the EPA and the Corps to jointly develop an action plan, released in 1994, for expediting review of dredging permits in the harbor. The plan calls for clarification of testing required in the permit process, evaluation of possible near-term alternatives for sediments that may be unsuitable for ocean disposal, and development of long-term strategies through a broad participatory process.

4. This law also allows localities to take over regulation of wetlands within their boundaries. While this has rarely been done, conservationists feel that towns might not strongly enforce wetlands regulations.

5. Adjacent property owners also have the right to wharf out to navigable waters and may apply to lease or purchase underwater lands for private use.

6. The $1.5 million eventually endowed the Hudson River Improvement Fund, administered by the Hudson River Foundation. The fund supports projects that will enhance public use and enjoyment of the natural, scenic, and cultural resources of the river.

7. One engineering study suggested that pumping 300 mgd from the river at Chelsea would shift the salt front two miles north, though New York City acknowledged a great deal of uncertainty in this estimate. The effects of the larger withdrawals envisioned by the high-flow skimming plan are not known.

8. This effort will extend metering to the 75 percent of accounts, mostly residential customers, not metered at the time the program started. The 25 percent already metered were mostly commercial (stores, office buildings, restaurants, etc.) and industrial users.

9. The Estuarine District stretches from the Troy Dam to the Narrows, including adjacent tidal wetlands, tidal portions of tributaries, and associated shorelands.

10. The greenway legislation also established a Greenway Heritage Conservancy to provide financial and technical assistance for projects—land acquisition or environmental studies, for example—that would further Greenway goals.

12. Is the Hudson Getting Cleaner?

Robert Boyle's *The Hudson River: A Natural and Unnatural History* provided historical information on pollution of the Hudson. *The Hudson River Ecosystem* by Karin Limburg et al. offered a well-researched case history of the PCB issue through 1984. Barry Commoner's *Making Peace with the Planet* was helpful in developing the section on pollution prevention.

Given the contemporary nature of such issues, full-length book treatments can become outdated quickly. Up-to-date information is scattered through a wealth of reports, impact statements, periodicals, and agency bulletins. Among sources of this type, a particularly valuable reference is the "Hudson River Estuary Quarterly Issues Update and State of the Hudson Report," available from the Estuarine Management Program, DEC-Region 3 (21 South Putt Corners Road, New Paltz, NY 12561). The quarterly newsletter *Water Bulletin* covers a broad spectrum of New York State water quality and resource management programs and issues (DEC—Division of Water, Room 310, 50 Wolf Road, Albany, NY 12233-3501). In this chapter, statistics on the success of these programs came from the *Bulletin*, especially from the issues of August 1991 and February 1992, and from the DEC's report, *New York State Water Quality 1990*.

The perspectives of advocacy groups came through personal communication with Clearwater environmental staff and their reports, "Toxic Tides: Your Right to Know" (October 1989), "Polluting the Hudson: A Gentlemen's Agreement" (February 1983), and "Polluting the Hudson: Business as Usual" (July 1985). Discussion of oil pollution prevention depended on the study, "No Safe Harbor: Tanker Safety in America's Ports" (Natural Resources Defense Council, New York, 1990). The EPA's Region 2 office in New York City publishes fact sheets updating the status of cleanups of cadmium in Cold Spring and PCBs in the upper Hudson; these were helpful in discussing Superfund. The most generally useful of the many reports and fact sheets examined in writing about PCBs was John E. Sanders's paper, "PCB-Pollution Problem in the Upper Hudson River: From Environmental Disaster to Environmental Gridlock," *Northeastern Environmental Science*, vol. 8, no. 1 (1989).

1. The dissolved oxygen used by aquatic microorganisms feeding on sewage and other organic matter is measured as biological oxygen demand (BOD). High BOD indicates the presence of large amounts of organic matter in the water.

2. Until 1984, federal grants covered 75 percent of construction costs, states typically another 15 percent. Localities covered the remaining 10 percent. New York State voters should be credited for earlier attention to sewage cleanup; a spate of treatment plant construction began soon after they passed a billion dollar bond act for the purpose in 1965. Currently the federal government allots construction money to the states on a loan basis; the types of construction eligible are more limited and the federal share can only be up to 55 percent of costs.

3. The plant was originally to be constructed farther south on the West Side. Moving it to Harlem, some observers claim, reflects a tendency to inequitably site sewage plants, hazardous waste treatment sites, incinerators, and similar facilities in low-income neighborhoods, often with high minority populations, where opposition will likely be less organized, vocal, and powerful.

4. Health agencies do not routinely count the numbers of pathogens; it is a demanding and expensive task given their variety and relative scarcity.

5. In a 1989 draft report on its industrial pretreatment program, New York City stated that sludge from all of its sewage plants met state land application standards for chromium and zinc, almost all met standards for nickel, and all but four met standards for cadmium. Copper remained above the limits at almost all plants, not due to industrial discharges but to leaching from plumbing.

6. However, along the tidal Hudson only ten recognized swimming beaches were monitored by county health departments during 1992. These sites were in Ulster, Rockland, and Westchester. In Rockland, swimming is not allowed even at tested sites due to the water's poor visual clarity. At many other informally used swimming beaches, no official testing is done.

7. The Clearwater study, "Toxic Tides: Your Right to Know," also reported that up to 75 percent of toxic discharges in the Hudson basin were not covered by the SPDES system; they were piped into sewage systems, and discharges to sewers do not require SPDES permits. The report emphasized the need to continue and accelerate progress in establishing pretreatment programs.

8. The DEC's Region 3, which covers ninety miles of the Hudson from Westchester and Rockland to Columbia and Greene Counties, oversees 1,500 SPDES permits, 250 of them considered significant. As of 1991 its staff conducted five or six inspection visits yearly at each; funding constraints may reduce these to one or two annually, and may also cut all money for actually sampling the discharges.

9. The DEC's Nonpoint Source Management Program, approved by the EPA in 1990, identifies New York waters adversely impacted by non-point pollution, categorizes the forms of such pollution, maintains a catalog of corrective and preventive practices, and sets up working relationships with other agencies to correct problems both in individual watersheds and statewide. New Jersey has a similar program.

10. In 1988, 324 spills were reported; in 1989, 368; by early March of 1990, 112. Spills under 1,000 gallons are often unreported and not cleaned up.

11. New York's DEC has three spill response teams for different sections of the Hudson and New York Harbor; New Jersey also has such teams on the harbor. While the Coast Guard has primary responsibility, cleanups are coordinated efforts including the Coast Guard, state response teams, and industries involved in oil transport and storage. State agencies identify sensitive habitats that need prompt protection during spills, and inspect oil storage facilities.

12. The EPA must also consider taking no action, an option that may be appropriate if, for example, the environment or public health risks posed by cleanup outweigh those associated with the contamination.

13. Commercial fishing for blueback herring, alewife, Atlantic tomcod, and blue crab reopened in 1978.

14. The quote is from Limburg et al., *The Hudson River Ecosystem*. Based on concerns over exposure to contaminated

dust, the EPA did call for capping deposits of PCB-laden sediments left high and dry after destruction of a dam in Fort Edward, and in a 1990 consent decree it directed GE to pay $10 million for the task.

15. The reasons for revaluating the 1984 decision included new advances in treating PCB-contaminated sediments, a policy of reviewing Superfund records of decision every five years, and a preference—established when the law was reauthorized in 1986—for remedies that permanently and significantly reduce the volume, toxicity, and mobility of hazardous substances.

16. It was during this period of the Reagan Administration that the EPA officialin charge of hazardous waste cleanup, Rita Lavalle, was found guilty of improperly linking cleanup funding decisions to political considerations. Anne Gorsuch Burford, the EPA administrator responsible for impounding the PCB cleanup funds, was forced to resign due to similar allegations.

Glossary

adipose fin: a fleshy fin lacking rays; found behind the dorsal fin on some fishes.

aesthetic: a sense or taste for the beautiful; a love of beauty.

amphipod: a small, vaguely shrimplike crustacean, usually flattened from side to side, with a thorax in segments instead of a single piece; also called scud or sideswimmer (order Amphipoda).

anadromous: describes fishes that live in the sea (or large lakes) as adults but move into freshwater streams to spawn.

anal fin: an unpaired fin located on the underside and toward the tail of many fish.

arachnid: an arthropod that typically has eight legs and two body sections, one combining the head and thorax, the other an abdomen; spiders and water mites are examples (class Arachnida).

arthropod: an animal characterized by paired, jointed legs and an exoskeleton made of chitin; crustaceans, insects, and horseshoe crabs are examples (phylum Arthropoda).

barbel: a fleshy sensory appendage of some fishes, catfish "whiskers" for example.

benthos (adj. *benthic*): organisms living underwater on or in the bottom.

bioaccumulate: to build up quantities of a contaminant in the body of an individual organism.

biological concentration: process by which contaminant levels increase in the organisms along a food chain, reaching highest concentrations in top predators.

bivalve: a mollusk with two shells (valves) joined at a hinge; clams are examples (class Bivalvia).

bloom: a rapid and sizable increase in a population of microscopic aquatic plants.

bouweries: farms or plantations owned by early Dutch settlers.

calcareous: containing calcium carbonate.

carnivore: an organism that eats animals.

cartography: the science of mapping.

catadromous: describes fishes that live in fresh water as adults but move into salt water to spawn.

caudal fin: tail fin.

chevaux-de-frise: obstacles of wood, wire, or spikes placed in a pathway or waterway to prevent an enemy's advance.

chitin: a horny, flexible substance that is the major component of arthropod exoskeletons; in crabs and other crustaceans chitin is hardened by deposits of calcium carbonate.

chlorophyll: found in green plants, this chemical gives such plants their color and captures light energy for conversion into chemical energy.

chloroplast: a structure, found in many plant cells, in which chlorophyll is concentrated and which provides energy necessary to the workings of the cell.

chromatophore: one of the specialized cells in a fish's skin which contain pigment and cause color changes.

cilia: tiny hairlike structures which, arranged in groups and beating rhythmically, provide locomotion and other functions for living things.

cladoceran: one of a group of tiny crustaceans characterized by a nonsegmented body, a pair of large antennae used for locomotion, and, in most, a bivalvelike shell covering the abdomen and thorax; also called water fleas (order Cladocera).

cold-blooded: describes animals that do not maintain a set internal body temperature.

comb jelly: *see* ctenophore.

community: in ecology, an assemblage of organisms living and interacting in a given habitat.

compound eye: an eye composed of many separate units, each with its own lens and light-sensitive cells.

consumer: in ecology, an organism that obtains energy by eating other organisms; primary consumers eat plants, secondary consumers eat the plant-eaters, tertiary consumers eat secondary consumers, etc.

copepod: one of a group of tiny crustaceans that most commonly have elongated, segmented bodies, a pair of prominent antennae, swimming legs on their undersides, and a pair (or two sets) of tail-like spines (subclass Copepoda).

critical zone: in estuaries, a highly productive, low salinity region important as a nursery for larval and juvenile fishes.

crustacean: one of a group of arthropods that are primarily aquatic and very diverse in form; typically the body has three sections (head, thorax, and abdomen) and a calcified chitinous exoskeleton; crabs and water fleas are examples (class Crustacea).

ctenophore: one of a group of small jellyfish-like creatures which lack stinging cells and have eight rows of cilia used in locomotion; comb jellies (phylum Ctenophora).

cyanobacteria: photosynthetic single-celled organisms; also called blue-green algae, but their simple cell structure is more like that of bacteria than that of algae (division Cyanophyta).

DEC: New York State Department of Environmental Conservation.

decomposer: an organism that obtains energy by breaking dead organic matter down into simpler components; usually refers to bacteria and fungi.

delta: a deposit of sediment, often triangular in shape, laid down where stream currents enter and slow in relatively still water.

DEP: New Jersey Department of Environmental Protection.

dermis: in fish, the underlying fibrous layer of skin.

detritivore: an organism that feeds on dead organic matter; usually refers to organisms other than bacteria and fungi.

detritus: cast off or dead and decaying plant and animal matter.

diatom: one of a group of algae with a cell wall made largely of silica; they are often yellow in color (division Bacillariophyta).

dinoflagellate: one of a group of microorganisms that usually possess both chlorophyll and hairlike flagella for locomotion (division Pyrrophyta).

dorsal fin: unpaired fin(s) with rays; found on the backs of most fish.

dredging: digging up sediments from the bottom of a water body.

ebb current: a tidal current moving toward the ocean.

echinoderm: one of a group of marine animals that possess tube feet connected to a system of vessels carrying water through the body; sea stars and sea urchins are examples (phylum Echinodermata).

ecology: the study of relationships between living organisms and their environments.

ecosystem: a functional unit of ecology, encompassing interacting living organisms and the physical environment they inhabit.

EIS: environmental impact statement.

emergent: describes aquatic plants that have erect stems, leaves, or other parts that project above the water.

energy: the ability to do work, to power activity; takes several forms: light energy in solar radiation, chemical energy in food, for example.

EPA: U.S. Environmental Protection Agency.

epibenthic: living underwater on the substrate's surface.

epidermis: the outer layer of skin in fish.

epiphytic: living attached to submerged plants, but not deriving any nutrition from them.

estuary: a body of water freely connected to the sea and partially surrounded by land, in which salt water is diluted by fresh water running off the land.

ethnocentric: believing in the superiority of one's own group.

euphotic zone: in water bodies, the area near the surface in which there is enough sunlight for plants to grow.

exoskeleton: an external framework that contains and supports the tissues of many invertebrate animals.

fecal coliform: bacteria found in the digestive tracts of warm-blooded animals; elevated levels of these bacteria in water often indicate pollution by sewage.

filamentous: a habit of growth in which cells are arranged in a line; often describes algae.

fission: a process by which one cell divides into two.

fix: in ecology, to capture energy or nutrients and convert them into forms usable by plants and the animals that depend on plants.

fjord: a valley eroded below sea level by glaciers and later submerged by rising seas.

flat: a level area of sediment in subtidal shallows or in the intertidal zone.

flood current: a tidal current moving in from the ocean.

flushing rate: the time necessary for water to move from the upstream end of an estuary to its mouth.

fly boat: a fast sailing vessel used chiefly in the sixteenth and seventeenth centuries for the rapid transportation of goods in coastal trade; usually a Dutch flat-bottomed boat.

food chain: a linear pathway by which food energy moves from plants to plant-eating animals to predators; in grazing food chains, animals feed directly on green plants; in detrital food chains, dead organic material from plants and other organisms nourishes decomposers and detritivores eaten by other animals.

food web: interconnected food chains in which each organism has several sources of food and, except for top predators, is in turn eaten by a variety of other organisms.

gastropod: a mollusk distinguished by a well-developed head, a broad, muscular foot, and a radula; snails and slugs are examples (class Gastropoda).

green algae: microscopic, single-celled plants with nuclei and chlorophyll concentrated in chloroplasts (division Chlorophyta).

habitat: the place or setting in which an organism lives.

herbaceous: nonwoody.

herbivore: an organism that eats plants.

historical associations: enhancement and celebration of a landscape's identification with local, regional, or national history.

home rule: a legal doctrine giving local governments responsibility for land use decisions within their communities.

hydroid: the attached, polyp form of a hydrozoan.

hydromedusa: the planktonic, jellyfish-like form of a hydrozoan.

hydrozoan: one of a group of small jellyfish and sea anemone-like animals (class Hydrozoa).

intertidal: within the zone between average low and average high tide level.

Knickerbocker: a descendant of the Dutch settlers of New York.

larvae (adj. **larval**): an early life stage or immature form of an animal.

lateral line: a sensory system, attuned to vibration, appearing as a series of pores or canals arranged in a line along the side of many fish.

limiting factor: of factors necessary for an organism to survive and grow, the one in lowest supply relative to need.

luminism: a style of painting that emphasizes the transcendent quality of pure and constant light.

mantle: in mollusks, a fold in the body wall that secretes the calcareous shell.

marsh: a wetland dominated by emergent herbaceous plants; in tidal areas, low marsh is found below the mean tide level, high marsh above.

mean tide level: the water level determined by averaging high and low tide.

medusa: free-floating form of a jellyfish or related organism; resembles an open umbrella with tentacles hanging below.

metamorphose: in biological development, to change profoundly in form when moving from one life stage to the next—caterpillar to butterfly, for example.

mgd: million gallons daily.

midden: a refuse heap, often one left by early inhabitants of an area.

mollusk: one of a group of animals characterized by having a mantle and a muscular foot; clams and snails are examples (phylum Mollusca).

molt: to shed a body's outer covering and replace it with a fresh one, as a bird replaces feathers or a crab its shell.

nares: nostrils.

nationalize: the act of identifying an object, event, or place with a country's history and identity.

neap tide: a less extreme tide—a lower high tide or a higher low—occurring when the moon is in its first or last quarter.

nektonic: capable of swimming strongly enough to move against the current.

nematocyst: one of specialized cells used by jellyfish and their relatives to sting or ensnare prey.

NEPA: National Environmental Policy Act.

non-point source pollution: pollution carried in runoff from an area of land rather than being released through a pipe from a factory, sewage plant, or similar facility.

nuclei (singular *nucleus*): in cells, specialized bodies that contain genetic material and direct cell growth and metabolism.

nutrient: an element—nitrogen or phosphorus, for example—required for an organism's growth and development.

nutrient trap: a phenomenon in which large amounts of nutrients are retained in an estuary by salt water pushing into the system.

nymph: an immature insect, similar in form to the adult, which attains adulthood by molting rather than by metamorphosis.

oligochaete: a segmented worm characterized by bristles that grow singly from a sac in the skin; the earthworm is an example (class Oligochaeta).

omnivore: an organism that eats both plants and animals.

operculum: in fish, the gill cover; in snails, a flap that is attached to the foot and seals the shell opening.

ostracod: one of a group of tiny crustaceans with body parts enclosed in a bivalve shell (subclass Ostracoda).

pathogens (adj. *pathogenic*): organisms, such as certain bacteria and viruses, which cause disease.

patroon: a member of the West India Company who was given manorial rights to lands in exchange for planting a colony of fifty settlers.

PCBs: polychlorinated biphenyls, a class of chemical compounds in which chlorine atoms are attached to two connected phenyl rings.

pectoral fins: in fish, the paired fins closest to the head or highest on the body.

pelvic fins: in fish, the paired fins located on the underside either below or behind the pectoral fins; also called ventral fins.

photosynthesis: the process, energized by sunlight and aided by chlorophyll, in which green plants convert carbon dioxide and water into sugar and oxygen.

phytoplankton: microscopic plants that live drifting in the water.

PIPC: Palisades Interstate Park Commission.

picturesque: interesting in an unusual way; irregular.

plankton: aquatic organisms which, unable to swim strongly, drift at the mercy of currents.

point discharge: pollution released via a pipe from a specific factory, treatment plant, or similar facility.

polychaete: a segmented worm with bristles that grow in a bundle from a sac in the skin; the clam worm is an example (class Polychaeta).

polyp: the attached form of a jellyfish or its kin; hydroids and sea anemones are examples.

ppm: parts per million.

ppt: parts per thousand.

pretreatment: in pollution control, treatment of industrial wastes prior to their release into a sewage system.

primary producer: an organism capable of converting light energy into chemical energy that can serve as food for other organisms; green plants.

primary production: in ecology, the energy accumulated by plants through photosynthesis; net production is primary production minus the energy used by plants in meeting their own needs.

primary productivity: the rate at which energy is accumulated through photosynthetic activity by plants.

projectile points: commonly called arrowheads, but more often spearpoints and knives; important archaeological indicators of time and culture.

protoplasm: the semisolid and liquid component of a cell.

public trust doctrine: in common law, ownership of certain waters and lands by the state in trust for its citizens.

pupa (plural *pupae*): a resting, usually immobile stage or form occurring during some insects' transformation from larva to adult.

radula: in mollusks other than bivalves, a toothed tongue or ribbonlike organ used for feeding.

rays: thin, bony structures that support the fins of fish.

reach: the stretch of water visible between bends in a river channel.

reef: in the Hudson, a partially or fully submerged ridge of rocky substrate.

respiration: uptake of oxygen in organisms, a process that breaks down organic molecules, produces carbon dioxide and water, and makes energy available to the organism.

rhizome: the underground portion of a plant's stem; it usually grows horizontally, and from it spring erect stems and true roots.

Romantic: the primacy of thoughts and feelings of the imagination; the subjective experience.

sachem: a chief of a tribe or confederation of native Americans.

salt front: in estuaries, the leading edge of dilute saline water moving landward from the sea.

sessile: living attached to the substrate.

shaman: a priest or medicine man among certain North American tribes.

simple eye: in arthropods, a primitive eye in which a single lens refracts light for sensory cells in the retina.

SPDES: State Pollution Discharge Elimination System, a pollution control program established by the Clean Water Act.

spring tide: an extreme tide (higher high or lower low) occurring when the moon is in its full or new phase.

sublime: grand, majestic, noble, and awe-inspiring.

substrate: an underlying layer of material; the mud or sand on a river bottom, for example.

subtidal: pertaining to portions of tidal waters below low tide level and thus always submerged.

succession: replacement of one ecological community by another over time.

swamp: a wetland dominated by woody plants.

swim bladder (also air or gas bladder): a gas-filled sac located in the body cavity of many fish; provides buoyancy and in some species serves as a sound-producing or sensing organ, or as a primitive lung.

technological sublime: the beauty and majesty in machinery and mechanical progress.

terminal moraine: a deposit of glacially eroded soil and rock marking the limit of a glacier's advance.

thermodynamics: the study of energy flow and transformation in mechanical and chemical systems.

topography: the physical features of an area's landscape.

transpiration: loss of water vapor by land plants.

tributary: a stream that flows into another stream or body of water.

tunicate: a primitive chordate (backboned animal), usually sessile and possessing a tough, translucent outer layer of body wall—a tunic; sea squirts are examples (subphylum Urochordata).

turbid: clouded with sediment.

water column: the portion of a water body between the surface and the bottom.

water flea: see cladoceran.

watershed: the area of land from which water runs off into a given body of water.

wetland: land and submerged land supporting aquatic or semiaquatic plants.

zooplankton: animals, mostly tiny, which are unable to swim strongly and thus drift in the water column.

Suggested Readings

A thorough study of the Hudson River should encompass history, literature, art, architecture, political science, biology, chemistry, geology, and many other fields of knowledge. This brief reading list can include only a fraction of the valuable reference books in river-related disciplines; but it does cite those most useful in preparing this book.

General overviews of the Hudson ecosystem and its inhabitants can be found in Robert H. Boyle's *The Hudson River: A Natural and Unnatural History* (W. W. Norton & Company, New York, 1979), *An Atlas of the Biological Resources of the Hudson Estuary* (Boyce Thompson Institute for Plant Research, Yonkers, NY, 1977; out of print, but remainders available from Clearwater), and *The Hudson River Ecosystem* by Karin Limburg, Mary Ann Moran, and William H. McDowell (Springer-Verlag, New York, 1986). Widely available, Boyle's book is engaging, informative, and well suited to the layperson. The *Atlas* is more disjointed, inconsistent in its assumptions of a reader's scientific background, and partly outdated. However, good drawings and descriptions of important organisms of the estuary make it a worthwhile reference. *The Hudson River Ecosystem* is intended for an audience comfortable with formal science writing. For such readers, its opening chapter provides an excellent overview of the Hudson ecosystem.

For readers who want their science embedded in lyric prose, or for language-arts teachers involved in curriculum focused on the estuary, Rachel Carson's *Under the Sea Wind* (NAL/Dutton, New York, 1992) is an excellent choice. While not specifically about the Hudson, this book describes the lives of creatures common in the area in very literate style.

General histories of the Hudson tend quickly to wander from the river into the wider setting of the valley's communities. We still do not have a history of the river per se but rather histories of the river valley. The most focused of the recent works and one filled with new ideas is Raymond O'Brien's *The American Sublime: Landscape and Scenery of the Lower Hudson Valley* (Columbia University Press, New York, 1981). But the touchstone for histories of the river is Carl Carmer's *The Hudson* (Fordham University Press, New York, 1993). This work, originally published in 1939, has a timeless quality that still provides inspiration for river lovers. A more journalistic account is Allan Keller's *Life along the Hudson* (Sleepy Hollow Press, Tarrytown, N.Y., 1985). Finally, D. W. Meinig's innovative geography of early American history, *The Shaping of America: A Geographical Perspective on 500 Years of History: Atlantic America, 1492–1800*, vol. 1 (Yale University Press, New Haven, 1986), describes patterns of settlement that are clearly observed in Hudson Valley history.

One can supplement these traditional histories with firsthand accounts from Roland Van Zandt's *Chronicles of the Hudson: Three Centuries of Travel and Adventure* (Black Dome Press, Hensonville, N.Y., 1992), images from Jeffrey Simpson's *The Hudson River 1850–1918: A Photographic Portrait* (Sleepy Hollow Press, Tarrytown, N.Y., 1987), and river guidebooks including Arthur Adams's *The Hudson: A Guidebook to the River* (State University of New York Press, Albany, 1981; out of print but worth a search) and Wallace Bruce's *The Hudson by Daylight* (Walking News,

New York, 1982, a reprint of the 1907 edition). Finally, Clearwater's *Panorama of the Hudson River from New York to Albany* (Clearwater, Poughkeepsie, N.Y., 1979) reprints William Wade's 1845 series of maplike drawings depicting the river's shores, accompanying them with old prints, current photographs, and commentary.

Chapter 1. Those interested in Hudson Valley geology will find *Geology of New York: A Simplified Account*, ed. by Y. W. Isachsen, E. Landing, J. M. Lauber, L. V. Rickard, and W. B. Rogers (New York State Geological Survey, State Education Department, Albany, 1991), a valuable reference. The forces that cause tides are described in many books on oceanography; *An Introduction to the World's Oceans* by Allison B. and Alyn C. Duxbury (William C. Brown Publishers, Dubuque, Iowa, 1989), has particularly clear diagrams of these phenomena. Tidal information, invaluable to anyone planning trips on or along the Hudson, can be found in two annual publications from the National Ocean Service (National Oceanic and Atmospheric Administration, Distribution Branch, Riverdale, Md.): *Tidal Current Tables, Atlantic Coast of North America* and *Tide Tables, High and Low Water Predictions, East Coast of North and South America*. More compact and less expensive is *Hudson River Tide and Current Data, 1 April–30 November*, distributed annually by Sea Explorer Ship 168 (contact Jack Feldborg, 63 South Gate Drive, Poughkeepsie, NY 12601, or Clearwater).

Chapter 2. Energy flow, food webs, and nutrient cycles are covered in ecology texts such as Eugene P. Odum's *Fundamentals of Ecology* (Saunders College Publishing, Troy, Mo., 1971). Limburg's *The Hudson River Ecosystem* (cited above) provides an overview of these topics more specific to the estuary. Aldo Leopold's description of nutrient cycling in the essay "Odyssey," from his classic *A Sand County Almanac* (Ballantine Books, 1986), merits the attention of those teaching both science and literature.

Chapter 3. River habitats and plant communities are well described in *Hudson River Significant Tidal Habitats: A Guide to the Functions, Values, and Protection of the River's Natural Resources* (New York Department of State/Division of Coastal Resources and Waterfont Revitalization and the Nature Conservancy, Albany, 1990). More generalized treatment of these habitats is available in *The Ecology of Tidal Freshwater Marshes of the United States East Coast: A Community Profile* by W. E. Odum, T. J. Smith III, J. K. Hoover, and C. C. McIvor (U.S. Fish and Wildlife Service, Washington, D.C., 1984). John and Mildred Teal's classic of nature writing, *Life and Death of the Salt Marsh* (Ballantine Books, New

York, 1983), may have more appeal to the layperson. Helpful in identifying wetland plants along the Hudson is *A Field Guide to Coastal Wetland Plants of the Northeastern United States* by Ralph W. Tiner, Jr. (University of Massachusetts Press, Amherst, 1987).

Chapter 4. A fine general introduction to the invertebrates is Ralph Buchsbaum's *Animals without Backbones* (University of Chicago Press, Chicago, 1987). More details on aquatic invertebrates are available from scientific reference works such as Robert Pennak's *Fresh-water Invertebrates of the United States: Protozoa to Mollusca* (John Wiley & Sons, New York, 1971) and Kenneth L. Gosner's *Guide to the Identification of Marine and Estuarine Invertebrates: Cape Hatteras to the Bay of Fundy* (look for used Wiley & Sons editions, or contact Books on Demand, in Ann Arbor, Mich., for an expensive photocopy version). Gosner's *A Field Guide to the Atlantic Seashore* (Houghton Mifflin Company, Boston, 1982), with the beautiful illustrations typical of the Peterson Field Guide series, is useful to laypeople interested in invertebrates of the Hudson's saltier regions. While its focus is not the Hudson, William W. Warner's *Beautiful Swimmers: Watermen, Crabs, and the Chesapeake Bay* (Viking Penguin, New York, 1987) evocatively blends the natural history of the blue crab and the human interests of those who catch them.

Chapter 5. C. Lavett Smith's *The Inland Fishes of New York State* (New York State Department of Environmental Conservation, Albany, 1985) is an excellent reference, with a section devoted to the Hudson estuary's fishes—hence the adjective "inland" rather than "freshwater" in the title. There are many helpful field guides. Mervin Robert's *The Tidemarsh Guide to Fishes* (1985; available from the author in Old Lyme, Conn.) covers freshwater and saltwater species found here in a light-hearted, anecdotal manner, with asides on fisheries and ichthyological research, but its species descriptions vary in thoroughness. *McClane's Field Guide to Freshwater Fishes of North America*, ed. by A. J. McClane (Holt, Rinehart, and Winston, New York, 1978), offers full-color illustrations to go with descriptions of many species likely to be familiar to anglers. Robert G. Werner's *Freshwater Fishes of New York State: A Field Guide* (Syracuse University Press, Syracuse, N.Y., 1980) adds an identification key and good descriptions but few illustrations. Url Lanham's *The Fishes* (Columbia University Press, New York, 1967) is a good choice for the layperson interested in general fish biology; more detail is provided in texts such as *Ichthyology* (John Wiley & Sons, New York, 1977) by Karl F. Lagler, John E. Bardach, and Robert R. Miller. Finally, a number of books about fish and fishing enter the realm of literature; John

N. Cole's *Striper: A Story of Fish and Man* (Lyons and Burford, Publishers, New York, 1989) is a worthy choice, interweaving the life histories of fish and fishermen.

Chapter 6. There is a wealth of general reference works dealing with amphibians, reptiles, mammals, and birds—the *Audubon Encyclopedia of North American Birds* (Outlet Book Company, Avenal, N.J., 1991) by John K. Terres, for example. But for recent information specific to the Hudson, one needs to dig into scientific literature, the newsletters and species lists of local organizations interested in these creatures, and regional periodicals that deal with natural history topics. For field identification, the Peterson Field Guides are good choices, starting with series originator Roger Tory Peterson's *A Field Guide to Eastern Birds* (Houghton Mifflin Company, Boston, 1984) and including *A Field Guide to the Mammals* by William H. Burt and Richard P. Grossenheider (Houghton Mifflin, 1976) and *A Field Guide to Reptiles and Amphibians of Eastern and Central North America* by Roger Conant and Joseph Collins (Houghton Mifflin, 1991).

Chapter 7. There has been a modest renaissance in the history of the native peoples of the valley, exemplified by Herbert Kraft's thorough *The Lenape: Archaeology, History and Ethnography* (New Jersey Historical Society, Newark, 1987) and Julian Harris Salomon's more specialized *Indians of the Lower Hudson River: The Munsee* (Rockland County Historical Society, New City, 1983). Henry Hudson has been the subject of many biographies, but *Juet's Journal: The Voyage of the Half Moon from 4 April to 7 November 1609* (New Jersey Historical Society, Newark, 1959) is still the best account of his exploration of the river. A good, detailed recent study of early Dutch settlers is Charlotte Wilcoxen's *Seventeenth-Century Albany: A Dutch Profile* (Albany Institute of History and Art, Albany, 1984). The Bicentennial failed to produce a definitive regional history of the Revolution. Lincoln Diamant's *Chaining the Hudson: The Fight for the River in the American Revolution* (Carol Publishing Group, New York, 1989) is as close as we come to an account of the Hudson's role in the Revolution.

Chapter 8. The glorious age of the romantic Hudson is best approached through the work of the painters and writers. John K. Howat's *The Hudson River and Its Painters* (Outlet Book Company, Avenal, N.J., 1991) gives a good basic overview, while Barbara Novak provides a framework for interpreting the paintings of the Hudson River School in *Nature and Culture: American Landscape and Painting 1825–1875* (Oxford University Press, New York, 1980). The more personal relationship between artist and river valley is examined

in *Charmed Places: Hudson River Artists and Their Houses, Studios, and Vistas* (Harry Abrams, New York, 1988), ed. by Sandra S. Phillips and Linda Weintraub. A selection of the pertinent literature is available in Arthur G. Adams's *The Hudson River in Literature: An Anthology* (Fordham University Press, New York, 1988). The remarkable legacy of the nineteenth century's frenzied estate building is lavishly presented in John Zukowsky and Robbie Pierce Stimson's *Hudson River Villas* (Rizzoli, New York, 1985).

Chapter 9. Nineteenth-century industrialization of the river valley has not been treated fully in a single detailed work. The catalog of a Bard College exhibit, *Industrial Transformations: Nineteenth-Century Business and Industry in the Mid-Hudson Valley* is helpful. Regional industrialization is best studied through histories of individual business activities such as brickmaking, ice harvesting, lumbering, and shipyards. The Romantic impulse was not limited to the arts but extended to technology as well. Images of technical progress are examined in Kenneth W. Maddox's *In Search of the Picturesque: Nineteenth-Century Images of Industry along the Hudson River Valley,* another Bard College exhibit catalog (Red Hook, New York, 1983). River steamboats were among the most celebrated objects of Romantic technology. Donald C. Ringwald's *The Mary Powell* (Howell-Norton, Burbank, Calif., 1972) is a study of the queen of river steamers. The impact of the railroad on river travel and the valley landscape is one of the main themes in John Stilgoe's *Metropolitan Corridor: Railroads and the American Scene* (Yale University Press, New Haven, 1983).

Chapter 10. The Hudson's twentieth-century history has seen an increased emphasis on conservation and preservation. To study these forces one should begin with Boyle's *The Hudson: A Natural and Unnatural History* (cited above), a work that changed the way we look at the river. Allan R. Talbot's *Power along the Hudson: The Storm King Case and the Birth of Environmentalism* (Dutton, New York, 1972) is out of print, but the first chapter of his *Settling Things: Six Case Studies in Environmental Mediation* (Books on Demand, Ann Arbor, Mich.) reviews the resolution of the issue. Frances F. Dunwell's *The Hudson River Highlands* (Columbia University Press, New York, 1991) provides the most recent review of environmental issues in the Hudson Highlands, along with much information on the natural and human history of the river. Roderick Nash's *Wilderness and the American Mind* (Yale University Press, New Haven, 1982) places the modern environmental history of the river in the context of its historical background. Thomas Berry's *The Dream of the Earth* (Sierra Club, San Francisco, 1990), a good example of the eco-theology movement, contains several chapters that focus on the Hudson. Berry sees the valley as a bio-region, a natural community in which we are functioning members.

Chapters 11 and 12. With ongoing disputes over Hudson River environmental concerns, the most timely information comes from newspaper reports, articles in periodicals, reports from agencies and organizations involved in the disputes, and scientific literature. Given the degree of research and the logistics involved in producing books about these battles, such longer works tend to reflect the history and basic science involved rather than the most up-to-date information on progress toward resolution. However, Boyle's *The Hudson River: A Natural and Unnatural History* must again be cited here for its descriptions of political and legal clashes along the river and its statement of values held by one of the river's most outspoken environmental advocates. Limburg et al., *The Hudson River Ecosystem* (cited above), presents more objective, detailed reviews (through 1985) of three major controversies—Westway, PCBs, and power plant operations—and the roles played by scientific research in attempts to resolve these disputes. The New York Department of State publication *Hudson River Significant Tidal Habitats* (cited above—Chapter 2) provides a broad overview of human impacts on the river and of the roles of specific agencies in resolving issues raised by these impacts. While its perspective is national and global rather than regional, Barry Commoner's *Making Peace with the Planet* (Pantheon Books, New York, 1990) offers a well-documented and provocative critique of environmental improvements—or lack thereof—under the Clean Water Act and other relevant laws.

Index

Page numbers in boldface refer to illustrations.

About the Authors

Stephen P. Stanne is education director for Hudson River Sloop Clearwater, a job that has immersed him in the Hudson both literally and figuratively since 1980. He has taught aboard the sloop, lectured widely about the river, and produced a variety of resource materials for Hudson River education. Mr. Stanne holds a B.A. degree from Amherst College and a Master of Science Teaching degree from Antioch/New England. He resides in New Paltz, New York.

Roger G. Panetta is an assistant professor of history at Marymount College. The Hudson has been a central subject of his teaching and consulting work with museums and historical societies. Through the College of New Rochelle, Mr. Panetta has offered teacher training courses in Hudson River Studies. He holds a B.A. degree from Columbia College and an M.A. in American History from Fordham University. Mr. Panetta makes his home in Hastings-on-Hudson, New York.

Brian E. Forist is an environmental educator whose twenty years of teaching experience include six years as an education specialist with the Hudson River Sloop Clearwater, teaching on the boat and leading workshops on land. Mr. Forist holds a B.S. degree from Huxley College of Environmental Studies and an M.S. in Environmental Studies and Elementary Education from Antioch/New England. He lives in Massachusetts.

Development of this book was a project of Hudson River Sloop Clearwater, Inc., a not-for-profit, member-supported environmental education and advocacy organization dedicated to restoration and protection of the Hudson River and similar waterways. Its members own and operate the 106-foot sloop *Clearwater,* launched in 1969, as a floating classroom on the tidewater Hudson. In addition to educational sail programs, the organization provides land-based field trips and classroom presentations, teacher workshops, and curriculum resource materials. Clearwater staff also conduct grass-roots environmental action programs with the goal of cleaning and preserving the Hudson. Royalties from sales of this book go to Clearwater to support these programs. For more information about the organization, contact: Hudson River Sloop Clearwater, Inc., 112 Market Street, Poughkeepsie, New York 12601; telephone (914) 454-7673.